THE COAST OF WEST
CORK

N

riff

•Reenadisert

•BANTRY

as

Ballinascarthy

•Shannonvale

•Clonakilty

Leap   •Rosscarbery
•Glandore
lydehob   ×Castle Freke   •Clonakilty
                  Copinger's Court ×Rathbarry Castle   Bay
Famine   •Unionhall
graves
×   Kilcoe
sbrin   ×   Castle   Dromberg Circle
Horse   •SKIBBEREEN
r I.   •Castletownshend   Spanish graves   •Galley Head
        Lough
        Hyne   •Reen
re I.
        •Baltimore

Sherkin I.

To Will
for Christmas
1973

May this aid in
many hours of
enjoying Ireland!

With
love
Gordon & Elizabeth

THE COAST OF WEST CORK

THE COAST OF
WEST CORK

by

PETER SOMERVILLE-LARGE

LONDON
VICTOR GOLLANCZ LTD
1972

ISBN 0 575 00739 7

Printed in Great Britain by
The Camelot Press Ltd., London and Southampton

CONTENTS

———————————

LIST OF ILLUSTRATIONS

ACKNOWLEDGEMENTS

Plates 1, 2a, 3a, 4, 6a, 8a, 11, 12a, 13a, 13b, 14, 15, 16a, 18, 19a, 19b, 22a, 22b, 23a, 23b, 24 are reproduced by kind permission of Bord Failte.

Plates 5b, 6b, 7a, 8b, 9a, 17a, 17b, 21 are reproduced by kind permission of the National Library of Ireland. They are from the Lawrence Collection, and were taken between 1895 and 1905.

The remaining photographs were taken by the author.

PREFACE

The man who sold me my bicycle had been surprised that anyone should want to buy one. Only a few years ago he could remember at least four bicycle shops in Skibbereen. Now there was only his own, filled up to the doorway with rusty old machines that had seen a lifetime of use.

"It's a disgrace to be seen on one nowadays," he said as he screwed on the saddle.

I set out into the country. The sun had filtered through after rain, making the tarmac steam with moisture and sending up towering clouds off the mountains into the sky. Cattle stood motionless in the boggy fields and water dripped from the leafless sycamores.

For the first time I noticed how rural life had changed since I last went at a proper pace to observe it. Dogs still chased the postman, but now he had a van in which to take refuge. In the farmyards the piles of dung had changed to neat plastic bags of fertilizer. Farmers herded their dairy cows from the wheel of their Ford car or scarlet tractor; the donkey cart and the trap had gone to take their place beside the iron bedstead, filling a hole in the fence. Only the old men, and those unfortunates who were unable to rely upon the security of the milk cheque, had kept their beasts of burden, donkeys and white and piebald horses.

Even in snow a bicycle was an invaluable way of travelling. The appearance of a lone figure in winter pushing uphill with a rucksack bulging on the carrier of his machine made people hospitable. Perhaps, now that so many cars sped past, the opportunity to talk to strangers had become rarer. I was asked in for endless cups of tea and plates of bread, in return answering questions about my journey.

I travelled along the coast of West Cork, through Carbery, from Clonakilty to Roaring Water Bay with its fringe of islands and castles, and north to Bantry and the Beare peninsula. Much of the land near the coast consists of bog and mountain with headlands like lines of slanting spears thrust into the Atlantic. But there are parts that are sheltered, with a tropical lushness that is partly ascribed to the benign influence of the Gulf Stream. Ruins are soon covered with thick ivy and it takes only a few trees or slips of fuchsia to make a protective wall. Some valleys and hillsides have pockets of moss-covered oak-trees which are survivors of the ancient forest that covered the country three hundred years ago.

This part of the country remained largely outside the mainstream of Irish contemporary life, that is, outside the spheres of invasion and war. It was settled very early; many important Neolithic remains are to be found in the area. Stone circles, standing stones, dolmens and ring forts are abundant. For thousands of years men chose to settle here because they expected to find peace and a simple prosperity. The shores of Carbery and Beare overlooked a series of exceptionally rich fishing grounds. The islands and deep inlets provided safe harbours for the fishing fleets of Europe which paid dues to the men of West Cork for the privilege of trailing their nets off-shore. The O'Driscolls, O'Mahonys, O'Sullivans and others who established themselves along the coastline over the centuries have left their castles, strategically and romantically sited on rocks along the edge of the sea. In addition to the fees collected from visiting ships, they profited more directly from the abundant shoals of pilchards which they caught themselves and preserved and pressed for oil as part of their winter diet. Since most of the land was forested, herds of swine were kept, which lived on acorns from the oak-trees. Wolf and otter skins from the animals that roamed the forests and proliferated beside the rivers were exported and traded for the luxuries of the Continent. The castles, small chilly editions of the imposing Norman strongholds in east and central Ireland, could not have been comfortable. But their inhabitants, traditionally hospitable to strangers, upholders of an ancient aristocracy and religion, lovers of music, story-telling and dancing, lived more or less in a pleasant and civilized manner until they were driven away.

Throughout the seventeenth century, at times when the battles and massacres seemed to have halted, large numbers of Englishmen flocked here to settle. Other more easterly parts of Ireland had been exploited, but in West Cork there was land that no planter had yet touched. It was nearer than North America and to reach it did not entail a long sea journey. Although the newcomers destroyed most of the ancient forests, they made vigorous attempts to establish their settlements by improving the land and introducing more sophisticated methods of agriculture and fishing. They built towns and cultivated their estates so that today the countryside is full of ruined demesnes. Something defeated them. It was not only the latent hostility of the people around them or the soft yet harsh climate which could induce lethargy and despair. Part of their ultimate failure in integration was the fact that England was too near. The land was no more difficult to cultivate than the wildernesses of America. But it was much easier to be an absentee from here than from estates in Rhode Island or Connecticut. Those Anglo-Irish who had the means never severed their roots with English society. Even if they were not absentees in fact, England was at the back of their minds as a place of escape. There was always the feeling that if the crops were bad this year, or it rained non-stop for three months, London or Bath offered an easy retreat. And although as the generations passed they became increasingly attached to the land, they were fatally distant from the people their ancestors had dispossessed. Separated from them by religion and race, they remained apart, and perhaps their refusal to integrate has contributed to their quick decline.

West Cork never recovered from the potato famine of 1847, and its effects linger like clouds of fall-out. It gave the push to the emigration that has never halted. After a hundred and thirty years of departure the bare headlands with their ruined houses, the schools emptied one by one, the old people living in lonely places are remnants of the communities that populated every corner of the coastline. West Cork, of course, is hardly unique in Ireland, but its decline is striking; the percentage of loss is greater than practically anywhere else in the devastated country. Both the countryside and the towns continue to lose their people. In Schull recently, when the Bishop of Cork made his annual confirmation visit, it was observed for the first time that there was no need to go early to church to find a seat. There were more than enough places for all.

In the last decade the region has benefited from tourism. Motorists spill over from the Ring of Kerry to experience the remote grandeurs of south-western scenery. After seeing it for the first time, many visitors return to buy houses with views of the sea, finding compensation in the beauty of their surroundings for wet weather and Ireland's expensive economy. Their presence is one of the few signs that the long era of stagnation which resulted in so many people leaving may conceivably be coming to a close.

To view a country from a bicycle is to see it in selective detail which makes no attempt to be comprehensive. I have tried to fill in the broad outline of its history and to describe a wild and remote region which is the far corner of these islands, and, indeed, of Europe. Some of the history is familiar, like the story of the siege of Dunboy and the invasion of Bantry Bay by the French in 1796. I have quoted from the comments of strangers who visited the area, beginning with Sir George Carew. These were not a very attractive lot. They included the eccentric Bishop Pococke whom Mrs Delaney unkindly described as "the dullest man who ever travelled". He sped through on horseback in 1758, noting down details of landscape and society with the detachment he had shown when viewing Constantinople and Acre. Thackeray passed this way and liked little of what he saw; his jaundiced comments on Ireland must have put off tourists for half a century. A more affectionate picture of West Cork is to be obtained from the writings of one of its most remarkable inhabitants, Edith Somerville. In addition to the comments of these and other writers, I have consulted local histories, beginning with Charles Smith's *History of Cork* published in 1750, and including Dr Donovan's *Sketches in Carbery*, 1876, and the modern histories of Jeremiah O'Mahony and Father Holland. More important has been the information that many people whom I met conveyed to me with patience and kindness everywhere I travelled. In particular I am indebted to Paddy O'Keefe in Bantry, Dan O'Brien in Eyeries, Mr William Kingston in Skibbereen and Father Coombes in Courtmacsherry.

My affection for West Cork was initially inspired by my uncle, Becher Somerville-Large, who loved the area all his life. I am grateful to my aunt, Mrs Beatrice Somerville-Large, for lending me his notes.

Finally, I would like to thank my wife, who has given me invaluable help in the preparation of this book.

ONE

Clonakilty to Castlefreke

THIN SHOWERS OF rain were falling over Clonakilty. A butcher's
van filled with carcasses waited patiently while two lorries, one
carrying drink, the other sheep whose wet fleece bulged outward
through wooden slats, struggled to pass through each other in the
narrow main street. The cars parked carelessly along both pavements
threatened to clog Clon's main artery completely. They looked an-
achronistic, lined up bumper to bumper in front of solid rows of
nineteenth-century houses and shops, many of which still retained old
arched windows and a faded air of withdrawal behind lace curtains.
Signs anticipated the summer: BED AND BREAKFAST, REFRESHMENTS AND
BOARDERS (BACON, EGG, COLD MEATS). Some windows displayed
portraits of the Pope, or Pope John, hands pressed together in blessing;
others presented coloured profiles of the Kennedy brothers, garlanded
in black crêpe or touched with a dash of surrounding light in the
Italianate style in which saints are represented.

The gents' hairdresser contained hard-backed shaving chairs and a
long gilt mirror which could reflect a whole row of clients. Numerous
little pubs that also acted as general stores continued their struggle for
existence, although they did a slack business since the closing of the
monthly fairs. Beside the tins of beans were stacked bottles of whiskey
as if drought were expected. A few stores had changed to self-service,
cramming food on high shelves between narrow passageways. They
were like the main street in miniature; customers had difficulty in
passing, and wire baskets clashed against each other with a noise of
jousting knights. In summer, all over West Cork tourists would
lament the high prices of these little shops as they watched the faint

ink of the cash registers writing up stupendous bills. Too many small
supermarkets, inadequately converted, were choked with untidy
expense. Two and sixpence written in purple on the heels of dying
cauliflowers. Sugar brushed over the floor, trodden with crunching
footsteps. Soups, Royco, Maggi, Erin, mushroom, tomato, kidney,
slopped off their stands and mingled with burst packets of Oxo cubes
and matches.

The neo-Gothic church of the Immaculate Conception is as big as an
Italian cathedral. Beside the door stands a collection box for the Peru
Mission, which has a considerable significance for West Cork because
it is Bishop Lucey's special preoccupation. Within, the line of red
marble columns and the varnished pinewood pews leading to the high
altar were paid for by the children of the parish.

There are few children belonging to Clonakilty's other parish,
represented by the thin spire visible over the town and the grey mud
flats where the Protestant church of Kilgariffe stands moribund, shut
and locked for most of the week. The Presbyterian chapel in the town
centre stopped functioning in 1924 when the congregation ceased to
exist, and the building was converted into a post office. Although
draughty in winter, it is considered admirably suitable for its present
purpose. Envelopes are stamped and parcels sorted out where choirs
sang. Not far away the Masonic Hall has become the new Town Hall.

The decrease and disappearance of the Protestant population mark the
final failure for Richard Boyle, the first Earl of Cork, who founded
Clonakilty in 1605 and settled it with a hundred English families. It
was modelled on Bandon, and was to be a Protestant town from which
Catholics were to be excluded. It formed a small part of the territory that
Boyle had acquired in Ireland since he first arrived, a poor adventurer
carrying with him twenty pounds, a diamond ring, a gold bracelet
given to him by his mother, a taffeta doublet, black velvet breeches, a
new suit, some underwear and a dagger. These were the assets which
he converted into most of Munster. Later, this self-made politician
and businessman, who has been described as Ireland's first capitalist,
set about transforming his forests and bogs. Fields were fenced, trees
cut down, towns built and industries developed, such as the fishing
which he encouraged all round the south coast, and the iron-mines in
the Blackwater valley.

Clonakilty was part of the overall plan for his widespread possessions.

The charter he obtained for it in 1605 was generous, and the town not only had the right to appoint twenty-four burgesses and a "sovereign" or mayor, but to send two members to Parliament at Westminster, a privilege it retained until the Act of Union. But Boyle never had the same affection for Clonakilty that he felt for his beloved Bandon. "My town of Bandon-Bridge is more in compass than Londonderry. My walls are stronger and thicker and higher than theirs . . ." Clonakilty had no walls. As a result it was quite indefensible during times of rebellion. In 1641 its citizens had to join the rural fugitives scattered all over West Cork in seeking shelter behind Bandon's elaborate defences. If Boyle had lavished the same care on Clonakilty that he had on Bandon, his losses in that year might not have been so extensive.

The town had recovered from this setback, when forty years later during the Williamite wars it had to be evacuated once again. Among the refugees was William Bird, who escaped carrying the records and town charter, a second one, granted by James II at a time when his fortunes were in the ascendant. Citizens loyal to his cause swore to "well and truly serve the King's most excellent majesty, his heirs and successors and the place and office of the sovereign of the borough of Clonakilty".

In 1798 there was again tension in the town. At the Battle of the Big Cross which took place three miles away, Teig O'Donovan and his followers tried to start a rebellion in West Cork on the pattern of the fighting which was taking place in Wexford. The engagement is commemorated by a monument at the cross-roads itself and by the centenary statue of the Pikeman in Clonakilty's main square.

> "Then here's to their memory
> May it be for us a guiding light
> To cheer our strife and liberty
> And teach us to unite.
> Erected by the Clonakilty Association, June, 1898."

Some people still talk about Clonakilty, God Help Us. The town is supposed to have acquired this mournful suffix during the famine, when it served as a focus for the starving. From all round the countryside ragged figures gathered here in the hope of relief or a respite before they fled on to Cork where the coffin ships waited. The workhouse which stands above the Cork road at the eastern entrance to the town was, in fact, built after 1847, but its gaunt all-purpose design is a reminder of those times, even though the typical workhouse layout—men's ward —laundry—wash-house—idiots' ward—has been transformed. Now it serves as the largest old people's home in West Cork. All day long the groups of old men who live there venture outside on to the road to view the passing cars or to pause in front of the grotto with its Virgin. Behind the modern buildings, the original workhouse has become a hospital. The nuns move among smells of polish and newly cleaned brass and disinfectant. Central heating soothes away the damp, and amid the pale opulence of blue tiled floors and litmus-coloured walls, rises the subdued chatter of old people lying in bed.

During the revolution of fifty years ago both town charters disappeared. Street names changed; Sovereign Street became Pearse Street, George Street Connolly Street, and so on. The great Earl's memory has been obliterated, and Boyle Square is renamed Astna after a saint. Symbolically, the Wheel of Fortune, a large metal pump erected before the famine and reputed never to go dry, still stands in its little square and is in constant use.

More personal memories of the past have also gone. The cry of the watchman recorded by Dorothea Townshend in 1895 has been superseded by the horn of the car.

> "Two of the Clock,
> A fine morning,
> Wind's in my back,
> All's well!"

Deasy's went thirty years ago. Just behind the Georgian houses of Emmet Square beyond the John F. Kennedy Park stands the old brewery of Deasy and Co. which once produced the famous Amber Ale and Wrestler Stout. "Rassler", which sold in half-gallon stone jars all over West Cork, was renowned for its potency. Bevelled mirrors advertising its excellence are still found in pubs round about, with information about past triumphs written across their surfaces. "Deasy and Co. were awarded the gold medal at Chicago World Fair, 1893, in open competition against all the breweries of the world. For Brilliancy: $15\frac{1}{2}$%. Flavour: 20%. Chemical Analysis: 45%."

The Wheel of Fortune, Clonakilty

On the road near Clonakilty

On the road to Galley Head

After the winning brew ceased to be produced in 1940, the brewery stood vacant for many years. But today the old buildings have been converted to broiler production and half a million frozen birds are sold annually. The handling of these broilers provides a certain amount of employment. Mr O'Regan, who converted Deasy's to the production of plucked chicken corpses, considers that the town is reviving after many years of depression and is becoming a centre for small industries. The old railway station has become a handweaving factory called Carbery Tweeds, employing over fifty people and exporting its products all over the world. Clonakilty has also become a centre for the horse caravans that tour West Cork. In appearance these are like tinker caravans, so that when you pass one you expect to see a brood of red-headed children. Instead it will be filled with London secretaries or Dutch hippies or bespectacled Malay students. The vehicles have rubber wheels and fresh paint and are fitted with four neat bunks beside a minute stove. So far as it is possible to cram four people into a tiny living space, they are moderately comfortable. Animal-lovers complain about the treatment of the horses, saying that they are inexpertly driven and that they tend to get parked like cars for long periods in hot sun by ignorant holiday-makers. But on wet days I would be sorrier for the drivers patiently dealing with the damp and obstinate beasts, holding their bridles as they plod through rain and traffic on a holiday for which they have paid twenty-five pounds a week.

I cycled to Shannonvale and Ballinascarthy, where a monument at the Big Cross recalls the events of 'ninety-eight. The road climbed above the grey rooftops of the town, and looking back I could see the estuary and the line of the sea. The hills were smooth and green, for Clonakilty sits in the centre of a rich farming area. The neat prosperity of the landscape fell into an ideal view with subdued colours, like an old print. A Prospect of Clonakilty was formed by the town beneath, the sea in the distance, and little farms all around linked by twisting roads. Overhead the clouds drifted past, evenly spaced in proportion to the composition.

I passed the stone circle which Dr Donovan, writing a century ago, called a "Druidical Temple". Five boulders surrounding a single stone rose up in a field, monumental and mysterious, and at the same time as casual a part of the landscape as a stone wall.

B

A few fields along were the ruins of an ancient church built beside a holy well and a pillar stone with some Ogham writing scratched on its edge. Beyond, in a dip of the hills, lay Shannonvale. The presence of two villages named Innishannon and Shannonvale in Cork, so far from the great river, has puzzled many strangers. They were both weaving towns established by the Earl of Shannon, a descendant of the great Earl of Cork. In 1780 Lord Shannon acquired twenty-five acres of land north of Clonakilty where a Public Bleaching Green was laid out at Shannonvale to improve the conditions for bleaching the coarse linen and yarn woven and spun around the countryside.

Clonakilty, like Youghal and Bandon, had been a staple town until the mid-eighteenth century when the wool trade collapsed after England virtually prohibited the import of Irish wool in order to protect her own wool producers. Then linen assumed increasing importance. Its manufacture had long been a cottage industry in Ireland; the women were skilful in dressing flax hemp and making linen cloth, as the traveller, Vincent Gooking, observed in 1663. In the late eighteenth and early nineteenth century the growing of flax and spinning of linen prospered. Linen spun in West Cork was of a coarse quality only considered suitable for home consumption or for export to the West Indies where it was made into clothes for slaves. By 1839 there were more than four hundred linen looms around Clonakilty which sent their produce up to Belfast. By then Belfast had replaced Dublin as a distributing centre for linen, and the great Linen Hall in Dublin had become little more than a ruin. "That huge useless lonely decayed place," Thackeray wrote, "in the vast solitude of which stands the simpering statue of George IV pointing to some bales of shirting over which he is supposed to extend his august protection."

Already in 1842, the time of Thackeray's visit, the linen trade was beginning to fail, killed by the manufacture of cheap cotton. "Formerly everybody wore linen," David Lonmore observed, "and now everybody wears cotton." The farmers who grew the flax and the weavers were badly distressed. In West Cork flax ceased to be grown altogether until the First World War when it reappeared as an emergency crop. The Second World War saw a similar revival of flax-growing and a small linen manufactory continued up until about 1950. For a while it appeared to be flourishing, but the lack of any price support and the introduction of synthetic fibres killed it. Today the linen trade has left few traces—an occasional washing pool or abandoned scutching mill, or the quiet decay of Shannonvale.

Shannonvale is bridge, mill, garage and line of rustic cottages running up the hill. The garage is prosaic, but the cottages built for the weavers by the improving landlord have a well-intentioned prettiness and charm. The valley, tucked away from main roads, envelops the village, dominated by its great mill. This mill was never actually associated with linen manufacture, which remained a cottage industry, but was built in 1788 as a flour mill, using the Arigadeen river for its power. The inhabitants of surrounding towns who used to buy their grain direct from farmers suddenly found that all the harvest was sent to Shannonvale to be milled. For this reason it was extremely unpopular for a time; and in 1791 a mob from Bandon attacked it.

A later proprietor was James Sadleir who, in addition to grinding flour, used his premises for weaving cotton. He was the father of George Foster Sadleir, reputed to be the first European to cross the Arabian desert on foot.

In an old mill you can follow the slow changes as its machinery progresses over the centuries. The waterwheel gives place to a turbine. You can see where the rails were laid over which a horse-drawn vehicle carried the flour to the nearest railway connection. Shannonvale was one of the last mills in Ireland to use horse-drawn wagons in this way. Perhaps this was the reason for its eventual failure. Today it is full of chickens. All over the country chickens are vanishing inside. It is becoming rare to see them wandering around a farmyard. Busy farmer's wives do not bother to rear them when they can buy their eggs in moulded cardboard boxes or cook a stiffened broiler without having to pluck it.

Stretching along the river was a meadow which the first Earl of Shannon had designated as a bleaching green, and it is still known as the Bleach. Behind it an austere golden-coloured Georgian house rose out of the trees. Snowdrops covered the grass in front and the stems of daffodils were forming buds in the mild January sun. Within lived Mrs Bennett, an elderly Protestant lady whose family had owned the mill for a spell of ninety years until the Cork Milling Company bought it in 1935 to conduct it to its final staggered demise.

I wheeled the bike away up the road past the line of rustic cottages, outside one of which I met an itinerant chimney sweep carrying a

bundle of brushes under his arm. For a few minutes we passed the
time of day. He travelled round the countryside from house to house,
but with the electric, people used chimneys less and he was finding it
harder to get work.

A little further east from Shannonvale was the cross-roads of
Ballinascarthy where the battle was commemorated by an elaborate
monument in multi-coloured brick, too fussy for the savagery it
recorded. As a memorial it compared unfavourably with the simplicity
of the stone plaque erected at the birthplace of Michael Collins five
miles away. The inscription in Irish and English read that "on the 19th
day of June, 1798, the principal engagement in the south took place in
this area. Over a hundred United Irishmen lost their lives in the fighting. They rose in dark and evil days to right their native land." It was
a brave desperate fight, less of a battle than a massacre.

In 1798, when the prospect of rebellion was imminent throughout
Ireland, West Cork was heavily settled with military. Not only was the
local yeomanry called out, but militia were assembled from all over
Ireland and from England. Among these regiments the Westmeath
Militia had a large contingent quartered in Clonakilty and a smaller
one in Skibbereen. The lower ranks of the former were disaffected,
and a number of troops were planning to join the local United Irishmen in a general uprising supporting the rebels in Wexford. The plot
was discovered, and the regiment's commanding officer, Sir Hugh
O'Reilly, was ordered to march his men eastward to Bandon out of
harm's way. This news, received late in the evening of June 18th,
spread through the surrounding countryside, and before daybreak on
June 19th a huge untrained force of local men had converged on
Ballinascarthy to await the arrival of the Westmeath who would pass
that way.

The rebels expected only a token resistance from the militia. But the
Westmeath, obedient to discipline, did not join with them. They had,
in addition to their muskets, two six-pounders which they brought to
bear on the scattered ambushers assembled along the heights above the
road. The United Irishmen fought bravely with their pikes, but had
little chance, particularly when a detachment of the Caithness Legion,
on their way to Clonakilty to relieve the Westmeath, marched
straight into the battle. The Irishmen "retired without precipitation
and reformed again and again. Some lost their lives in recovering the

dead bodies of their comrades." But the body of their leader, Teig
O'Donovan, who, according to one account, had started the engagement by seizing the reins of Colonel O'Reilly's horse, was taken by the
local yeomanry down to Clonakilty and left for some days outside the
market house. Later it was dragged down to the shore and thrown into
the tide at a place called the Crab Hole.

The skirmish was a fiasco for the cause of the United Irishmen and a
stroke of fortune for the government, which could have been presented
with an uprising on the Wexford scale. If the Westmeath with their
muskets and six-pounders had joined the assembly at Ballinascarthy,
the combined army would have been stronger and better equipped
than that of Father Murphy which fought on Vinegar Hill two days
later.

From Ballinascarthy I rode down to the town and then south to
where two roads ran along the side of the estuary. Across the mud flats
and the narrow bottle opening of the estuary was straddled Inchdoney,
still known as an island, although the mud had silted up the gap
between it and the mainland over which a causeway had been built.
It was another of Clonakilty's misfortunes that it could never have a
harbour. Smith noted in his history of Cork that "the river affords the
town more pleasure than profit. The mouth of the river, being choked
with sand, prevents vessels coming up into the town."

At low tide the flats were alive with birds, sandpipers, oyster catchers,
a heron and a pair of swans having a feast on an overspill of garbage.
Behind them rose the island of Inchdoney, a sleek round shape covered
with squares of woods and fields that ended on the south side with the
Virgin Mary's Rock overlooking the sea. Once some sailors saw a vision
of the Virgin kneeling there at prayer. They scoffed at the sight, and
Our Lady caused their ship to founder. In the words of Jeremiah
Callahan, Clonakilty's poet and recluse:

"Loud from all the guilty crew one shriek rose wild and high
  But the angry surge swept over them and hushed their gurgling cry."

The uncharacteristically vindictive behaviour of the Virgin was
possibly a legend relating to the goddess Cleena; westward beyond
Colghna Head is Carraig Chliodhna, Cleena's rock, which lies off shore
and is said to be haunted by the goddess. Below Rosscarbery the tides

rushing into sea caves produce a sound which is said to be caused by Tonn Chliodhna (Cleena's Wave), one of the three magic waves of Irish mythology. At Inchdoney it is difficult to see where Mary assumed her vengeful role among the lines of bungalows and the hotel that overlooks the Bank. But holy shells can still be found on the sand at the east side. Among the piles of seaweed and the skeletons of crabs lie the fragile tests of the cake urchin, *echinocardium cordatum*.

"They are found in the sand there in front of the Bank," a pious man in Clonakilty had told me, "and nowhere else. They are full of holy marks. Look to one side and you will see Our Lady set in a star. A little figure like those carried in the front of cars." With only a small burst of imagination one can follow his imagery set in the stencilled starfish outline. "And on the other side of the shell, for extra measure, where it bulges, you will see an outline of the Sacred Heart. Below that there is a hole similar to the spearmark that entered Our Saviour's body."

Past the Bank is the place where Lord Forbes and his men slew six hundred Irishmen in 1642, driving them into the sea at high tide, so that the waves were dyed red with blood. Further on, a small stone building on Mr Hayes' farm is believed to have been used as a mortuary chapel for some Spanish sailors whose bodies were washed up here after the battle of Kinsale. People do not like to pass it at night.

In the nineteenth century this melancholy place was owned by a family who were known as the Hungerfords of the Island to differentiate them from other Hungerfords in West Cork. They lived in the manse surrounded by high stone walls, situated above an overgrown graveyard; the property is now turned into a convent and disinfected with clerical grey paint. Here they acquired a reputation for being unpopular landlords. Miss Mary Sandes Hungerford is still remembered for her ruthlessness towards her tenants. Within her gloomy house she sat and devised a new and instantaneous method of lacing boots which was patented and in due course appeared in a Victorian journal of inventions. At the same time she showed firmness in collecting her rents. There were at one time sixteen families living among the five hundred acres that comprised the island, but by 1886 only a few tenants remained. One of these was Pat McCarthy, who held thirty-one acres of her land for which he paid £54. When he came into arrears she declared that she had as much right to her rent as Pat McCarthy had to his coat. It was a gentler comment, perhaps, than that of her neighbour, Mr Bennett, who in the same year, at the height of the land war, was declaring that if there were seven years of famine and the people were dying in the ditches, he would not grant one penny reduction in rent: "Devil a penny; devil a penny!" However, her convictions were similar and Pat McCarthy's stock was seized and taken to the town pound. Later, with the assistance of the parish priest the cattle were redeemed and the landlady was paid off. When the priest, Fr. Lacey, went to the pound and released the animals, the whole town turned out to form a procession behind them; they were decorated with rosettes and green ribbons and escorted in triumph back to the Island.

West of Inchdoney, stretching out into the sea, is the long arm of Galley Head with the upright finger of the lighthouse at its end. It is a strange little peninsula, more like Connemara than Cork, with its lines of stone walls and isolated stone cottages sheltering under hedges of New Zealand flax and fuchsia. Near the lighthouse lie the ruins of a coastguard station burnt in 1920. Their present owner told me how, after news that the buildings had been wanted by the British to accommodate Black and Tans, the coastguards had been amiably invited out to a pub for a drink while their station was burnt down.

At the Red Strand three crude new chalets named Dolphin, Mermaid and Neptune shattered the impact of the wild scenery. At the end of the Head overlooking Dirke Bay are the ruins of Dundeady Castle, which consists of a piece of wall and keep surrounding a little farmhouse. Dundeady is a Norman stronghold, built in 1275 by Nicholas de Barry. Practically nothing is known about it for the following four hundred years until it passed, along with its extensive lands, from the de Barry family into the possession of the new settlers. Sir Phillip Percivale purchased it in 1649; writing to Captain John Hodder he wondered what he could do with his new acquisition, which still had some de Barrys living inside it. "Downedeady is a pretty strong place, and I would have you advise me how to make use of it. . . ." Hodder made suitable arrangements, and later wrote that "Colonel Searle had set Percvalle's lands to some Englishmen at Bandon for a small rent and will be accountable for it. He intends to turn John Barry out of the castle and put English into it. The castle, by report, is an old ruined thing. . . ."

I cycled to the far end of the point, to Galley Head lighthouse, built with the same squat solidity as Dundeady. Inside, the keepers kept everything spick and span in an atmosphere of nineteenth-century ingenuity involving a lot of brass instruments and white paint. There was a suggestion of Jules Verne about the system of pressurized paraffin for the light which had been in use since 1904. Each evening after the blowlamp was lit, the weights were wound up like the works of an enormous grandfather clock. But this piece of machinery, so lovingly tended by generations of keepers, was at last considered obsolete, and later in the year would be superseded. The light would go fully automatic. I climbed the spiral staircase with its brass rails to see where it beamed out from the tower, sweeping eastward towards Kinsale, westward to the Fastnet and fifty miles out to sea.

I spent the night in a farmhouse. The next day snow came. Its appearance was quite sudden. The day before had seemed like spring with the movement of crows against the fields. The song of thrushes rose above the deep throb of a tractor cutting its furrow in the smooth green face of the soil. Now the sky had become a steel grey shot through with bars of light and the ploughed fields were striped black and white. The dusting of snow turned to thick drifts along the lanes, where it gathered at the roots of the fuchsia hedges which in winter resembled bundles of dry sticks. Boggy pools were frozen and icicles hung from rocks. Galley Head looked like a Christmas cake with the light-house as a candle stuck on the end. The wind roared among the trees and crackled through the clumps of New Zealand flax and the plastic coverings of the open hayricks.

A trap came bowling along the hill with two wild unshaven tinkers holding on to their hats. Behind them were snow-covered mountains, ahead the extraordinary ruins of Castlefreke, once the seat of the Earls of Carbery. This assembly of walls and towers was erected about a hundred years ago in the Gothic style. Many English architects, such as John Nash, Edward James Goodwin and Thomas Hopper, came over to Ireland at this time to practise building Gothic buildings in suitable surroundings. Ireland had mountains, lakes and cliffs over the sea; but somehow the castles already here with their ruined utilitarian dis-comfort were insufficient for the Romantic imagination. Dundeady is far less picturesque than the crenellated walls of Castlefreke, designed by the Cork architect, Sir Richard Morrison, a pupil of Gandon. Morrison built the pro-Cathedral in Dublin and built or remodelled many country houses. In his exteriors he imitated medieval castles and abbeys or Tudor mansions, or combined the two. His interiors were full of ornamental carving, tracery, windows filled with stained glass, carved beams and gilt pendants on the ceilings. Castlefreke was quite typical of his style.

The ruin seems as large as Camelot and looks as if it had suffered all the troubles of Ireland. But it came to decay in a more prosaic fashion than is usual for such buildings. In fact it was destroyed twice. The first time was in 1910 when it was burnt down. I encountered Patrick Santry, who worked on the estate as a boy of fifteen, and could remember the morning in March when he noticed smoke pouring out of the windows. A plank over one of the chimneys had taken fire. He had helped the servants to rescue some of the effects. Lord Carbery was away at the time, but as soon as he was informed of the blaze he hurried back to see the damage. A pioneer motorist living in days of privilege, he was able to ring up the police in Bandon and Clonakilty to order the roads cleared so that his car could bowl along unimpeded at thirty miles an hour. Subsequently the house was rebuilt with insurance money, said to amount to over two hundred thousand pounds. There were a few changes: wooden floors, for example, were replaced by pressed concrete, and electric lights were installed.

The earls of Carbery, whose family name was Freke, belonged to a second creation, the Vaughan family, ennobled by Charles II, having become extinct. The Frekes were among the biggest landowners in Cork, which was a county of big landowners. A hundred years ago, when fifty men owned one third of Cork's total acreage between them, the Frekes' share was 13,700 acres. The Land Acts reduced their possessions, but left quite enough for the last earls to live in flamboyant style. Mr Santry remembered his former employers with affection. "They weren't the worst of all, but nearly the best." James McCarthy, once a gardener on the estate, recalled nostalgically the party given to all the tenants around Rosscarbery at the coming-of-age of the last earl. Thompson's of Cork supplied a vast quantity of buns which were eaten to the accompaniment of a pipe band playing at the long table. For refreshment a horseload of drink was brought in from Clonakilty, most of it "Rassler" beer.

This last Lord Carbery was mad on shooting, married to three different wives, and one of the first Irishmen to fly his own plane. He did the loop at Clonakilty and Bandon shows. The *Skibbereen Eagle* of July 18th, 1914, wrote in appreciation of his generosity in agreeing to one such exhibition:

> "His Lordship has modified his demand to one of £40 which is reasonable, considering the enormous amount of expense attendant to aviation. The people of the district . . . will now have an opportunity of witnessing the daring and youthful aviator performing in the air feats which it would be impossible to describe, and must be seen to be believed."

Shortly after his majority, at a time when landowners were in an increasingly uneasy position, Lord Carbery decided to abandon his mansion, renounce his title and be known as plain Mr Carbery. He emigrated to Kenya and joined that hard-living East African society whose members were able to enjoy themselves well into the Second World War. On his old estate the oak woods were destroyed and all that remained was a small area claimed by the Land Commission. From that time on, the castle had a sort of half-life. In the Second World War the army took it over, but at other times it was used for social events in the area. Dances were held in the ballroom on the fine teak floor and parties assembled in the hall, where, between the great mahogany-panelled doors and stained-glass windows, lion skins were splayed on the walls.

During the depression of the fifties the roof was pulled off for the lead and timber. A few years afterwards the tourist boom began. If Castlefreke had survived, its situation overlooking the sea and its abundant accommodation would have made it the perfect hotel. But perhaps that would have been too prosaic a destiny for a building of such pretensions, and it is better suited as a vast and noble ruin.

All around stood the remains of a planted wood, palms, monkey puzzles and oaks with tangled branches furred in lichen. Behind were lines of firs where the foresty had taken over the old park. The walled garden, which once required a dozen men to maintain it, was full of weeds growing out of the snow. South of the wood the church of Rathbarry with its fine turreted tower stood roofless and cloaked with ivy. Built in 1832, it was abandoned a century later when its congregation ceased to exist. Trees had grown up in the centre of the aisle. The ivy surrounding the Gothic windows and climbing the walls had not yet obliterated the mosaic at the east end, whose motto in curly Art

Nouveau lettering stood out against the dark green: "Till He Come".

Rathbarry Castle, beside the church, crumbles away three centuries after Captain Arthur Freke, ancestor of the barons of Carbery, withstood a siege of "rebels, rogues and Papists". Rathbarry, which had been built in the fifteenth century by Randal Oge Barry, was first rented and then bought by Captain Freke from Lord Barrymore, the Earl of Cork's son-in-law. In the summer of 1642 the Irish besieged the Captain and his family for several months, during which it seemed that they might take the castle at any time. Even the arrival in July of Lord Forbes, who had slaughtered his way through Clonakilty, was only a temporary check on the rebels. Forbes had to leave the Freke family to its fate while he hastened to fight against a renewed Irish attack on the English garrison at Rosscarbery. Rathbarry was not relieved until October 7th, when a force arrived under the command of Sir Charles Vavasour. Captain Freke's journal, which is preserved in the British Museum, describes the occasion:

"Ye next day being Sunday, ye army approached the castle and divers doubted it was ye Irish army, yet at ye sound of trumpets we threw down the walled gate, when we discovered of friends. Ye appeared to us like ye angels of God whose mercy is most felt and magnified in extreamist misery."

All the action, all the fighting and emotion belong to the past. Today it seems that nothing much can ever happen again on these lonely headlands with their ruins. Setting a stamp on the surrounding desolation, the large Celtic cross to the memory of Algernon William George, ninth Lord Carbery, stands on a hill looking out to sea. Someone has constructed a large concrete water tank just beside it. According to local rumour the ashes of this lord were scattered by thieves who believed that they were contained in a golden box.

TWO

Rosscarbery to Drombeg Circle

IN THE HOTEL in Rosscarbery I read the *Southern Star*. "Pony Cart in Collision at Drimoleague" . . . "Middleton is experiencing a severe wave of rowdyism and blackguardism. It is like Chicago on a Saturday night" . . . "Fat Sows, Fat Sows, Fat Sows—I will attend at the weigh-bridge, Bantry, to buy Fat Sows" . . . "The price of cock turkeys has dropped eightpence a pound. . . ." But most news was given over to the weather, so unusual in a soft south-western climate. COUNTRY IN GRIP OF SNOW AND ICE ran the headlines on the front page.

A thin film of heat wavered above the storage heater and the smell of frying percolated from the kitchen. Because of the cold the pipes had frozen for several hours; then a trickle of water, followed by a gush of something like soup, came bursting out of the tap. At ten o'clock the curtains round the bar and lounge were still tightly drawn. I sat among piles of unwashed plates and empty bottles, surrounded by funereal urns of artificial flowers, facing a long panoramic cut-out of white mountains in Switzerland which did nothing to dispel the chill and gloom. In the plastic box for donations for the handicapped were a few pennies and numerous pieces of paper and cigarette ends.

Outside snow had choked the main square. It was Sunday, and except for the place where newspapers were sold the shops were shut . . . Kelly, the hairdresser, Fitzpatrick's Lounge Bar, the undertaker, cluttered with plastic wreaths, Patrick Hayes, Harness Maker. Yesterday I had watched Mr Hayes patiently stuffing a horse collar with coconut fibre; when he began work forty years ago, he told me, horsehair was used. Down the street more shops with Victorian fronts and interiors . . . Callaghan, Walshe, Draper; Kingston, Chemist;

and the Rossa Bar, named after Rosscarbery's most famous son. His birthplace was a little grey house further down with a plaque on the wall: "O'Donovan Rossa, Fenian and Patriot. That brave and splendid Gael, unconquered and unconquerable."

Light fell across the bay in shafts that threw the causeway into focus. Beyond, the sea was deceptively smooth, its corrugations like grooves of silver-grey silk. In the lanes streams of people were coming towards the town to church. Women and children walked the treadways in groups, men went singly. Some were on tractors that splattered the snow. Gobbets hung on the hedges, while the rest lay feet thick along the sides.

"Good luck!"

"'Tis wicked!"

The church for which they were making was huge, like most churches in country towns, but it failed to reflect sufficiently the splendid ecclesiastical tradition of Ross which had brought it fame over the centuries. St. Fachtna, a disciple of St Finbarr of Cork, founded a monastery here in A.D. 570 which soon became famous as a place of pilgrimage and as a school which attracted students from all over Europe. With Glendalough, Clonmacnoise and the other great monastic foundations of the early Christian period, the monastery at Ross shared in Ireland's supreme period of civilization until its destruction by the Danes in A.D. 979. Later in the twelfth century the Benedictine priory of St Mary was founded here by Nehemias Scotus, formerly a monk of St James in Wurzburg in Germany. This priory, besides carrying out its traditional function as a hostel for pilgrims and wayfarers, supplied recruits to the order of Irish Benedictines which flourished in Germany, particularly at Wurzburg. St Mary, situated at a focal point for pilgrimage, became rich; before its dissolution in the closing years of the fifteenth century, the priory contained a church, a buttery, a bakery and kitchen, in addition to surrounding farmhouses.

In 1653 Cromwell granted "Abbey Ross in West Carbery" to an adventurer, Captain Robert Gooking, who proceeded to fortify the buildings as an outpost of English power in the south-west. Over three hundred members of various settler families lived within musket-shot of this fort. Already, in an effort to dim the old glories of Ross, the Protestants had founded their own cathedral in 1612. Transformed at a later date, it is an undistinguished eighteenth-century building, full of relics of the ascendancy.

When I visited it the central heating was working. For anyone who has suffered through a chilled Morning Service in a country church, these wafts of warm air on a February morning were pleasantly unexpected. In the entrance nave beneath a large royal coat of arms stood a life-sized marble statue of James Evans Freke, sixth Baron Carbery, in Elizabethan fancy dress. It had formerly stood in the hall of Castlefreke which he had built, and had been moved here after the sale of the estate. The Baron, who died in 1845, founded schools in various parts of his property and clothed the surrounding hills with trees. A typical improving landlord, whose rents, in the days just before the famine, amounted to £20,000 a year.

Looking disapprovingly across at Lord Carbery's marble doublet and hose was a bust of St Fachtna stuck high on the opposite wall. Local tradition states that a sufferer from toothache can be cured by kissing this head, but to reach it he would need a ladder.

In the burial vaults below the building Mrs Goodman was laid to rest two hundred years ago. On the evening after the funeral her butler, remembering the valuable ring she was wearing, went down to steal it. In the darkness he wrenched it off her finger, and Mrs Goodman awoke and sat up. She went home, lived for many years afterwards and even bore a son.

In the small vestry were kept various objects pertaining to the diocese. There was a case filled with the seals of previous Deans, some fine eighteenth-century chalices, and pictures and prints of the Bishops of Ross. The Irish Bishops began with Neachlain in 1085 and continued for five hundred years until 1582, when William Lyons made his appearance and took over the inheritance of St Peter. There is a tradition that this first Protestant Bishop of Cork and Ross was appointed by Queen Elizabeth in recognition of his success as a naval captain fighting Spanish ships. On the death of his royal patron his valedictory sermon included these words: "Let those who feel the loss deplore with me on this melancholy occasion. But if there be any who hear me who have wished secretly for the event (as perhaps there may), they have now got their wish, and the Devil do them good with it!" After a long ministration which covered many of the turbulent years of the counter-reformation, William Lyons died in 1619. His portrait can be seen in the Bishop's Palace in Cork, a crafty Renaissance face with a long beard falling over his chest.

Today the Protestant Bishop of Cork has jurisdiction over Cloyne as well as Ross, for the three dioceses have been united since 1617. In the Catholic Church Ross continued to be a separate diocese until very recently. Its disappearance is still a matter of deep-felt regret for people round about. "It was gobbled up by Cork!"

An Act of Consistory dated 1517 states that "the town of Ross is situated in a fertile plain on the sea coast, rich in corn, and is surrounded by a wall with two gates and contains about two hundred houses". The Cathedral has a drawing of Ross made for Lord Riversdale in 1788 when such defences were gone and the town sprawled above the estuary much as it does today. There have been a few changes: the departure of the eel fishery and flour mills, the addition of the causeway built in 1863, and the Catholic church and convent, but Ross is much the same, and Lord Riversdale would have little difficulty in finding his way about.

The biggest changes are out of sight. West Cork has very few long sandy beaches, and one of the best is within a mile of the town. Here the results of the tourist boom are evident. Along the sands rows of chalets have sprung up, new hotels, seaside villas, converted railway carriages, bundled together and toppling over each other to be as near as possible to the sea and the tar-strewn sand. The absence of planning, the sense of rivalry among the disporportionate buildings and the surrounding snowy silence suggested an abandoned gold-rush town in the Klondike.

In 1970 a bulldozer revealed a series of prehistoric chambers beneath a tourist caravan site.

Rosscarbery has always been a place of pilgrimage. Even before the arrival of St Fachtna, the site was known as *Ros Ailithir*, the Pilgrim's Promontory, after a pilgrim named Colman. Today two pilgrimages are held here annually. In June people go to the graveyard on the site of the old priory where stands the tomb of the Reverend John Power, a nineteenth-century priest who performed miraculous cures. The corners of his sarcophagus are worn to hollows by hands rubbing the edges. On August 15th, St Fachtna's Day, groups of pilgrims walk two miles east out of the town to visit the saint's cell and the holy well beside it. (But their numbers grow less as enthusiasm declines for the traditional pilgrimage and for the "pattern", the minor pilgrimage where the devout tour a group of holy places in one locality. Increasingly the shrines are left to the old people to visit.) The tiny cell is the place where St Fachtna was reading his breviary and forgot to take it home. Rain came on during the night and the little oratory sprang up over the precious book to save it. Smith mentions that the building was repaired around 1700 "by a person who, in a fit of sickness, vowed if he recovered to build a church; and the old foundation of this oratory, being but twelve foot long and eight broad, he fixed on this spot to fulfill his vow".

In the surrounding area there were many signs of a flourishing communal life long before St Fachtna settled here. Two ring forts overlooked the harbour; further on stood a dolmen, and across the steep valley a stone circle topped the far hill. These ancient remains had withstood the passing of time better than the relics of the saint. The graveyard where the oratory stood was hidden in dead bracken, and the well had almost disappeared under the snow—even with the help of a farmer who lived beside it, I could not find it. He told me that someone must know where it was; they opened it up every year on the eve of the saint's day, and anyone who saw a live fish swimming in it would be cured of his illness.

West of Rosscarbery beside the main Skibbereen road are the ruins of Derry House, the early home of Charlotte Payne Townsend, wife to George Bernard Shaw. Her father, Horace Townsend, a member of a prominent West Cork family, was reputed to have made a fortune out of the stock exchange. He married an English woman who disliked Ireland and West Cork in particular, and worried about her social position. Charlotte had a lonely upbringing at Derry. In a letter to T. E. Lawrence she wrote: "I had a perfectly hellish childhood and youth after I had got old enough to take things in at all." As an early suffragette in London she met Sidney and Beatrice Webb, and through them was introduced to the Fabian Society and G.B.S. Mrs Webb's first impressions of her had been unflattering . . . "Charlotte Payne Townsend is a wealthy unmarried woman of about my own age. Bred up in a second-rate fashionable society without any education or habit of work, she found herself at about thirty-three years of age alone in the world without ties, without any definite creed and with a large income."

Castlefreke

Drombeg Circle in summer

Glandore

Charlotte and G.B.S. were married on June 1st, 1898, at the age of forty-one and forty-two respectively. In 1905 they paid a visit to West Cork, an occasion which caused much anxiety to Charlotte's relatives and friends there. They feared her husband's socialist opinions and the trouble that his vegetarian meals would cause their servants. During his stay Shaw was working on *Captain Brassbound's Conversion.* A cousin of mine went to Derry House to meet him; she remembered him wearing his famous knickerbockers and spending all the afternoon playing with the children.

Derry was built by Horatio Townsend, Charlotte's grandfather, the author of a *Statistical Survey of the County of Cork*, published in 1810. In his book he described the demesne as "lying on an agreeable variety of hill and dale, and enjoying the advantages of a sea view". After he had improved it, he hoped that it would possess "no inconsiderable share of rural beauty". It was well planted, and the surrounding wood had reached maturity when the house was burned down during the Troubles. A few years ago the farmer who bought the estate knocked down the shell. There were fifteen chimneys, and seven hundred tons of debris had to be removed. The trees were cut down, and after much work with a bulldozer the stumps were dug up and the wood transformed to tillage. The walled garden remains with the yard and outbuildings, and the little office where Charlotte's father used to sit and collect the rents.

Another estate which used to be famous for its fine surroundings was Castle Salem, or Benduff Castle, as it is known today. The long L-shaped Dutch-style house, fused to the truncated tower of a castle, lies in a secluded valley about a mile north of the Skibbereen road. The present owner, Mr Daly, seeing me push my bike through the snow, invited me in for tea. He told me that his father had bought the place in 1895, and he had heard that at one time there had been enough land for a man to do a day's hunting round about. In those days there was a large wood, like the wood at Derry, and a deer park. (Donovan, writing in 1870, described the grounds as being laid out in the Dutch manner, "with ponds and little islands full of shrubs and yew trees, and so sheltered and warm that fig trees grow and flourish there in the open air".)

The castle of Benduff had been the property of Florence McCarthy whose estates were forfeited after the rebellion of 1641. According to

Smith it was built by the O'Donovans, but others assert that it was built by Catherine, daughter of the eighth Earl of Desmond, the "Black Lady". This would give its date as about 1470.

After 1641 it was acquired by a soldier named Major William Morris who obtained a grant of the estate from Cromwell, and on the restoration of Charles II succeeded in having this grant confirmed to him. He changed the name to Castle Salem, knocked off the roof of the tower, which was originally seventy feet high, and replaced it with a slate roof which still covers the large barn-like main room of the castle, now unused. Among his furnishings was a stern portrait of Oliver Cromwell in full armour.

Later William Morris had to abandon a successful military career when he became a Quaker. The Society of Friends came to Ireland at an early date, its first meeting house being established in 1654. According to Rutty's *History of the Quakers*, Major Morris had originally been "an Elder amongst the Baptists of great repute, Captain of a Company, Justice of the Peace, Commissioner of the Revenue, Chief Treasurer in that Quarter, also Chief Governor of three garrisons. . . . He became a Quaker, and because of this was discharged from his command."

He had six ornately named children, Fortunatus, Tribulation, Appolos, Temperance, Phoebe and Patience. Fortunatus, his eldest son, built the yellow house in 1682 upon the occasion of his marriage. It was placed at right angles to the castle tower, forming an L with the high outside chimney and two gables.

Fortunatus' son, another William, was a good friend and correspondent of William Penn, who often came to Ireland and stayed at Benduff. Later, however, when William Penn had founded his colony in America (with the support of many Irish Friends), this second William Morris ceased to be a Quaker and reverted to the established church. At the gate of Benduff there is still to be seen the little graveyard founded by his grandfather, which was in use for over a century. Quakers from as far away as Cork chose to be buried here. But its use ceased abruptly after the death of the second William Morris in 1763, when he was buried here in a tomb which, although simple, was considered too ostentatious. The community was so horrified that it abandoned the graveyard and no further burials took place. Today the Quaker graves are no more than gentle mounds in the turf; William

Morris' tomb still rises above them, a stone vault with a tree growing out of it.

All round the castle are the remains of extensive slate quarries, Froe and Benduff. The sides of the hills glisten with the exposed slate, and empty cottages testify to the numbers of people who found work here. More than a hundred men were employed digging out the slate, which had the reputation of being better than Welsh slate from Bangor. Now the quarries are derelict and the slopes are covered with fragments like heaps of black postcards.

South-west of Rosscarbery, towards the sea, a crumbling eighteenth-century house and tower, once a mansion with servants, made an inconvenient farmhouse. An old woman with wild white hair stepped out from beneath a doorway topped with a fanlight, carrying a red plastic bucket. Picking her way in gumboots through the mud, she looked up as I hurried by, following a path between two stone walls down to the battered walls of Doneen Castle. Once Doneen must have been joined to the mainland by a bridge, but now it is cut off and stands on its own island above grey cliffs. The castle seems to have no history; it was never besieged or sacked or involved in a battle. Invaders made no attempt to settle or claim this ruin on the edge of the water. Was it ever lived in? Or even used as a place of refuge? Or was it merely a reassuring bulwark for people on the mainland?

"I often wonder about them. . . ." A farmer whose land overhung Doneen speculated as he leaned on his spade. "A very different sort from ourselves." He directed me towards Millcove and the eastern Pouladav. There are two Pouladavs west of Rosscarbery, great caverns which have been gnawed out of the cliffs by the action of the sea. Not easy places to find, even with directions. After a tiring walk plodding over bog and snow I found an isolated farmhouse and knocked. A window on the upper storey opened and a man in a long nightshirt peered out.

"What time is it?"

"About three o'clock."

"The evening is it!" he shouted and banged the window down.

I stumbled on and found a track across a hilltop looking out to sea from Toe Head to Galley Head. Distracted, I nearly tumbled down the eastern Pouladav, which opened at my feet just beyond a mangel field. It was a fissure in the ground, deep and unexpected as if it had been caused by an earthquake; only if you looked carefully over the precipitous cliff that falls two hundred feet could you make out a tiny beach at the bottom lapped by a gentle sea whose action carved out the cliffs. A length of barbed wire fenced off grazing animals. Pouladav means the Hole of the Ox—ox, one assumes in a collective sense, for it must have been a hazard to ancient cattle for many thousands of years. The chasm has three separate entrances connecting it with the open sea; one of them is more than a mile in length. On a calm day a boatman can row round from Rosscarbery and explore these narrow passages.

Next day, in another little snow-filled valley I found the ruin of Coppinger's Court. In building Castlefreke Lord Carbery was indulging himself in Tudor and Gothic fantasy, while only a few miles west stood the real thing. Coppinger's Court is a mixture of mullioned stone windows, high Elizabethan chimneys and castle defences. There are ruins of a number of other fortified houses in West Cork, but this is by far the most spectacular, its outline perfectly preserved. Like other builders of fortified houses, Sir Walter Coppinger was in two minds as he designed his Court early in the seventeenth century. He wished to reproduce the comforts of English manorial life and at the same time provide protection for himself and his family in a wild country. It would have been better to concentrate on defence, for the Court was destroyed in 1641. The shell remains, large enough to engender the usual myth about such buildings, that there is a chimney for every month, a door for every week and a window for every day in the year.

Sir Walter Coppinger came west soon after Kinsale, laying claim to what he could get hold of, including the town of Baltimore. Because of his unscrupulous dealings and contempt of court, he was confined in Dublin Castle for a time. He had intended to develop the fertile valley where he had situated his mansion. The Roury river ran through it and the hills round about gave shelter; he would build a market town and a canal leading through the hills at one end of the valley to the sea. The rebellion put an end to his plans, and the people around must have felt satisfaction in burning him out. "No Russian nobleman lorded it over his serfs like Coppinger", Donovan considered. A yardarm extending from one of the gables of the Court served as a gallows, a melancholy sort of house flag.

From Roury Bridge a steep road led into a nest of hills. It was cold weather for cycling and the ice-encrusted road was slippery. Coming down the far side with my heels stuck into the ground for balance, I looked across to the grey stones of the Drombeg circle standing out against glittering snow; behind them white-ribbed fields stretched towards the sea, blue and sparkling in sunlight.

In the south-west strip of Cork bounded by Clonakilty and Bear-haven with Mallow and Millstreet to the north, at least sixty stone circles have been identified. Ten of them have the distinctive features of Drombeg—a recumbent stone or slab lying horizontally on its side situated on the western curve, faced by two portal stones, larger than the others standing directly opposite to the east. The axis of Drombeg's portals with the opposite recumbent stone is aligned to the mid-winter sunset. The circle is almost perfect, and the height of the fourteen evenly spaced stones surrounding the small area which measures a little more than thirty feet in diameter, gives it the compact appearance of a crown. It is situated on a ridge overlooking a bowl-shaped valley beyond which lies the sea. Behind there are hills on three sides and to the west a broken view of the cliffs of Glandore harbour. It resembles other West Cork recumbent circles in its location on an elevated position open to the western horizon.

Circles like Drombeg, so precisely positioned, have inspired much speculation about their origins. Some theories have been prosaic, like the suggestion that they were merely used for stacking corn like the stone mushrooms found on farms. At the other extreme was the Victorian emphasis on Druidical mysteries, and such images as that conjured up pleasantly by the historian Froude in an over-romantic mood: "Were the circles magic signs? And did here stand the chair of justice of some Brehon, half rogue, half sage that sat in judgement there in the quarrels of the glen?" But Froude's ideas are less singular than the conclusions of modern archaeologists.

When Drombeg was excavated fifteen years ago the cremated bones of a young adolescent were discovered almost at the centre of the circle. They had been carefully pulverized and contained in a half-broken pot, which in turn had been placed in some sort of wrapper before burial. Over them a handful of charcoal had been sprinkled, a ritual echoed many ages afterwards in the "ashes to ashes" of the prayer book. The burial pit was concealed very carefully beneath a spread of clean sub-soil so that the ground appeared to be undisturbed.

The stone which stands two places away from the northern portal is smaller than the others and taken to resemble a phallus; the one next to it, in contrast, is large and lozenge-shaped. At Avebury in Wiltshire thin and plump stones like these have been found in association, and presumed to represent male and female elements. These facts, together with the alignment of the portal and recumbent stones to the winter solstice, strongly suggest that among the people who lived near Drombeg in the late Bronze Age, about two thousand years ago, a fertility cult formed a major part of religion. Their ceremonies took place over the bones of a young man or woman which were left undisturbed after the initial ritual of burial. In fact, their place of worship had been consecrated with death. Many of the findings at Drombeg have been confirmed by more recent examinations of other stone circles in the area.

I happened to meet Dr Fahy, who excavated the circle, standing outside a pub in the neighbouring village of Glandore. Over a glass he described an excavation which had taken place in 1960 of the remains of two stone huts fifty yards away from the Drombeg circle. They were ranged near a cooking pit with a large stone basin which could hold seventy-five gallons of water. It had presumably been used in the Bronze Age equivalent of a church social. Dr Fahy had emulated ancient large-scale cooking methods by filling the stone basin with water into which hot stones were thrown, bringing it up to boiling point within fifteen minutes.

THREE

Glandore to the Rough Quarter

THE ORIGINAL NAME for Glandore was *Cuan Dor*, the harbour of the oaks, and even today the hills across the harbour are covered with dusky grey woods. Three hundred years ago most of West Cork consisted of similar forest. One of the most important of domestic economies was pig-keeping, and herds of swine roamed among the trees looking for acorns. The clearing of large areas of the Munster woods began at the end of the sixteenth century as a result of the need for arable land and the practice of exporting oak to England for ship-building. The trees were felled by settlers, uncertain of their tenure, determined to make a quick profit on the land. The peasants also destroyed many young trees because they were afraid that their growth would raise the value of their holdings and subject them to confiscation. But the total destruction of the forests did not come until a century later when the new iron-smelting forges—many of which owed their origin to the enterprise of the Earl of Cork—were insatiable in their demands for charcoal. By the beginning of the eighteenth century Munster of the oak-clad plains was unable to produce sufficient oak bark for local tanners. People stopped making wooden household utensils and used iron ones instead. The memory of the old forests lingers in a few tracts of wood like the trees opposite Glandore and in the names of townlands and estates. For example, Derry, the the name of the Townsend estate at Rosscarbery, means "oaken", and the name Derry, with its derivatives, is very common.

Outside Glandore harbour there are two small islands called Adam and Eve. "Avoid Adam and hug Eve", the old sailing directions used to say. Within, the bay has more the atmosphere of a lake than an

arm of the sea. Daniel Corkery described the eastern shore of Myross
as "one of the most secret places in Ireland, without traffic, almost
without the pulse of life". Glandore Bay was not always so peaceful.
Sir Richard Cox in his *Hibernia Anglica* states that the Munster rebellion
of 1642 first broke out here "when the Irish gagged several English to
death, then seized a Scotch minister, broiled a piece of his flesh and
forced him to eat it . . ." Here in 1675 six Irish pirates brought in a
Dutch ship which had been bound from Hamburg to France. Having
embarked as passengers, they murdered the crew and took shelter in
Glandore with their prize. But five were caught and hanged, and their
heads were exposed in various ports along the coast as an example.

Dean Swift stayed at Unionhall on the other side of the bay in 1623,
a guest of his friend, the Reverend Thomas Somerville, who was rector
of nearby Myross and Castlehaven. Swift was grieving over the death
of Vanessa, and had come "to hide in the south of Ireland". He wrote
a Latin poem about West Cork, *Carberiae Rupes*, the Rocks of Carbery:

> "*Ecce ingens fragmens scopuli, quod vertice summo*
> *Desuper impendet nullo fundamine nixum*
> *Decidit in fluctus . . .*"

and so forth for forty lines. The Reverend W. Dunkin, M.A., an
admirer of the Dean, ponderously translated the poem in 1760:

> "Lo: from the top of younder cliff that shrouds
> Its airy head amidst the azure clouds
> Hangs a huge fragment; destitute of props
> Prone on the waves the rocky ruin drops . . ."

Swift occupied much time during his visit in sailing round the coast,
and it is believed that *Carberiae Rupes* was composed while he sheltered
in Castlehaven during a storm. Certainly the images of grandiose
scenery and the calls to Jove seem more appropriate to the rugged
coastline further westward than to the atmosphere of Glandore harbour,
which is perhaps better invoked by a poem written over a century
later by a visitor named Dr Morris:

> "Of all the gems which deck our isle
> And stud our native shore
> None wears for me a sunny smile
> As bright as sweet Glandore."

I stayed in Riviera View, which had rooms hanging over the water's edge. It was a place to see spectacular sunrises and sunsets, and in the visitors' book an exuberant entry described the village as "an Irish Venice". I took the narrow twisting road down to the tiny harbour. Out of a cottage a fat white cat gazed across to where three old ladies, warmly wrapped in tweeds, sat immobile in a Morris Minor before the dilapidated front of the King's Hotel, which had been built in 1828 with just such winter visitors in mind. Glandore was the first holiday resort in West Cork; the regatta held there in 1830 was the first ever held west of the Old Head of Kinsale. The eastern shore of the harbour had many gentlemen's residences where the elderly could enjoy the soft climate. Even today the bay does not attract the active tourist; it lacks any beaches and its pretty views are perhaps a little enervating.

In 1828, when the King's Hotel was rising on its foundations, Glandore was a miserable overcrowded village in a part of Ireland where there was endemic poverty. The area was fortunate in having two landlords who made efforts to relieve the distress around them. They were quite dissimilar, but for many years James Redmond Barry, the Catholic, and William Thompson, the atheist, vied with each other to improve the lives of their tenants and the people living round about. Recently there has been controversy about their efforts; the model farms ascribed to Thompson have been proved to be the idea of Barry. There is even doubt as to whether the two men were acquainted, although living within a few miles of one another they must have been aware of each other's efforts.

Undoubtedly the more practical and benevolent philanthropist of the two was Barry, who spent much of a long lifetime of ninety years in efficiently organizing charities.

He was born nearby in the parish of Barryroe, east of Galley Head, in 1789, a member of a family which had made its imprint on West Cork for nine hundred years. The Barrys, of Norman descent, but Hibernicized over the centuries, had once owned castles at Timoleague, Rathbarry, Dundeady, and in Glandore itself. They were among a number of Catholic families in the area around Clonakilty who had kept their wealth and prospered; James Barry was a prosperous landowner. He also had an active social conscience.

He is remembered most of all for his activities in improving the fishing around the south-west coast of Ireland. In 1819 he was appointed to the newly-formed Board of Commissioners for the Irish fisheries, responsible for fisheries from the Suir to the Shannon. He revived the decayed fishing industry in Glandore, had quays and wharfs built and the four rocks at the mouth of the harbour known as "the Dangers" marked out so that they would no longer be a hazard to shipping. Under his supervision boatyards were constructed at Baltimore and Unionhall.

At the same time these results of his public appointment were supplemented by a private experiment on his estates in Barryroe, where he set out to improve traditional methods of agriculture. For selected tenants he laid out model cottage farms, fenced and stocked with fruit trees, provided with beehives, dairy and pigsty. The land was broken up into allotments whose acreage depended on the size of the family. The cottages were slate-roofed, and each tenant was given a plough and a harrow; household furniture and other artifacts were lent to the tenants and could be purchased by annual instalments. In 1833, out of sixty families aided by Barry fifty-seven had paid their rent to a farthing and the remaining three had only failed because of some family misfortune.

In Glandore he provided schools for both boys and girls where the children of landless labourers could attend free of charge; unlike so many free schools of the day, the pupils and their parents had no suspicion that they might be tempted to change their faith. At the School of Industry founded under his auspices there was a model farm and carpenter's shop where boys could learn agriculture and a useful trade. This building with its flaking yellow walls still stands, an incised inscription above its door reading: "Glandore National Schools of Industry, 1835". It was in use as a primary school until 1966.

In 1822 Barry was appointed Commissioner of the Peace, but was later deprived of his position because of his activities during the Tithe War when he sympathized with the people of Myross who demonstrated against paying tithes to the Protestant clergy. During the famine, when hundreds of people flocked to Glandore for food, he did considerable relief work. He agitated for public works, attacked absentee landlords and demanded that they should be made to pay for relief schemes.

The activities of his neighbour, William Thompson, lacked his humanitarian drive, but Thompson has a more universal claim to fame. A follower of Saint-Simon, he was perhaps the most outstanding theoretician among early socialists; his ideas antedated Marx by fifty years. Sidney and Beatrice Webb once described Marx as "the illustrious disciple of Thompson and Hodgkin". Harold Laski considered that the writings of Thompson and his colleagues were superb and that "no one could read them without a sense that their case against capitalism must be answered and that it was not easy to answer".

He was born in Cork in 1775, the son of Alderman John Thompson, one of the richest merchants in Cork. When his father died in 1814, William inherited an estate of fourteen thousand acres at Cargoogariff, a few miles from Glandore. Determined to break with the custom of absentee landlordism, he spent most of his life in this remote spot, and here he founded a co-operative community on some sort of philanthropic lines. Very little is known about it although mysterious rumours about communal living seem to have filtered through the neighbourhood. Thompson has been credited with providing his tenants with ideal improvements remarkably similar to those of Barry; whether the efforts of the two men were mistakenly confused or whether one neighbour was influenced by the example of the other is not clear.

Much more important than Thompson's communal experiments were his writings, which had a profound influence on socialist philosophy. They included *Principles of Distribution of Wealth* and his gospel of co-operative political economy published in 1830 under the cumbersome title of *Practical Directions for the Speedy and Economic Establishments of Communities on the Principle of Mutual Co-operation, United Possessions, Equality of Exertions and of the Means of Enjoyment.* (This title alone provides a clue to what he tried to establish at Cargoogariff.) He foreshadowed Marx with the consideration that individuals are activated by class interest and the view that the profit motive was the only incentive to labour. He attacked the current system of capitalism, at the same time feeling guilt that as a landlord he derived his income from the sweat of poverty-stricken peasants. He advocated mass education at a time when the ruling classes were as a whole bitterly opposed to it. He championed women's rights, approved of birth control and condemned existing laws of marriage which were "conducive to blind animal increase". An avowed rationalist, he was confident that reason must ultimately triumph over dogma. Priests he considered "rapacious parasites, ghostly dealers in creeds and spiritual brimstone".

His atheism deprived him of much local sympathy. The villagers regarded him with some bewilderment which was increased by his eccentric behaviour. He walked around Glandore with the Tricolour at the end of his walking stick. He gave chemical experiments in public so that he was regarded as a wizard. For the last seventeen years of his life he was a non-smoker, a teetotaller and a vegetarian, declaring that he could read and write better without meat. His breakfast would be bread, and lunch consisted of potatoes and turnips, as he would not take eggs or butter.

When he died in 1833 he was given a church funeral. Afterwards, when his will was read out, it was discovered to the general dismay that he had forbidden "any priest, Christian, Mohammedan or Hindu, to meddle with my remains". The body then had to be exhumed from Drombeg cemetery to comply with his instructions. It was put on public display "to aid in conquering the foolish and frequently most mischievious prejudice against the public examination of corpses". Other directions were more bizarre. His skeleton was to be preserved, the ribs tipped in silver "so that it might present a fashionable appearance", and sent "as a memento of love" to a lady in England, Mrs Anna Whelan, an early believer in female emancipation and mother-in-law of Edward Bulwer-Lytton. A phrenologist named Monsieur Baume came across from London to collect the cranium.

Most of his fortune was bequeathed to the Co-operative Movement, but the will was fought by his nephew, one of the Whites of Bantry. Evenually after years of litigation it was overturned, but nearly all the money had gone in legal fees.

Thompson's behaviour and convictions drove him into bitter conflict with his own society. The final outrage, in the view of his peers, was his support of Catholic emancipation. He is remembered chiefly by students of early socialism, and his fame has earned him a bust in the International Communist Museum in Prague. But otherwise, when his name is recalled, his eccentricities tend to be exaggerated and his importance disparaged. The co-operative on his estate did not survive his death.

Other notables connected with Glandore were Colonel Hall and the

Earl of Glandore. (Many small villages on the coast were honoured by being incorporated in noble titles—at one time or another there were a Lord Kinsale, Lord Bantry, Count of Bearhaven, Lord Glandore, Lord Kenmare and so forth.) John Crosbie, Earl of Glandore, a member of the Irish parliament and Master of the Rolls, appears like a caricature of an Ascendancy nobleman in Lady Louisia Stuart's description of him as "a strange absent staring sort of being" who "seemed hardly in his right senses", with a wife who was considered "a dissipated fine lady . . . flirting and gaming, etc., beyond her fellows".

Colonel Hall introduced a new industry to West Cork when he observed that turf collected in a bog on the east side of Glandore burned with a blue flame. He collected the ashes, found that they were thickly impregnated with copper, and sent them by ship to Swansea. This venture earned him ten to twelve pounds a ton in 1819. Soon he was burning copper-tinged turf all over the neighbourhood. His zeal for discovering new lodes of ore took him westward; by 1823 he had opened no less than thirteen different mines between Skibbereen and Schull. He was also responsible for the discovery of the great mines at Allihies on the Bearhaven peninsula. According to his son (the author, with his wife, of an early travel book on the south of Ireland), Colonel Hall's enthusiasm got the better of common sense, so that eventually he lost a great deal of money. But from his efforts sprang a century of copper-mining in Carbery and Beare.

A great lode of manganese was also discovered running east from the Head of Glandore towards Rosscarbery. It has long been worked out, but the farmer on whose land the mine was situated still claims to benefit from it.

"My land is the best for miles around. The manganese is great for the cow. The metals heat up the ground, and because of this heat the grass comes up earlier than elsewhere."

I took the road which led across the inlet and down to Unionhall in its shaded corner of the bay. From far off it looked an idyllic spot with its old stone harbour, its line of houses and skeletal slate-walled mansion after which the village was named at the time of the Act of Union. But once across the iron bridge, the air was impregnated with the stench of mud and seaweed from the dried-up harbour abandoned by the ebbing tide. Irish place-names are usually graphically descriptive, and I have been told that before 1800 Unionhall had an even more unfortunate name which meant Dirty Strand. The village, positioned so that it faces north and east, avoiding the sunlight for most of the day, is gloomy enough. I inspected the lines of crumbling empty houses pervaded with the odours of the exposed beach, and the shed with the old tin notice tacked on its side, BELLS GREAT CURES SOLD HERE. The coastguard station was burned in 1921. So was Unionhall house itself, and only its shell remained. An enamelled finger on a shop pointed to an ancient trading list, Coal, Cement, Manure. Traffic was a horse and cart tied up outside a pub.

I parked my bike nearby. Fortified by stout, I was in better humour to tackle the steep hills leading westward through Myross. From the church a burst of Westminster chimes rang out, echoing across the bay. They came from an electric carillon given to Unionhall by an American lady who had once lived in the neighbourhood. The house where Swift stayed, Rock Cottage, was unrecognizable as a simple Georgian retreat, since it had been entirely reconstructed in recent years. The owner, who erected the present house, told me that he worked from the foundations of a single storey building, which, like so many places connected with Swift's life, had been levelled to the ground.

In the late nineteenth century the poet Sean O'Coileain, "the silver tongue of Munster", lived near Myross. He was born near Clonakilty and sent to Spain to study for the priesthood. This discipline he rejected to come to Myross and run a hedge school. Here he had a roistering sort of existence, drifting to towns in the neighbourhood, Unionhall, Rosscarbery and Skibbereen, at the same time struggling to support a large family. He died wretchedly poor in Skibbereen in 1817. His best known poems are the Jacobite song, *An Buachaill Ban* (The Fair Boy), and his lament for the ruined abbey of Timoleague.

The hills sloped to Lough Cluhir, whose golden circle of reeds divides its waters from the sea. Overlooking the lake was the fragment of a castle, Castle Eyre, originally named Castle Ivor, built in 1251 by Ivor Donovan, a celebrated trader who had a reputation as a magician. Long after his death his enchanted ship was to be seen floating in Lough Cluhir below his castle, all her sails set and colours flying. She was last observed in 1778.

On the banks of a small estuary was the little village of Carighilly which in pre-famine times had a thriving population made prosperous by fishing and smuggling. After emigration set in the fishermen left and the houses fell down. Among the handful of people who live there today, I found two sturdy old brothers named Glanton, seventy-six and eighty-six years old, but still active men dressed in blue jerseys and dungarees, their faces burnt by the sea. Behind the bank of rushes at the back of their house some boats were pulled up on the beach, which faced towards two craggy islands known as Rabbit Island and the Stack of Beans.

Con Glanton, the younger brother, described how they used to go fishing when they were young men. They went out to sea in open boats eighteen foot long and fished with the long lines. Long lines haven't been used for years; they took a terrible amount of work and a line could stretch out as much as two miles through the water with thousands of hooks on it. They caught ling, which they called The Bacon of the Sea, and herring, known as The King, and whiting, The Chicken. The fish were salted and they ate them together with potatoes and milk. He showed me the field known as The Cloche situated behind the few remaining houses. The Cloche had once contained the whole village, and it was easy to make out ridges where cottages had once stood. Although he did not remember seeing them, he had heard that there were once three hundred pipes smoking there. The only new houses were put up for tourists.

I rode along the road in the sun. Children were walking home from school, and an old man carried a couple of loaves in a bag. The sun shone on Blind Harbour and Squince, an island joined to the mainland by a causeway. Out on the horizon where the blue sea and sky quivered in reflected light, were the distant shapes of two more islands, whose names had been prosaically anglicized to High Island and Low Island.

Over the causeway on Squince were the ruins of ancient Myross church and a building which a local man told me was once a leprasorium. The graveyard was old, he said, but there was an older one over on Low Island. He had been across once, and seen the skulls there like daisies on the ground.

From Glandore I set out for Leap at the northern end of the bay, a village once known as *Cean Mara*, or the Head of the Sea. Leap—pronounced Lep—is small, just a twist in the Skibbereen road, a line of houses, the *garda* station, the Catholic church, open, the Protestant church, shut, craft shops, a sprinkling of pubs. But it is famous because of the Leap itself—a steep gorge over which the road passes from East Carbery to West Carbery. (Together the two Carberys form the largest barony in Ireland.) West Carbery was considered a wild place, and the old saying was: *"Beyond the Leap, beyond the Law."* The gorge is now spanned by a bridge over which the road passes, but I climbed down the steep sides which Smith compared to a staircase, "so that few horses but those who are well used to it attempt it with courage". Two village dogs pursued me as I made my way up between the rocks to a small waterfall, the foot of which appeared to be the local dump, heralded by the cheerful gleam of empty tins. Later, they would harmonize into chestnut-coloured rust. Bottles and bones lay among newspaper-wrapped parcels of decomposition, which, protected from snow and rain by the high walls of the ravine, incubated their sweet rotting smells. Over them a number of rats ran silently.

On the road west of Leap I came to Cononagh, where, by the side of the road, could be seen the remains of the last flax mill in West Cork, started in 1942. The sheds full of rusting machinery seemed more decayed than the mill at Shannonvale. Near the bridge was an attractive little Georgian house covered with creeper in which lived Mrs O'Donovan. She told me that the inconspicuous building opposite had been built as an inn for Bianconi cars. Here relays of horses used to be changed and the animals washed down in the neighbouring stream. With the introduction of the rail service to Skibbereen, Cononagh was left forgotten, and the Morris Arms—named for the family at Benduff Castle—sank into obscurity. But the railway has gone, and the road is once more in use. Hardly a month passes without some accident on the sharp bend outside her house.

Like many people around here she knew all about William Thompson. She gave me the address of Miss O'Callaghan, who lived in the vicinity of Cargoogariff where the philosopher had conducted his communal experiments. I cycled inland through the hills towards the mysterious and magical lake of Adereen, which was once noted for its floating island of reeds. It is almost dried up and all that remains is a weedy depression which provides a favourite breeding ground for wild duck. Nearby Miss O'Callaghan had her house. Over a cup of tea she told me that she had been born here and all her childhood Thompson had been a source of local interest. No trace remains of his community,

Main Street, Castletownshend

Market Square, Rosscarbury, *circa* 1900

Sycamores at Castletownshend "walled in their barbaric stone flower pot"

The harbour, Baltimore, with herring barrels stacked on the pier, *circa* 1900

where, Miss O'Callaghan believed, even the wives were shared. But there was a field still known as the Model Field near the site of his house at Cargoogariff, which means the Rough Quarter. Somewhere among the little fields huddled around the rocks is the spot where Thompson built his round tower. It was a well-known landmark, a hundred feet tall and thirty-five feet in diameter with a canonic roof and a distant view of Glandore Harbour. But even this has disappeared since it was pulled down for roadmaking.

D

FOUR

Castletownshend to Lough Hyne

THE ROAD APPROACHING Castletownshend winds through humpy little fields set among outcrops of rock, bogs and open ditches; there are views of low furze-covered hills and the sea. It is recognizably Flurry Knox country, and no one has ever described it better than Edith Somerville and Violet Martin. Their books about West Cork were designed to amuse a public seeking for laughter in the rural scene, which they depicted with a patronizing accuracy that has infuriated many Irishmen. But they did not attempt to describe the curious atmosphere of Castletownshend itself. There was little comical material to be found in the seigniorial isolation so proudly cultivated by a handful of families that lived together and intermarried over the centuries beside the sheltered harbour of Castlehaven.

The Ascendency usually chose to build their mansions far away from villages or towns where barefooted peasants walked the muddy streets. But at Castletownshend ("C.T." to the initiated), the Protestants were all herded together side by side in the English manner. Many of the charming houses look over a precipitous main street leading down the hill to the harbour. Half-way down it divides and circles two fine sycamores "walled in their barbaric stone flower pot", according to Edith Somerville, "the distraction of the village". There is a walk at right angles to the main street called Boulevard, or the Mall. The old coastguard station has been restored and is lived in by a retired naval captain. Down in the harbour the Gothic castle has become a guest house. This castle, the home of the Townshend family, is not particularly old or distinguished, most of it being rebuilt on the site of an older building burnt down in 1856. In its grounds is the

Nelson Arch, overlooking the harbour, under constant threat of being daubed or destroyed. After Nelson was blown up in Dublin, it seemed certain that the arch at Castletownshend would go. For weeks a guard kept constant watch hidden in the trees, and it survived. But it remains a target for vandals and patriots.

Elsewhere a whalebone arch emphasizes a seafaring tradition. One of the houses used to be known as Laputa, recollecting the visit of Swift. Drishane, Edith Somerville's home, stands on the top of the hill at the entrance to the village, a slate-covered early Georgian mansion whose austere outline is relieved by the generous curve of the fanlight over the door.

Overlooking the estuary rises the Protestant church of St Barrahane. (The Catholic church is well out of sight, a good three- or four-mile walk in the direction of Skibbereen.) In the carefully tended grave-yard Edith Somerville and Violet Martin are buried beside each other in simple graves. Protestant places of worship are usually locked, but this church is kept open nearly all the time. The interior, beautifully maintained, smelling of polish and newly applied Brasso, is like a Shinto family shrine. All the fittings recall the memory of ancestors, for everything has been presented in honour of someone who has died—the altar rail, the bellrope, the organ, the electric light. In the north transept one entire wall is taken up with a tablet on which is inscribed, not the Ten Commandments, but a very detailed history of the Townshend family.

There are three Harry Clarke windows, full of jewelled colours and baleful faces. Harry Clarke windows trouble the spirit in churches of all denominations all over Ireland; his designs, which were strongly influenced by Beardsley and the fairy-tale illustrations of Arthur Rackham and Edmund Dulac, are seldom suitable for holy themes. But they are very beautiful, and the Epiphany scene above the altar and St Louis and St Martin on the south wall are aglow with shafts of violet and Prussian blue light, which fall on the brass plates and marble tablets in memory of military men. The British army and navy were well served with brave and successful recruits from Castletownshend, and the high-ranking bemedalled soldiers and sailors whose virtues are here extolled encompass the expansion of the British Empire. Among them is remembered Lieutenant Coghill, who won his Victoria Cross when he died trying to save the colours at the Battle of Isandlwana in

1879, where a force of seven hundred and seventy-two soldiers were overwhelmed by twenty-five thousand Zulus. As a child Sean O'Casey used to be regaled with details of this action . . . "Melville an' Coghill cutting their way through the blacks, thick as bees around them, gallopin', gallopin', gallopin' away with the colours tied round their middles, sweatin' with the ceaseless slash slash of their swords, reddenin' the black back 'n breasts of the Zulus with their blood, fallin', fallin', sliding down dead under the gallopin' horses . . ."[1]

Typical of all this passionate family pride is the name of the village itself, whose location was originally known as Glen Barrahane after a local saint. Anglicized to Castlehaven, it eventually took on the name of its most influential family. Before any of the invaders arrived, the harbour had been considered one of the three most important along the coast, on a par with Baltimore and Bearhaven. For many centuries previously it had been an important base for fishing vessels. Its settlement by planter families was heralded, appropriately enough, by a naval engagement, the Battle of Castlehaven, which took place just three weeks before the Battle of Kinsale.

In 1601 Castlehaven Castle, on the north side of the harbour, was in the possession of a branch of the O'Driscoll family represented by Donogh O'Driscoll and his brothers. The Spanish had finally sent a force to the aid of O'Neill and Red Hugh O'Donnell in their long struggle against the English crown. It set sail with the blessings of Catholic Europe and a phoenix feather from the Pope as a symbol of the forces of the Counter-Reformation. The main body of the Spanish fleet put into Kinsale in September, 1601, under the command of Don Juan D'Aquila. At the same time a smaller group of six ships equipped with stores, ordinances and ammunition and commanded by Don Pedro de Zuibar, D'Aquila's naval colleague, set out for Castlehaven. They arrived on November 28th, and were guided into the harbour by the O'Driscolls, who gave de Zuibar possession of their castle. (This procedure of ceding their castles to their allies was repeated by Irish chieftains at Baltimore and Dunboy.)

When news reached Kinsale that the Spaniards had landed in Castlehaven, Admiral Levison sailed out to attack de Zuibar. Sir Richard Levison had been appointed a month previously as "Captain General and Admiral of certain of Her Majesty's ships to serve against the Spaniards lately arrived in Ireland". He reached Castlehaven on

December 6th, 1601, and immediately fired on de Zuibar's ships, which were not adequately equipped for fighting, but were transports somewhat the worse for wear after a long sea journey from Spain. One of them was sunk and three others were driven on the rocks. But the Spaniards were saved from disaster by the arrival of various Irish reinforcements, principally Donal Cam O'Sullivan Beare, who arrived on the scene with five hundred men. "Elated and emboldened", Don Pedro took the cannon from his battered ships and fortified a redoubt on the highest position on Reen point at the eastern side of the harbour.

For Levison the position abruptly changed. Now he found himself under the direct fire of Spanish guns, and his ships were unable to move out of the harbour because of the prevailing west wind. For two days they were bombarded. There is a conflict of opinion among contemporaries as to the losses incurred by both sides. Stafford in his *Pacata Hibernia* emphasized that except for one ship all the Spanish ships were sunk. The Irish historian, Phillip O'Sullivan, maintained that Levison's ship was completely destroyed and that five hundred and seventy-five Englishmen were killed, including a group of sixty who were sitting on board at a table when they were hit by a cannon-ball. What is certain is that eventually Levison was able to seize the opportunity afforded by the wind to limp out of the harbour and escape.

This engagement was eclipsed by the Battle of Kinsale, which virtually put an end to further resistance by the Irish. The Spanish capitulated and their forces were withdrawn. A few days before the actual surrender, Hugh Roe O'Donnell sailed away from Castlehaven to Corunna to solicit further aid from the King of Spain, and to meet his mysterious death at Zimincas.

After the surrender, the Spanish evacuated Castlehaven Castle in accordance with the treaty made at Kinsale. The O'Driscolls promptly reoccupied it. When Captain Roger Harvey arrived on 10th February, 1602, to take possession on behalf of the victorious English, he found the Spanish commander, Pedro Lopez de Soto, engaged in assaulting the castle and its owners in order to get it into Spanish hands again. The appearance of the English put an end to the fighting: the O'Driscolls surrendered to de Soto, who in turn delivered up the castle to Harvey.

The Battle of Kinsale on Christmas Eve, 1601, was a watershed, and it finally confirmed the English in their conquest of Ireland. Afterwards

newcomers arrived in increasing numbers. At Castlehaven the
O'Driscolls lost their possessions to Alderman Phane Becher. He had
come to Cork a quarter of a century before as an undertaker, that is, a
well endowed settler who guaranteed to occupy a large tract of Irish
land with Englishmen brought over under his sponsorship. His "under-
takings" brought him fourteen thousand acres of Munster, including
the town of Bandon, which he actually founded, but sold to Boyle,
later Earl of Cork, before he moved westwards. He settled down in
Castlehaven, and there are Bechers there to this day.

The Bechers were soon followed by others. In 1616 George Touchet,
a Dutchman, and former governor of Utrecht, who had taken part in
the Battle of Kinsale, was granted a title and became Lord Audley,
Earl of Castlehaven. (The title became extinct in 1777.) A little later,
during the parliamentary wars, Colonel Richard Townsend, an officer
of the Long Parliament, found himself in West Cork where he was
granted large estates under the Act of Settlement. In 1690 the Reverend
William Somerville, a Church of England minister in Scotland under
pressure from Scottish dissenters, crossed the Irish Sea to the north of
Ireland and made his way down here. To the initial number of families
that gathered at Castletownshend were added the Coghills and, a
century later, the Chavasses, a north-country family of French origin.

The settlers weathered the difficult years, twice experiencing the
paroxysms of rebellion and civil war. They had come for adventure
or greed, or, ironically, to escape religious persecution, motives that
sent people across the Atlantic. Ireland was regarded as untamed as
North America, more so, perhaps, for there was the devastation of war.
Others besides Lord Grey had left Munster a ruin of "ashes and carcasses".

In the seventeenth century life was fairly rough. "There was not a
pew in the Church, only Benches . . . there was only one genteel
family in the parish. . . . Revenue men and farmers were in constant
attendance . . . (and) . . . invited to dinner. . . . On Sundays a boat was
ready to fetch the Captains of every vessel that came in." But even in
the early years Castletownshend society solidified. By the mid-
eighteenth century the "genteel" families had increased and become
prosperous; elegant houses were built and the village took on the shape
it has today. Estates were improved and the fishing industry revived.
The Bechers were immensely rich, while the Townsends owned
adequate property in the area. In the mid-eighteenth century the

Somervilles acquired money through the activities of a member of the family who became an enterprising shipowner, known disparagingly ever afterwards as "Tom the Merchant". His ships traded mainly in the West Indies, and in addition he made a fortune carrying "salted provisions" to places like Newfoundland and the East Indies. Another source of revenue was the thriving smuggling trade in which most landed families were not too proud to take part.

Although considerable energies were spent in organizing their vast tracts of land, inevitably the families were aloof from the poverty of their tenants. They clung together in this small village, occasionally setting out to visit cousins and connections elsewhere in West Cork. They formed their own aristocracy, intermarrying constantly so that the same names reappear on family trees.

The Irish had a passion for genealogy. "The people in general are great admirers of their ancestors," wrote an English traveller in 1647. "It is two hours' work for them to repeat their names." They regarded their conquerors as upstarts, an opinion repeated in modern times by Daniel Corkery. The planter "had no learning . . . he lacked breeding. . . . He was not fit to be named in one breath with the Gaels on whom he had trampled."[2]

Notwithstanding the contempt of those they had supplanted, the Anglo-Irish soon acquired that characteristic absorption in geneology and family history. In West Cork particularly, in the enclosed society that they had created, this interest became obsessive. It was justified with quotations from the Bible. "Look unto the rock whence ye were hewn, the hole of the pit whence ye were digged." "Children's children are the crown of old men; and the glory of children are their fathers." (This verse from Proverbs is incised at the foot of the Townshend memorial in Castletownshend church.) Even today the few survivors of that society spend much time drawing up family trees and privately printing books of family histories. The past is gathered up and preserved in miniatures, daguerrotypes, and the thick albums with their brass clasps in which, between silk-covered cardboard, the cocoa-coloured photographs are identified, names pencilled in by a modern hand. Old letters written from dark candlelit houses are usually full of bad news—tuberculosis, unhappy confinements, sick children. There are glimpses of contemporary Ireland seen with the narrow vision of the landlord.

The famine destroyed much of the old prosperity as the land which had brought them their money became a liability. Later, under the Land Acts, they lost much of it. Increasingly younger sons, usually men of ability, ventured abroad in the armed services of England, to return only at the end of their lives to Castletownshend where people continued to pass their time in preoccupied leisure, planning to avoid the frustrations of comfortable idleness. In their isolation the pattern of Victorian day-to-day existence was closer woven; their numbers were so small, their outside interests so far away. Summers passed in boating and regattas, tennis parties, excursions from house to house. There were quarrels; a good quarrel between two families might last a decade. Much time was spent contemplating small problems, as, for example, whether or not the Townsend family should add an "h" to its name. In 1870 they wrote to Lord Townshend in England asking him if he would mind. ("Do what you like!") There was hunting, and for a long time Edith Somerville was Master of the Carbery foxhounds. She is still remembered sitting side-saddle and formidable on her white horse as the meet assembled at the cross in Skibbereen. People improved their estates, took an interest in amateur archaeology and the supernatural. Edith Somerville had a fairy shoe on display at Drishane, its heel worn down by a heavy-footed leprechaun. She developed the fashion for table-tapping, which had been prevalent in village society, by continuing to collaborate with Violet Martin long after her friend had died. She summoned up the spirit of her ancestor, the Reverend Thomas Somerville, to help her write the history of her family. "My dear Descendant," she quoted him as saying, "I esteem your aspirations, and will strive to draw from the Well of Memory. . . ."

They continued unruffled in Castletownshend well into the twentieth century. They came through the revolution and civil war unscathed; no house in the village was burnt. Edith Somerville attributed its preservation to spiritual assistance . . . "Castletownshend has escaped by dint of special help and effort from the other side. Martin says that there has been an unwearied cordon of spiritual protection around us, provided by my father, Egerton, Uncle Kendal and many others . . ."

Not until fifteen years later did the changes bring violence with the murder of Admiral Boyle Somerville in 1936. He was Edith's brother, and had retired to his home after a lifetime in the British navy. Such a tragedy might shake them, but still the encroachment of the twentieth century was ignored. I can remember being taken to Castletownshend in the nineteen thirties, and seeing the ladies in long dresses carrying their antique wooden tennis rackets. To gain an entrée into their society, you had to have some connection with one or more of the families, preferably by blood. "People always go into each other's houses without knocking, unless they are 'outsiders'."

Lionel Fleming, who, like myself, had relations living in the village, has written about it as "one of the most curious phenomena in Ireland. For there until quite recently . . . the rise of Nationalism and the decay of the Ascendency had been arrested. The world remained stable. Any idea of change was an illusion, butlers and family pictures continued placidly and unchallenged."[3]

"There's a hotbed of gentry in Castletownshend," I was told this year. But they are dying out now, along with the rest of the Protestants, the farmers and shopkeepers in Skibbereeen from whom they kept their distance. In winter a few proud old people remain to tend the memorials in the church. In summer, when scattered relatives return, regattas are still held, and races take place in the little harbour where Admiral Levison was trapped by the Spanish guns. The boats are clinker built, of ancient design. The races are organized with military precision and etiquette: flags are raised, guns boom and members of the families race against each other to win.

The atmosphere of a mini Valley of the Kings is oppressive, and I was glad to wheel my bicycle up the long hill and out to explore the surrounding area. I went up to the Three Fingers—long grey columns of stone dramatically placed on the summit of a hill. "They are sudden and strange," Edith Somerville wrote, "breathtaking in their unexpectedness. One feels they are like three stern priests of a forgotten religion." She described how she and her brother, Admiral Boyle Somerville, a keen amateur archaeologist, waited beneath the stones one midsummer morning. "Our archaeological hearts beat, and then precisely at the sunrise hour in the gap, the first gleaming spark of the sun's rim appeared. The Fingers had been truly aligned." There used to be a fourth finger, but this was removed by Madam Townsend, a nineteenth-century chatelaine of that family, who wished to decorate her rock garden in an unusual fashion. It still lies somewhere in the castle grounds, lost in a tangle of ivy and briars.

Close by on a hill overlooking the harbour in Knockdrum Fort, is a fine ring fort with thick stone walls enclosing a circular area seventy-five feet in diameter. At its centre is a roofless clochan, a dwelling with a chambered souterrain hewn out of the rock. Boyle Somerville, one the first people to describe Knockdrum accurately, felt that although this was a pre-Christian structure, it was probably used as a lookout post right up to the time of the Battle of Castlehaven. Certainly, from this point you can see any approaching ship which might threaten the estuary.

Little remains of the old O'Driscoll castle which de Zuibar had defended. Unlike the majority of Irish castles, this one was lived in right up until the end of the nineteenth century. For many years it was used as a Protestant rectory, after the Reverend Thomas Somerville took it over in 1732 from a tenant of Lord Audley. He lived in state in tapestried rooms with handsome brass fireplaces surrounded by blue Dutch tiles, and built an annexe to contain his large family. Here his friend Dean Swift came to stay on his second visit to West Cork in 1735. Years later the last tenant of the castle, the Reverend Robert Morrit, pulled the roof off and let in the weather. What was left finally collapsed on February 25th, 1924. "Our men working on the farm above the strand heard a slow rumbling roar," wrote Edith Somerville. "They looked down south over the cliff of Fyle Dick towards where the sound had come from, and there, where for some five centuries the castle had dominated the harbour, was nothing but a grey heap of stones."

To get to the peninsula of Reen on the far side of the harbour, one must take a detour around the upper end of the estuary and what is called the Rineen river—really an extension of the estuary. A more direct route would have been through Townsend land; during the nineteenth century the county authorities planned to make a road by the water's edge through the demesne. This scheme was frustrated by the imperious Madam Townsend who sent off to her friend, Lord Bantry, for a few fallow deer. The presence of these animals in her demesne turned it into a deer park, and thus inviolable by law. To have it walled, as was necessary, Madam Townsend took away the masons who were engaged in building the Catholic church and employed them in erecting the great wall that finally put an end to the aesthetic ideas of the council. The building of the church was delayed for some time.

The detour, however, leads through pleasant country. The land through which the narrow neck of the Rineen river winds has remained unchanged since Charles Townsend described it in 1760 . . . "The river, alternately contracting and expanding its winding channel, now collects into a narrow strait, now spreads into an expansive lake. The hills which rise from the shores at either side—sometimes rocky and abrupt, and sometimes with more gradual acclivity—are for the most part thickly wooded . . ."

In comparison to this lush setting, the Reen peninsula is stark, a long rocky ridge of land covered with furze and small trees. At Reen village there are just a few cottages, a pier and what appears to be an incomplete causeway extending into the harbour. It is bleak compared to Castletownshend whose Gothic castle, church and tiers of big houses are visible across the bay among grey trees.

Standing on the water's edge in an isolated position behind the harbour bar is the fine ruin of Raheen Castle, an O'Donovan stronghold. The east wall has fallen down; the west wall is pitted with the mark of shot and cannon, and according to Donovan there are cannonballs still embedded in its masonry. This castle probably met its destruction in 1649 when the lands around Raheen were ravaged by Cromwellian soldiers and the castle was pounded into ruin by the bombardment of ships in the harbour.

At the end of Reen the far-off silhouette of Toe Head is visible and the curiously shaped rocks known as The Stags. Many rock formations off the coast were called *cruach* or *ben* in Irish, translated to *stacks* in English; the word was often slurred to stags. On Horse Island just outside the harbour are the remains of a tower which Tom Somerville, the merchant, built as a landmark for his ships on their return from the West Indies.

In 1970 four green-encrusted bronze cannon were discovered by a skin diver near this spot, and brought to shore at Castletownshend. Their marks were Spanish, and they were evidently all that remained of a wrecked ship. However, the date on one of them, 1642, precluded any idea that the wreck formed part of de Zuibar's fleet.

At a lonely place beyond Reen village is Reenlegena, the "little graveyard", where the Spanish sailors who died in the battle of 1601 lie buried. According to Edith Somerville, they numbered seventeen sailors and one great lord. In 1928 Boyle Somerville, who shared his sister's interest in the occult, summoned up one of these men with the aid of a medium. She caught sight of a wild figure with tangled hair and tattered cloak. He spoke to her in Spanish, which she could not understand, but automatically transcribed in English. He gave details of the battle which Boyle checked for accuracy in the British Museum. He was very unhappy at not being able to leave Reen and return to Spain, whose bells he could hear. Possibly, they thought, he was guarding buried treasure. From the medium's description Edith drew a picture of him, which she reproduced in *Notions in Garrison*, together with an account of the séance, which took place in the graveyard.

Pat Sullivan, a farmer on Reen, showed me the place, almost invisible now, where the grass and the cattle had moved in. You had to look carefully before noticing the stones sticking out from low grass-covered mounds. The sailors are supposed to lie boxed from the hips up with stones weighing down their legs.

"Perhaps they were in a hurry or short of timber when they buried them," Mr Sullivan said. "They are all forgotten. There should be something done to commemorate them. For they were trying to help us Irish here!"

Scattered around were other reminders of the battle. Outside his house lay two large cannon-balls from Admiral Levison's guns which he found down on the strand. After heavy storms they had been shaken down from the cliffs in which they had been embedded. Near the graveyard a ruin was still known as "the general's house", and overlooking the point was the line of Spanish entrenchments and a place called "the ovens" where the cannon-balls were heated up.

West of Castletownshend the high wooded shoulder of Knock Caima overlooks Lough Hyne. The lake is surrounded on all sides by wooded hills. Because of its seclusion, it has been used for secret activities like smuggling and prayer. Behind the old coastguard station there is a tiny penal altar, a carefully constructed ledge of rocks completely hidden from view. St. Bridget was particularly venerated here. Near the lake the remains of an ancient chapel and a well are dedicated to her.

Thackeray was taken over swampy roads to view Lough Hyne with its island on which stand the ruins of an O'Driscoll castle. It was a romantic sight, but the novelist was unenthusiastic. "I felt not sorry to have seen this lonely lake, and still happier to leave it."

Lough Hyne is an arm of the sea. If you gaze into its clear blue waters you can see whelks and periwinkles and clusters of the same reddish spiny sea urchin which torments bathers in the Mediterranean. The entrance to the lake from the sea is a narrow channel about twenty feet wide through which the tidal waters surge in an out from the bay of Barlogue. It comes and goes with the speed of a fast torrent, and mackerel and herring are often carried in with it. Shooting the rapids assisted by this remarkable tide race was at one time a daring local sport; if you got the time of the tide right, you could be in and out of the lake within a quarter of an hour.

The structure of Lough Hyne and the effect of this tidal current make it a centre of study for marine biologists. Within a small area there is the perfect microcosm of coastal marine life in ideal sheltered conditions. The distribution of species, their numbers and the effects of environment can be observed in a natural laboratory. The rapids and creeks are ideal for studying the effect of current on distribution, and the lake, which is very deep at certain points, provides controlled contrasts between deep and shallow water.

The first person to take a serious scientific interest in Lough Hyne was Richard Southern, a director of Irish fisheries, who noted the unique advantages of the lake in 1916. He was followed in 1922 by Professor Renouff from University College, Cork, who put up three laboratories on the slopes at the southern side. In 1938 Professor Kitching—now at East Anglia University—came to Lough Hyne for the first time. The laboratories built there under his supervision, one called Glannafeen, the other Dromadoon, are also situated at the southern end of the lake close to the rapids. They are so well hidden that no stranger could suspect that there was a centre of scientific interest hidden behind the rocks. A cable running out into the lake gives instantaneous readings of the temperature at its deepest points; within the laboratory there are mechanisms for measuring the amount of light and oxygen in the water, and specially made cages for testing the reactions of marine organism.

The presence of these laboratories provides amusement and mystery to local farmers. "They stick an unfortunate cockroach on a pin and see if it has two livers," was how one farmer summed up a quarter of a century of scientific endeavour. The work is little publicized and most people in the area know nothing about it. The summer tourists looking across the blue waters of the lake to the small boats drifting slowly over the surface are unaware that the oarsmen are not fishermen but earnest students studying something like the diurnal migration of sea urchins.

FIVE

Baltimore and Sherkin

EASTWARD OF BALTIMORE the land had predominated, the hills
and the winter fields whose mellow russet browns and greens gave the
country the colours of an apple-skin. But at Baltimore the sea took
over every view, and every point west along the broken coastline
had to be seen in relation to the seascape. The town should really be
approached by boat. I had been able to do this one previous summer,
sailing under the cliffs of Beacon Point which form precipitous grey
slopes that shelve into the water, their jagged edges worn through with
caves. Close to the shore we passed the curiously shaped Kedge Island
with its splinters of rock and its gulls' nests. The desolate headland of
Beacon Point was crowded with ruined cottages; everywhere there
were traces of old fields, the scars of ancient lazy beds and the outlines
of forgotten houses. The people gone, signs of life are confined to gulls
or colonies of seals lying on rocks under the cliffs.

Today, in winter, I looked out over Baltimore harbour and Roaring
Water Bay from Spain Point where a nineteenth-century signal tower
stands on a hill above the town. Probably there was another earlier
tower here, sited to watch Spanish fishermen. Towers and beacons were
planted in high places around the coast during the seventeenth century,
if not earlier. In 1632, after the Sack of Baltimore, the Lord President,
St Leger, gave instructions that warning beacons should be erected at
intervals along the coast right up to Dursey. But the present structure
was built after 1796, when the government took fright following the
unsuccessful invasion of Bantry Bay by the French. There are similar
towers standing on all the high points along the south-west headlands,
each within signalling distance of two others. If the French had invaded

again, the whole coastline could have been alerted within an hour. Messages were relayed by semaphore to shipping or sent as far away as Cork. *Tuckey's Cork Remembrancer* related that "on December 30th, 1803, Captain Maguire, R.N., arrived in this city to attend to the erection of Signal Posts along this coast". In March, 1804, it further recorded that: "The establishment of Signal Posts along this coast was carried on with expedition. Strong buildings capable of lodging the naval officer and his assistants as well as containing a detachment of armed men, were built in the most proper places contiguous to the signal posts. They were so constructed that they were entered by a ladder from the top." Later their walls were covered with slate and at each corner there were projecting *machicoulis*, giving practical structures some fashionable Gothic trimmings. In appearance they closely resemble the O'Mahony and O'Driscoll castles beside the sea.

During the emergency from 1939 to 1945 the Spain Tower was occupied by the army. Now it is a ruin with gutted windows through which the wind roars. The exposed position of these towers, subject to constant buffeting from wind and storm, brings them quickly to a forlorn, ruinous appearance. Many of them were inhabited until quite recently; the tower on Toe Head contained a family within the last dozen years. The grey silhouette at Spain Point looks over the whole of Roaring Water Bay westward to the sea. From here the smallest change of weather is immediately reflected in the sea and sky. I watched as the rain stopped and the sun came out across the water on the dazzling blue spectacle of bays and islands with the Fastnet Rock and the open Atlantic in the distance. The day was changed by flashes of sun falling through the clouds, charging the horizon with lemon light. The headlands shone out in an azure sea which might have been lapping the Peloponnese. Then a storm cloud, black and menacing, swept over the island of Cape Clear, the horizon became a band of silver, and in a few minutes the limitless stretch of water had returned to its habitual grey.

Standing above the entrance to the harbour is the white beacon marked on old maps as "Lot's Wife", although in more modern imagery its elongated shape suggests a rocket waiting for blast-off. It looks down into Baltimore harbour with Sherkin Island and its abbey visible at the west end, and the town of Baltimore on the east side. To the north the island of Ringarogy screens off the entrance to the Ilen river.

Baltimore has always been a centre for fishing and boating activities, and even in the middle of winter it has a busy nautical air. A narrow road twists down to the pier around which lines of boats are pulled up on the hard. The mailboat, the *Naoimh Ciaran*, waits her departure to Cape Clear. At Skinner's boatyard the Galway lifeboat, *RNLB Joseph Hiram Chadwicke*, is squeezed into a shed for her annual overhaul. There are a Mariner's Row, a Salisbury Terrace and a small grey Protestant church from whose windows stretches a fine view of the harbour's activities. Sermons have been interrupted by distracted clergymen watching the manœuvring of yachtsmen on a lee shore. "I knew he'd ram that rock somehow!"

For centuries the O'Driscolls, whose castle overhangs the town, controlled the fishing in this area. O'Driscoll appears to be senior to all other County Cork septs; it was once the most important of them. From a very remote period right up to the twentieth century it possessed all the land stretching from Kinsale to the Kenmare river. But gradually other families, such as the O'Sullivans and the western O'Mahonys, moved in and began to take over its possessions.

The O'Driscoll Mor division of the sept dominated this part of West Cork. At the end of the thirteenth century its territory was confined to Baltimore, Sherkin Island, Cape Clear Island and the coast eastwards to Castlehaven. Its castles included Dunasead, the Fort of the Jewels, at Baltimore, Dunalong, the Fort of the Ships, on Sherkin, and Duna-nore, the Fort of Gold, on the north side of Cape Clear. Others, like Castlehaven, have vanished or fallen down. The walls of Cloghane on the island at Lough Hyne were still standing in 1869 commanding the entrance to Barloge; today only the foundations remain. The stones of Dunagall on Ringarogy Island were shipped up the river to Skibbereen in 1826 and incorporated in the pro-Cathedral there.

The O'Driscolls were able to levy dues from the fishing fleets that sailed up to West Cork from all over Europe to harvest the rich fishing grounds with their pilchard shoals which lay off shore. The wealth of fish attracted the fishing boats of Spain and France, each of which had to pay exorbitant charges. In the fifteenth century the O'Driscolls declared that:

"Every ship that fisheth . . . between the Fastnet Rock and the Staggs is to pay ten shillings and two pence, a barrel of salt, a hogshead of wine and a dish of fish three times a day."

North Harbour, Cape Clear, 1900

Temperance meeting, Skibbereen

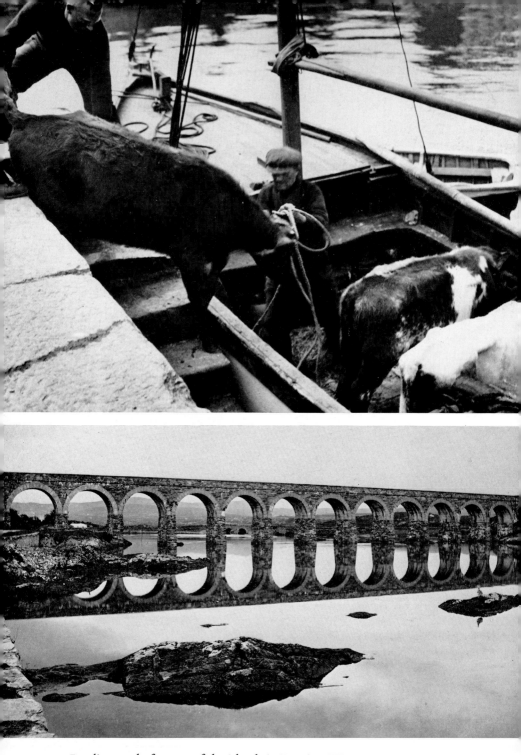

Loading cattle for one of the islands in Roaring Water Bay

Rail-viaduct, Ballydehob, 1900

Ten shillings was a great deal of money at the time. The prosperity of the O'Driscolls excited envy. In particular they had a long-standing quarrel with the citizens of Waterford. Waterford, which was an English settlement, constituted a rival fishing empire, and the feud stretched over centuries, studded with incidents like the kidnapping of 1413. This took place on Christmas Eve, when a party of Waterford men, headed by their mayor, treacherously captured the chief of the O'Driscolls and his family from their castle in Baltimore. The Carew MSS. gives an account of what happened:

". . . and so the Maior walked into the greate Hall where were O'h-Idriskoll and his Sonne, the Prior of the Friary, O'H-Idriskoll's thre bretheren, his uncle and wife, and leaving them in their daunce, the Maior commanded every of his men to hold fast the said powers. And so after singing a carroll came away, bringing with them aborde the said shipp the said O'h-Idriskoll and his company, saying into them that they should go with him to Waterford to synge their carroll, and to make merry that Christmas. . . ."

The feud reached a climax in 1537 when the O'Driscolls seized a Waterford ship. Four ships with cargoes of Portuguese wines had been driven off course along the south-west coast. One of them, the *Santa Maria*, laden with a hundred tuns of wine, was driven into a bay near the entrance to Baltimore. Fineen O'Driscoll and his son went on board and agreed to pilot the ship into the harbour for three pipes of wine. However, having sampled the liquor, they seized the merchants, put them in irons and plundered seventy-two tuns of wine which they divided up among their neighbours. In reprisal, a detachment of three ships from Waterford was sent against Baltimore. They reached the harbour at night, anchored under Dunasead and fired their guns at it throughout the night. The next day they landed on Sherkin, where they captured the fortress of Dunalong, running up St. George's standard above it. They destroyed all the island's villages and the Franciscan friary that stood near the castle. Fifty of the O'Driscoll pinnaces were burnt, and the great thirty-oared galley of the chieftain was captured and taken back to Waterford. Finally, as a flourish before their departure, the Waterford men returned to the fortress of Dunasead at Baltimore itself and burnt that down as well.

Not surprisingly, the O'Driscolls joined the abortive Geraldine

E

rebellion, when most of their lands were confiscated. But in 1585, under the Elizabethan policy of surrender and regrant, some of their territory was restored, and the last of a long line of chieftains, Finin or Fineen O'Driscoll, was given a knighthood. Sir Fineen, known as "the Rover", was adept at changing sides at the turn of fortune. He allied himself so closely to the English that before the Battle of Kinsale he was appointed High Sheriff of County Cork, a position which did not prevent him from joining his own people in the final struggle of 1601 and handing over his castles at Baltimore and Cape Clear to the Spaniards. After Kinsale he was able to obtain another pardon. It is said that this was a reward for supplying the English fleet with provisions when it was becalmed off Baltimore.

Before the pardon could take effect, Queen Elizabeth died and it became void. However, Sir Fineen held on to enough land to lease the harbour of Baltimore to Sir Thomas Crooke in 1608. A small English colony settled here, not where the modern town is situated, but a short distance away. Sir Fineen continued to live in his castle; this was the second Dunasead fortress on the site which he had built to replace the building burnt in 1537. The ruin survives today, dominating the harbour, a fortified house in the transitional style which became popular after 1600. Below it, Crooke strove to found his settlement, dividing the land into plots for each family with enough room for gardens. He gave leases and provided a patent for the new town. But his right to it was disputed by Sir Walter Coppinger, who maintained that Sir Fineen's land was confiscated, and claimed it for himself. For many years he sought through legal processes to have Crooke's patent dismissed.

No town could have started more inauspiciously. During the long period of litigation with Coppinger on one hand and Crooke on the other, there occurred in 1631 the famous Sack of Baltimore by Algerian pirates.

Throughout the seventeenth century and the early part of the eighteenth century the coast of Ireland was a prey to pirates. The Algerians gave endless trouble, but their biggest coup was at Baltimore. Piracy was a normal hazard for sea travellers of the time, who ran a small risk of being sold into slavery. In 1641, for example, the Reverend Devereaux Spratt, a Protestant clergyman who had lost his living during the rebellion, was taken off the ship on which he was travelling back to

England, which was captured in sight of land. In Algiers, where he became a slave, he estimated that the Algerians had seventeen hundred other captured slaves. After he was redeemed he implored that "the Lord stir up ye hearts of Christian princes to roote out ye neste of pirates!" In 1642 Edmund O'Dwyer, an agent from the Vatican, was taken as a slave and was ransomed for the sum of £60. As late as 1695 the *Ouzel*, a galley sailing from Dublin to the Levant, was taken by Barbary pirates. The crew recaptured the ship and returned to Dublin with the rich hoard of the pirates stolen treasure. The wealth—insurance money also having been paid—was applied to shipping in general, and the result was the beginning of the Dublin Chamber of Commerce.

Baltimore was attacked on June 20th, 1631, after two Algerian ships under the command of a Dutch renegade, Captain Matthew Rice, set out on a raiding party for the Cork coast. They first intended to enter Kinsale, but seeing that town well guarded, they drifted westward. Then they captured two Waterford ships, and one of their captains, Thomas Hackett of Dungarvan, agreed to guide them into Baltimore. Perhaps if he had not been a Waterford man the raid might not have taken place. But the Algerians entered the harbour, a scene described in Thomas Davis' poem:

"The yell of Allah breaks above the prayer, the shriek, the roar,
  Oh, blessed God, the Algerine is Lord of Baltimore!"

The town was looted and a total of a hundred and ten prisoners were taken away as slaves. Davis assumed that they were Irishmen, but this was not so. Apart from a housemaid and Dermod Mergey and his two children (Meirgeach was a surname of a branch of the McCarthys) all the kidnapped listed in official reports were English planters. Among them were the wife and seven sons of William Gunter, "a person of some credit". Eventually Thomas Hackett was caught and hanged, but his execution did the captives no good, for most of them were to pass the rest of their lives as slaves on the Barbary Coast. Fifteen years afterwards, in 1649, when the English Parliament sent a Mr Cason to Africa to redeem English captives at £30 a head, he could only secure the release of two of the Baltimore victims.

The Sack almost put an end to Baltimore. Although beacons were set up round the coast and armed vessels were commissioned to guard convoys of ships, the inhabitants felt too isolated and exposed for safety. Many of them moved inland to Skibbereen or sought to live elsewhere. Sir Fineen O'Driscoll, who had already lost his lands to Coppinger left Dunasead to retire and spend his last days in destitution in his castle at Lough Hyne. The rest of the once-powerful empire of the O'Driscolls slipped out of their hands into the possession of the new settlers.

The Coppingers were not to enjoy their acquisitions at Baltimore for long. They were involved in the uprising of 1641 and as a result their lands were forfeit. Although in 1652 James Coppinger succeeded in getting them restored because he was an "innocent Papist", they were forfeited again in 1690 when his brother, Walter, who had inherited them, was outlawed because of his part in the Jacobite wars. Eventually the estates at Baltimore passed into the hands of Sir Percy Freke. Besides adding to the wealth of the Barons of Carbery, the town was important to them as a rotten borough. Like Bandon and Clonakilty, its original charter gave it the right to send two Members of Parliament to Westminster, a privilege it maintained up to the Act of Union. For the loss of his two seats in Parliament, Lord Carbery received compensation of fifteen thousand pounds. (It is only fair to add that he voted against the Union.)

Baltimore has nothing to do with Baltimore in Maryland, as many people think. The right honourable John Calvert, Baron of Baltimore, who was proprietor of the province of Maryland and gave his name to the new town there, took his title from Baltimore in County Longford.

The town's main importance has always been derived from its excellent safe harbour which made it a centre for fishing. This has been true from medieval times up to the present century. Cycles of prosperity and depression have followed success or failure in marketing fish. However violence might impinge on the lives of the townspeople, there would always be those who earned their living from the sea. Forty years after the Munster rebellion the male population of Baltimore consisted of "a hundred and eighty-eight fishermen, eighty-four boatmen and two Papishes".

The fish from which they secured their income was the pilchard. Pilchards, salted and cured, had been a staple of medieval winter diet, and in later times they were exported to the continent. In addition, during the pressing of the fish a valuable oil called "train oil" was extracted which was used for a variety of purposes including lighting and curing leather.

In a field by the road to the Beacon there are still traces of a pilchard pallace or curing house, one of the many along the coast. The small rectangular holes drilled into the sides of a rock which held the beams used for pressing the fish can still be seen. When the road was dug thick deposits of fish scales were unearthed. The fish would have been caught in seine nets, which were said to have been introduced into West Cork by the first Earl of Cork. They resulted in larger returns of fish. "The nets are from 100 to 140 fathoms long," Smith wrote, "and from 6 to 9 fathoms deep; the nets being shot are dropt into the sea, they surround the fish, having two boats to attend them, one of which is called the seine boat, the other the follower."

During the early part of the eighteenth century the pilchards vanished. Some inexplicable change in currents or temperature drove the shoals away. The story goes that a house for curing pilchards was erected on the point of Coney Island, and when the fish caught sight of it they turned tail and fled. Mackerel and herring moved into their feeding grounds and gradually replaced them in economic importance. Foreign fishermen continued to visit the coast to catch them. Pococke mentions the French fishing boats in 1740. "They get chiefly Mackerel during the months of July and August. Herrings also come in . . . they salt and barell up the Mackerel and Herrings. The Mackerel sell well as they give only half a Mackerel to the Negroes which they call a fish with one eye."

Frenchmen continued to come to the fishing grounds off West Cork to well within living memory. Their presence was not always welcomed. Local fishermen resented their large numbers; for instance the fleet mentioned in *Tuckey's Cork Remembrancer* which was sighted on May 7th, 1770, consisted of three hundred French vessels whose successful catches were thought to be the cause of scarcity at the time. In August of the same year the Earl of Shelbourne stated in a memorial that a large number of French boats were fishing off the Kerry coast, "not only abetted, but encouraged by the Irish natives". A revenue cutter of April 24th, 1786, gave typical information of sighting a fleet of two hundred French boats fishing between Baltimore and Crookhaven.

Like the pilchards, the mackerel shoals diminished and almost vanished in the early years of the nineteenth century. But they reappeared sometime around 1860 and a steady industry of salting and exporting mackerel developed all along the West Cork coast, where every little port had its fleet of boats. This continued until after the First World War. Many older people can remember the pier in Baltimore as a scene of furious activity during the high season when mackerel were salted and packed for shipment to the United States. In Salter's Bar there are still some old photographs showing trestle tables set up on the pier behind which stand lines of girls with their sleeves rolled up surrounded by barrels. These were girls who came down to the southwest from Donegal and from Scotland to follow their chosen profession—gutting fish. Special fish trains carried loads of salted mackerel up to Cork. During the First World War as many as sixteen trains left Baltimore in one day, while as late as 1925 twenty thousand barrels of mackerel caught off West Cork were exported to America. In winter there was a demand for herrings, although not so large. Mr Salter, whose father was a fish buyer, at one time ran a small plant for smoking herrings. He remembered Russians coming to Baltimore to buy preserved fish.

The boom did not last. When the United States imposed tariffs to protect its own fishing industry trade slumped immediately. Thousands of men who had been dependent on making a living from the sea were forced to emigrate. Only now, forty years later, with the aid of government subsidies, has fishing revived, with the development of large-scale trawling. But the trawlers do not use Baltimore as a base.

In addition to fishing, Baltimore has long had a tradition of boat-building. There are three ship-building yards here still, two in the town and a third at Oldcourt on the way to Skibbereen. But the fate of the old fishing school, gutted by fire some years ago, illustrates the general decline in population. It was opened in 1886 with the aim of teaching local children skills in fishing and boat-building, but there were not enough boys to keep it going. For a time orphans and children in need of corrective training were sent here, but it was closed down in 1951, to the regret of those who had seen generations of boys learning a useful trade. Among the ships built here was the *Saorise* in which Cruise O'Brien and a man from Sherkin sailed around the world in 1923. Non-conformist round-the-world yachtsmen were rare in the nineteen twenties, and O'Brien, pacing around Baltimore in short trousers and bare feet supervising the construction of *Saorise*'s curious schooner rig, was considered unusually eccentric.

Skinner's large shed overlooks the harbour, facing the lines of yachts and boats drawn up on the hard. The inside is high and spacious choked with spars and coils of ropes, old blocks, anchor chains, pairs of rollocks, oars, flags and baskets of cork. A ladder vanishes in the direction of the musty sail-loft. Amid the smells of turpentine, wood shavings, canvas and paint, to the echo of constant hammering, rises the skeleton of a new boat.

A more recent and much larger boat-building yard was established by the Irish Fishery Board—*An Bord Iascagh Mhara*—in 1952 to build trawlers and lobster boats. Twenty-seven men are kept busy on the back-log of new ships.

But Baltimore's current air of prosperity is maily due to its being a centre for sailing small boats. Visitors come to sail in Roaring Water Bay and around the broad mouth of the Ilen, which provides one of the best and safest sailing grounds for small boats in the British Isles. The French are here once again, having taken over the old railway station and transformed it into the Glenans Irish Sailing Centre, a subsidiary of the club in France. Their sturdy *Mosquetiers* mingle with the Fireballs, Internationals, Mirrors and staid Enterprises which race each other all summer long. Pier and main street are flecked with the bright yellows and oranges of yachtsmen's anoraks and their children's lifejackets.

The islands within sight of the town form a contrast to the prosperity of Baltimore. Ringarogy is visible across the Ilen, but the causeway that connects it to the mainland is some way along the Skibbereen road, which passes the ruined seventeenth-century Protestant church. Within the shell stands the tomb of one of the Frekes who was the Deputy Governor of Cork as well as the owner of Baltimore.

The causeway across the Ilen to Ringarogy was built in 1836 by Sir Wrexham Becher, the island's owner. Steamships and three-masted schooners sailed up the river forty years ago; now nothing disturbs its surface except the occasional small boat with salmon fishermen spreading their nets.

Once Ringarogy held a large population, but today, I was told, there were only twenty families with their doors still open. All traces of the two castles, Dunagall, the O'Driscoll stronghold shipped up to

Skibbereen, and the fortress erected in 1215 by the Barretts, have vanished. The only large building left on the island is the shell of a corn store overlooking the Ilen. Along the coast, corn stores are a familiar sight, situated on tidal estuaries or on the edge of the sea. In appearance their high stone walls covered with ivy resemble the equally ruinous mills that abound all over the countryside. They were built during the Napoleonic wars when the price of grain in England began to rise, and continued in use until the repeal of the Corn Laws which was one of the direct results of the famine. Before the famine it was a seller's market for grain; foreign corn was prohibited from entering England, but Irish corn was exempt. Corn was the staple by which a poor man paid his rent. An old man told me that tenant farmers used to pay their landlords every third sack of corn and potatoes, but whether this was an accurate estimate or a convenient magical number is hard to say. The grain gathered in these stores was shipped to Cork and thence to England. Throughout the famine years it was sent away from Ringarogy.

From the pier at Baltimore I took the early-morning boat to Sherkin Island. A stout wooden ship that had once taken the mail to Cape Clear, its cargo included three coils of barbed wire, two sacks of fertilizer and some ladders. The passengers were the parish priest from Baltimore, the postman and myself. Later in summer the boat would be packed with visitors.

The journey across the harbour took about fifteen minutes; we landed in a tranquil world lacking cars and haste, dominated by the beautiful abbey that overlooks Sherkin pier. The grey lichen-covered walls and belfry tower have been left to decay slowly since its destruction in 1537 by the men of Waterford. It had only been in existence for half a century. Although the building is known as "Sherkin Abbey", it was in fact a friary, built around 1460 by a member of the O'Driscoll family for Franciscans of the Strict Observance. Its most famous alumnus was the scholar, Maurice O'Fihelly, who left Sherkin to go to Oxford and then to Padua, where he became a doctor of divinity and was known as *Flos Mundi* because of his learning. He wrote a number of books, including a commentary on the philosophy of Duns Scotus and a dictionary of the holy scriptures.

Inside the walls of the abbey the graves jostling for a place include that of Richard Coppinger, a brother of Walter, who wrote in his will, dated 1650: "I do bequeath my soul to Almighty God and my body to be buried in the Abbey of Sherkin." After the island had passed into the hands of the Becher family, Lionel Becher of Sherkin used the outside walls of the abbey as a curing house for fish, and the holes which contained the press for pilchards can still be seen.

There are two main roads on Sherkin. One follows the line of coast overlooking the harbour, passing a few farmhouses and Dunalong, the Fort of the Ships, now used as a barn. Beneath its wall the O'Driscoll fleet must have been anchored when it was fired on by the raiding party from Waterford. The castle, built at the same time as the abbey, was surrendered after the Battle of Kinsale to Captain Roger Harvey. Afterwards a fort was built around the ruined castle, which was already in disuse when Smith surveyed it in the mid-eighteenth century. Smith mentions that pieces of ordnance were lying scattered about on the rocks; in recent years there have been rumours of cannon glimpsed in the water below Dunalong.

In the late seventeenth century a number of Spanish gold pieces, reputedly from the Armada wrecks, were found buried in the sand on Sherkin by Colonel Thomas Becher, who kept them in his family, which preserved them as treasured heirlooms. This Becher was governor of the barrack behind the castle at a salary of ten shillings a day, and later he became M.P. for Baltimore. He served King William at the Battle of the Boyne. "What o'clock is it, Colonel Thomas?" asked that monarch as the noise of cannon died down. "Sire. I have not got my watch on me. . . ." "Accept mine as a reward for your good and faithful service!" Perhaps it had stopped. The watch is still in the possession of the family at Castletownshend.

The Bechers built a house somewhere near the fort which fell down. All around the tower of Dunalong there are pieces of massive dry-stone walls, but it is hard to say whether they belong to the house, the fort, or the O'Driscoll's "goodly castle and bawn".

The road ends at the pier and the abandoned settlement of Dock, on the north side of Sherkin, where the remains of some cottages look across the rock-strewn water towards Inishdriscoll, or Hare Island. Dock was once the location for a small boat-building industry. There is a story that during the famine a Sherkin-built boat filled with islanders set out from here to make the perilous voyage across the Atlantic to America.

I followed the other road—the main road—which crossed the island to the south. It started well on tarmac, but a little beyond the church became gravel, then grass, and finally ended in a beach of grey pebbles. There was a cottage with a faded calendar stuck in the window, a farmyard where hens scratched at a pile of manure, and boats pulled up on the beach. This end of Sherkin is separated from Cape Clear by the turbulent waters of the Gascanane Sound, whose fast-moving tides and treacherous fringes of black rock make it a difficult passage for shipping. Near the Gascanane in 1875, Paul Boyton, an American sea captain, decided to test the inflatable life-saving gear he had invented, by throwing himself off a United States mailboat into the sea. The current swept him out of sight in a moment, but after a twenty-minute swim he succeeded in making land.

To the south-west rose the gentle turf-and-heather slope of Slievenore Hill, from the summit of which could be seen most of the islands of Roaring Water Bay—Carbery's Hundred Isles. Between the hump of Cape Clear and the islands guarding the entrance to Schull harbour were the pancake shapes of the three Calves and the Skeams, the smoothness of their pastures broken by the walls and chimney stacks of deserted cottages.

Looking for somewhere to stay, I was directed to the house of Miss Eileen Donovan who lived up over Horseshoe Bay. The road went past Kinish Harbour, overlooked by a slab of rock ten feet wide by six feet in length. Mass was celebrated here in penal times. A cross would have been placed on it as people assembled here, walking from all over the island to attend Mass offered before the open sea and sky.

Horseshoe Bay was almost landlocked, a circle of blue sea with a narrow bottle opening cut through cliffs that fell to the water. On the far side, facing straight across the sound to the beacon on Cape Clear, was Sherkin lighthouse, erected in 1885. Formerly a keeper lived here, but now a farmer came every day to climb the spiral staircase in the tower and fill up the paraffin lamp.

The highest point above the bay was Miss Donovan's cottage, a lonely enough place for a single woman to live, particularly in winter, when the weather closed in and a journey to the pier or the post office meant a stiff walk in a gale. She seemed perfectly content. Nothing would budge her to join her relatives on the mainland; apart from occasional visits to them, she had lived here all her life. The house was warm and comfortable, there was electricity, and in the last few years she had installed television. On a place like Sherkin where newspapers might be a week old, she could listen to the latest news bulletin. From the windows in the back she could see liners passing on their way to America, the Q.E. II and the *Ile de France*, as well as giant oil tankers destined for Bantry Bay.

The atmosphere on Sherkin seems idyllic, neighbour befriending neighbour, living without rancour or competition. The islanders' houses, set in sunlit fields facing the sparkling Atlantic, always have their doors open. But it is the same story as elsewhere. The community is slowly dying. If people will not stay on the mainland, there is even less chance of them continuing to live in the isolation of an island. The present population of Sherkin is seventy, and most of those who remain are pensioners. When Miss Donovan went to school there were eighty children; now there are eight. Irish is rarely spoken, and the *ceilidhe* and traditional entertainments have been replaced by television.

The only new life is provided by tourism. In summer the two pubs —soon a third will be added—open joyfully, while the ferry boat rushes backwards and forwards from Baltimore bringing load after load of visitors to drink away the long evenings. Many of the cottages have been taken over by strangers in the last few years. It is easy to see why. Sherkin is only ten minutes away from the mainland at Baltimore, to which it is connected by a regular ferry service. The island is small, about three miles long by a mile wide, but it has a great variety of scenery which includes a series of beautiful high green headlands overlooking empty sandy beaches.

In the next valley to Miss Donovan's house there was a holy well where people suffering from illness used to go to be cured. She could remember the time when the house was filled on May Eve, and her mother would have baked a great heap of cakes for the guests. Her own sister, who had been going to the doctor without success, was cured at the well of a bad back. A pilgrim would make nine circuits of the well, and if he heard a bird sing inside it, his prayers would be answered.

I searched and found it with difficulty, only by the indication of a rough wooden cross stuck between some boulders on which was written in red paint, "My Lord and My God". The paint is chipped and fading; no one goes today to the little muddy pool hidden beneath a clump of fuchsia.

SIX

Cape Clear

From Baltimore I took the mailboat to Cape Clear. Most times passengers face the Gascanane with dread, and are swept through white and bilious, Atlantic rollers pounding behind them. In the old days those who made the passage for the first time were expected to improvise a short poem to bring them luck and to distract them from sea-sickness. Today, even though it was early March, the weather was admirable, and the *Naoimh Ciaran* made the journey under blue sky with only the suggestion of a roll. The long hump of Cape Clear rose out of the sea like a blowing whale, its steep sides scored with the pattern of fields that faded into bracken and gorse.

The Cape and Sherkin are roughly the same size, but quite different in atmosphere. The Capers have a unity which the islanders on Sherkin lack; they are remoter, proud of their isolation, and consider themselves to be living in a country of their own, where they have been able to preserve vestiges of traditional ways of life. They call the mainland "Ireland". Their houses, even after they are empty, are not sold to outsiders, and recent plans for a tourist hotel have been scrapped. Even the Youth Hostel is disapproved of; stories abound about unlicensed behaviour by hitch-hikers, but one feels that they may be exaggerated and that possibly the islanders resent them as intruders.

The Irish College, however, does flourish. Cape Clear, one of the few places in West Cork where Irish is widely spoken, has been classed as a Gaeltacht area. In 1966 President De Valera was flown here by helicopter to open the college, which takes in batches of students during the summer months. But the strength of the language remains in doubt. Contact with the English-speaking mainland and the summer visitors pouring in on day trips erodes the importance of Irish. As a result, the eastern end of Cape, centred around the church and the wooden bungalow of the college, has become the Irish-speaking area, whilst at the west end, where the main harbour is situated, English is largely spoken.

Coming up from the east I encountered the postman going on his rounds; he walked all round the island four days a week with the mail. Since so many islanders were named O'Driscoll or Cadogan, much time had to be spent sorting out which letters were for whom. (The name *Cadogan* is supposed to derive from a nickname bestowed upon an O'Driscoll who in one year reared a hundred calves *ceud gamhna*.) He told me that thirty-two of the houses on the east side were still occupied. They were sprinkled over green fields that sparkled in the sun with the same brilliance as the sea, divided by stone walls and continuing right down to the cliffs above the water.

In one field stood three standing stones, the largest of which had a hole cut through its centre where lovers used to pledge their vows by holding hands, a custom that probably echoed the stone's ancient cult significance. Stones elsewhere on the island had traces of Ogham writing. When I met Denis Hamish who "spoke the English strong", he pointed out a number of little lengths of stone with curious marks that formed part of the wall in a lane. They had recently been discovered when the lane was widened to accommodate the island's cars.

Hamish could remember when Irish was spoken generally not only all over the Cape, but as far away as Macroom. Like all men of his generation he had seen the slow eclipse of the old way of life, so many house empty, so many fields gone back to gorse. In spite of Gaeltacht grants, the population had declined to a little under two hundred, a tenth of the number here in the days before the famine. What one sees today is a ghost of the life there used to be. Once, the Capers had their own king and their own code of law which it was his duty to administer. If we are to believe Smith, they were bigger stronger men than those elsewhere, of noble character, living an ideal existence, rather like the Houynhnms. "The inhabitants here are generally very simple honest people, thieving being a vice unknown among them. If a person has been found guilty of a crime, he is directly banished to the continent, which is the greatest punishment they can inflict on a criminal who endeavours all he can to remain on the island."

Pococke, visiting Cape Clear in 1758, had less flattering impressions. "The great vice here is drinking spirits which they do excessively even some of them say to a gallon a day . . . They were alarm'd at seeing our boat thinking it was the Kings as they had laid in great store of Rum from the West India fleet which had lately pass'd."

Geographically the island is almost divided into two parts by the sea. An isthmus, overlooked by the main village of Cummer, divides the north and south harbours. The north harbour, by far the most sheltered, is mainly used now. But a century ago the south harbour was the scene of immense activity. During the American Civil War there was a telegraph station there with a submarine cable linked to Sherkin, Baltimore and Europe. Ships from America would stop off at the harbour, their first landfall after the Atlantic crossing, and throw the mails into the sea wrapped in waterproof cases. These would be picked up by the islanders' boats, the first there usually receiving a guinea. The latest bulletins about the war, or the assassination of Lincoln, would then be sent by cable to London.

The Protestant church and rectory also overlooked the south harbour. The rectory, now the Youth Hostel, survives, but the church was demolished some time after 1917 when the Protestant congregation was reduced to two families. The stones were carted over to Schull, where they were used to build the Munster and Leinster Bank, alternatively serving God and Mammon. The church had been built in 1850 by the Reverend Edward Rice, who had arrived on the Cape in 1846 when the distress caused by the famine had just begun. During the following years he made a number of converts. "They took the soup and ate hairy bacon", a Caper told me. The question of "souping" is a delicate and emotional one; many proselytizing clergymen have been unjustly accused of this unpleasant form of pressure. But Mr Rice's reputation as a souper has been maintained over the years.

The north harbour is an inlet completely hidden from the storms outside; boats slip through a narrow passage into the heart of the cliffs. Here is the centre of island life, a tranquil haven completely protected by a wall of gorse-covered cliff, its waters gently lapping against the little beach and the shrine of St Kieran. An inner harbour, constructed by the old Fishery Board, was for many years a safe anchorage for trawlers to weather out winter storms.

On the edge of the inner harbour stands the bird observatory established in 1959. The island's situation in the centre of a number of migratory routes makes it an ideal place for watching birds, and a detailed record of sightings has been kept for over a decade. The observatory, converted from a farmhouse, is not a luxurious establishment. Bunks are provided upstairs with blankets as rough as hair shirts. Outside the privy is tacked a notice: "Gentlemen. . . . If Possible Use the Bushes at the East End of the House. Not the Elsan, Thank-you." In the main room downstairs are kept the items of equipment indispensable to the ornithologist—nets, rings, weighing scales, clippers, maps —and the attractive postcards of birds and island landscapes, designed by Robert Gilmore, which are on sale to visitors. Reports and registers are filled in each day—the seawatch log, the daily census, the rarity log which shows the more unusual birds that have been sighted. A tin collecting box marked *New Species* has a label: "We hope that observers will join in the tradition of donating 6d. for each new species they see on the island."

Many of the ornithologists who come to the Cape are English, bird-watching being very much an Anglo-Saxon pastime. They record the passing of each day in minute detail. "A bout of gastritis put the Major out of action on the second. . . ." "The arrival of John Dixon and myself coincided neatly with the arrival of one of the most interesting birds of the period—a buff-breasted sandpiper which spent nine days on the island. . . ."

I stayed with Tom and Stephanie Green, who were the first ornithologists to spend a complete year on Cape Clear. Their enthusiasm might be gauged from the fact that during the first months of their stay Stephanie was expecting the birth of her first child. They did not live in the observatory, but away to the east in "The Glen", a valley once densely populated, but now full of empty houses and bracken-covered fields. The cottage they had found possessed the comfort of a bathroom. Outside on the balcony were strings of rabbit skins intended to be used for making clothes for the baby. The rabbits provided an unending substitute for the Sunday joint.

Tom worked from early dawn until the lack of light made bird-watching impossible. On successive days a different part of the island would be explored. Bogs, bushes, the few trees were minutely examined and each sighting tabulated. Robins, yellowhammers, wheatears, choughs. Occasionally a rarity would be sighted that sent a *frisson* through the ornithologist's world. Unusual birds seen on the island have included a rustic bunting, a blackbrowed albatross, a great shearwater, and once five eagles were observed flying in a group. In the evening Tom had further work filling up log books and adding to the collection of ticks which were being sent to a researching professor. Most of them came from the neck of a large grey cat.

For several mornings I accompanied him on his expeditions, setting off at dawn. Spring comes early in this south-west corner of the country; there were primroses already in the grassy banks and bird song everywhere. Above the cottage a track led to the ruined lighthouse and signal tower. The tower had been built at the same time as the one above Baltimore, and formed part of the same system of communication. The lighthouse, which came a few years later, was completed by 1810; its light could be seen for twenty-eight miles out to sea. Unfortunately the site proved unsatisfactory. It was too far inland and in foggy weather the light could not be seen clearly by passing ships. Its inadequacy was emphasized in 1847, when an American ship, the *Stephen Whitney*, struck a rock and went down with the loss of a hundred lives. Shortly after this tragedy, work began on the construction of a lighthouse on the Fastnet Rock.

The broken coastline was particularly dangerous, and in the nineteenth century hardly a year went by without some notable shipwreck on the cliffs of the island. In one year, 1867, for example, the *Cork Advertiser* reported two such wrecks. "The ship, *Czar*, of Glasgow was a few days ago found deserted off Cape Clear. She was loaded with iron and coal, and when picked up bore traces of having sustained a severe gale. Not a living creature was on board." A few weeks later: "Since Sunday 8th, several boxes and pieces of wreck have been picked up at sea by the owners of boats belonging to Long Island and Cape Clear, and it is feared from papers also found, that the vessel wrecked was the *Enoch Ebner* of Boston, commanded by Captain Jefferson Ebner. . . ."

Down the steep track to the west we passed through the village of Cummer, straddled between the north and south harbours, where among the line of whitewashed cottages were two pubs where groceries could be bought. On one day we made a detour to the north-west, past the observatory across the fields to Dunanore. The Golden Fort is perhaps the most dramatically sited of the O'Driscoll castles, set among

Main Street, Ballydehob, *circa* 1900

Ballydehob today

Road near Rosbrin

cliffs and sea birds on what is virtually a small island. At one time a narrow causeway linked it to the mainland; now it can just be reached by a hazardous climb over tumbled rocks. Built in the thirteenth century, it was a typical three-storeyed structure placed in a seemingly impregnable look-out position over the bay and the mainland. In later times, however, its situation proved no adequate defence from attack by land, and after the Battle of Kinsale, Captain Roger Harvey captured it by placing his guns on the high ground above it. Only the shattered tower and part of the original walls remain, while chunks of masonry dislodged by cannon and by centuries of storm are scattered among the rocks.

According to Donovan, there are many stories of treasure about Dunanore, as its name would imply. A ghost ship arrives there at night and a ghostly crew fills up the castle with treasure. In the early eighteenth century a soldier stationed on the island, excited by the stories he had heard, dug at the foot of the castle for gold. The pit can still be seen.

A few years later, a famous giant, Cruathuir O'Careavaun, retired here as a hermit, dying in the castle. He was over eight feet high and had great strength; once in Cork harbour he lifted up a ship's anchor which the whole crew had been unable to budge, even with the aid of a windlass.

On another day we took the path to the south-west past Lough Errul, on the edge of whose placid waters are a number of stone basins once used for cleaning flax. The lake is supposed to have special cleansing properties. At the far side of the hill overlooking the Atlantic are lines of stones known as the *Fir Breaga*, or False Men. *Fir Breaga* is a general term for standing stones; throughout the country many are known as False Men, possibly an indication of phallic associations. On Cape Clear the tradition goes further, and this line of unimpressive stones, so the story goes, was set up literally as false men to give the impression that the island was guarded. They look directly out to sea and, either painted red or dressed in red tunics and hats to resemble soldiers, they frightened off the French who were on their way to Bantry.

Below them were jagged cliffs speckled with yellow lichen and the droppings of innumerable birds that nested there. The steep gully of Foildermotycronacane dividing us from the long Bill of Cape was

F

swept by shrieking gulls. At Breen rock, another bare promontory, Tom had his hide, consisting of a wall of stones overlooking the sea. Here he settled to watch the birds. A line of gannets making a purposeful flight, their long white wings tipped with black almost touching the sea, disappeared due south. There were auks, terns and squalling herring gulls. In a few weeks the great westward passage would begin, when the migrating flights would pass in great numbers. On some days one or two thousand fulmars an hour pass this way.

In summer, in July, this would be a good place for watching the Fastnet race, when the expanse of sea is covered with yachts tacking towards the rock. After they wheel around the lighthouse, their multicoloured spinnakers are set to catch the west wind which will carry them past the Cape once more on their way home to Southampton Water.

I left Tom and my way to the north harbour where the arrival of the mailboat caused the daily flutter of activity. Bales of straw and corrugated roofing were unloaded and the few passengers stumped uphill towards uphill towards Cummer. Loaves of bread were transferred into a donkey-cart and taken away and within a few minutes the harbour was as deserted as before.

Against the pier lay the rotting hulls of the *Carbery Lass* and the smaller *St Patrick*. Once this small harbour was packed with ships. In 1920 there had been forty-three trawlers based on the island, including a schooner of a hundred and thirty tons. As elsewhere, the cessation of fishing sadly emphasizes the steady decline in population.

The majority of islanders always relied on fishing to augment their income from farming. They were equally at home on the rolling deck of a ship or behind a plough on their land. The famine was the first break in this pattern of life, and many of the emigrants who left the island after 1847 made their way to Newfoundland where they continued to employ their fishing skills by working on the dories. Thirty years afterwards fishing revived on Cape Clear and became a thriving trade. With the aid of grants men could buy new ships and fish on a commercial basis. The first fleet of new mackerel vessels arrived here in 1877 from the Isle of Man where they had been built. They were substantial ships compared to those formerly used, weighing twenty-four tons and carrying a crew of eight men. Their sails included a topsail, mainsail, foresail and mizen. Without engines the task of slipping

through the walls of the cliff into the shelter of the harbour must have
been formidable.

> "The harbour of Trawkieran
> I saw it in its pride
> With its fleet of yacht-like fishing boats
> Awaiting for the tide."

The men would fish mainly for mackerel and herring, which
were caught in long drift nets or by the obsolete long lines, laid out in
distant locations as far away as Dursey and the Bull Rock. It was slow
and laborious work in an open boat. Lewis, writing in his *Topographical
History of Ireland* of the previous generation of Capers in 1837, considered that "the men are expert and resolute fishermen, and the best
pilots on the coast; they are remarkable for discerning land at a distance
in snowy or foggy weather, possessing an uncommon sagacity in discovering the approach of bad weather and are exceedingly skilful in the
management of their vessels." Even today the old fishermen are
remembered with something like reverence: "Giants of men . . . not
like those of today. One of them could throw Cassius Clay over his
shoulder." As for their appetites: "For breakfast one would eat two
pounds of butter, six oranges, between nine and sixteen herrings and a
large crock of jam." In the evenings a man would swallow down a
bucketful of potatoes.

The Cape, along with the rest of West Cork, was hit by the American tariffs discouraging the export of mackerel. This move, coupled
with factors like emigration and the change in fishing methods—
trawling taking the place of drift nets—killed the old way of life. Some
people blame part of the decline on injurious government policy. "The
wholesale neglect of the pelegaic fisheries," wrote John Boland, a
Skibbereen man, in 1948, "robs the part-time fisherman of a source of
income which was essential to his well-being." On the Cape there are
four fishing boats left; all of these use Bearhaven as their base and
return to the island at the weekends.

But in the evening in the pubs the talk is still all about boats and
fishing. Nearly all Capers have a connection with the sea. Many
became merchant seamen and sailed all over the world before retiring
here. An old sailor showed me his souvenirs which included a pile of

pamphlets he had obtained on Hong Kong depicting Chairman Mao, whose bland features gazed up quizzically at the Sacred Heart and St Patrick which adorned his little kitchen.

Drifts of conversation come across the bar in Cottar's pub. "I was seven hundred miles off the Cape when the last war started. . . ." ". . . the man who built that boat had no conscience—it was designed like a submarine. . . ." Mick Donoghue, a big red-headed sailor, can remember the names of all the mackerel boats and who owned them . . . the *Gabriel*, *St Ultan*, *St Agnes*, and the *St Patrick* which he himself still owns and has completely rebuilt during the last few years. A man at the back complains that in England he was charged two shillings and sixpence for a mackerel, when once he used to sell them for one and six a hundred. He had asked the waitress for a receipt to prove it to his friends living here. . . .

Cape Clear is held to be the birthplace of St Kieran, whose feast day is celebrated on the fifth of March, a fortnight before the festival of St Patrick. Possibly the choice of an earlier date was made deliberately by those who believed that St Kieran preceded St Patrick in bringing Christianity to Ireland. He is said to have been born in A.D. 352, and therefore to have been thirty years older than the country's patron, with a good head start for missionary activities. But speculation about his life is unreliable. The dictionary of saints declares emphatically that "most of what is related about him, however entertaining or edifying, has no value as sober history".

On the Cape such austere rulings of scholars have been ignored. The island is filled with traces of him. Behind the strand of Kieran or "Trawkieran" in the south harbour is his holy well and beside it a standing stone engraved with a cross, said to have been incised by the saint's own hand. If this were so, the stone would be the earliest Christian relic in Ireland. A short distance away the shell of a Romanesque church, also called after St Kieran, stands on the site of a much older building. The islanders claim that on this spot was celebrated the first mass ever held in Ireland. In 1969 mass was said here again after a gap of four hundred and fifty years. Anyone buried within the walls of the churchyard goes straight to heaven. From the amount of tombstones that crowd every inch of space it would seem that the islanders have left little to chance. The giant, Cruathuir O'Careavaun, is buried here in a large grave.

On the evening of the fourth of March the first pilgrimage is made to the shrine. Up until Marian year this spot consisted simply of the stone and the well. But now the white figure of the Virgin stands under a wing of concrete, and the wall beneath her feet through which water trickles down to the beach has been boxed in. Around her are clustered some tins of flowers. She holds a battery and bulb in her outstretched hand, and a bicycle lamp shines up from the ground.

Pilgrims used to walk to the well from all over the island. Today many of them come in cars. On the one narrow tarred road, the islanders' cars and tractors tend to get congested. There are no police-men, and regulations about road taxation, maintenance and safety are not too stringently observed. Cars which would have been sent to the scrap heap long ago, find a new lease of life when they are shipped over the Gascanane. This evening all peace is shattered by the crackle of exhausts, as ancient Fords and Volkswagens drive down the hill from Cummer to the strand. On one the mudguards flap wildly as if at any moment it might take off and fly; another has a new plywood door, and a third hurtles through the dusk guided only by a pale flickering amber light. All are eaten away with rust, so that some fenders and mudguards look like old lace. Tonight they are parked near the shrine and families walk down to pray for a few moments. Beyond Cummer there is a flash from the Fastnet, and a ship, all lighted up, is swallowed by the sea.

Next morning another pilgrimage takes place before sunrise, but by the time I get down at nine o'clock only one man is kneeling by the standing stone, which is decorated with limp arum-lily leaves held down by pebbles. His name is O'Driscoll like so many of the islanders, and he has a thin hatchet face like an early saint.

After he has prayed I watch him fill up a bottle of water from the well. He says that it is used as a cure by most people, and moreover, because it is holy, it never goes bad. He has a bottle at home which was collected twenty years ago and is as fresh and sweet as the day it was taken. He tells me the story of the fishermen from neighbouring Long Island, who drew some of this water for their kettle.

"Naturally it wouldn't boil. And for months afterwards, as a punish-ment for them, their kettle wouldn't boil up any water at all."

SEVEN

Skibbereen

THE LIGHT WAS fading as I set out from Baltimore along the Ilen river. A red sunset glowed against the woods of Innishbeg, and the tower of Creagh church stood out against the trees, whose branches were crowded with roosting crows. Inside the church, the smell of mould, the dust-sheets on the pews and the dead butterflies in cobwebs indicated a reduced Protestant congregation.

Much of the road followed the defunct Baltimore railway line, along which the fish trains used to shunt up to Cork. At intervals on the grass-covered track the cross-road houses were converted for Englishmen. One was called "Hobson's Choice"; another had tubs of flowers all round it. At Oldcourt a boat-building yard flourished within the walls of an O'Driscoll castle overlooking the pier and river. Schooners and steamships used to anchor at this spot, the highest point they could travel up river. Here their cargoes of coal and other supplies were unloaded and placed on specially built lighters with a small draught that would be poled along a further sluggish turn or two upstream to the pier at Skibbereen. In this way cargoes of cattle were brought up by islanders to be sold at market.

Next day in Skibbereen I watched the rain slash across the window of my lodging in North Street. Further down the street was Becher's Hotel, outside which had been the regulation stop for coaches and Bianconi cars. Thackeray stayed at Becher's in 1842, having arrived on the coach, the *Skibbereen Industry*, which he nicknamed the *Perseverance*. He was depressed by the dirt and the swarms of beggars that crowded the narrow lanes of the town. Becher's he described as a "dirty coffee house with a strong smell of whiskey". He did allow, however, that "dirty as the place was, there was no reason why it should not produce an exuberant dinner of trout and Kerry mutton".

In 1858 the Prince of Wales, later Edward VII, stopped at Skibbereen and put up at Becher's along with his younger brother and a tutor. He was sixteen years old at the time and on his way to stay at Killarney. He drank some milk and the milky glass was kept unwashed in a glass case and shown to visitors. Afterwards the boys were taken for a drive in a jaunting car. When they saw a bog they made the jarvey stop and filled the car with pieces of cut turf which they threw at the donkeys and geese that they passed. Near Lough Hyne the horses bolted, and the heir to the throne of England was thrown out into a pool where he nearly drowned.

I saw that the bad weather was settling in. The downpour lashed the pavements and emptied the streets, as winds from all corners of the town swept around the Weeping Maid of Erin on her plinth. I went for a meal at the hotel which has superseded Becher's in prominence.

"It's a good place to commit suicide in," my landlady had considered. In the dining-room burly farmers made short work of the great T-bone steaks brought in from the kitchen. Dabs of ketchup lubricated the mounds of meat, which together with tea and brown and white bread-and-butter, were swallowed down to the sound of the radio. It was playing *ceilidhe* music very loudly, the amplified fiddle sounding like a neurosthenic bee.

Across the street some shops still carried signs which offered escape to a less gloomy life. "Cunard Atlantic Tours—Second Class, £29. Comfort and Economy." Within their seedy interiors there were brochures full of glib advertising. "You can do it in three weeks. Visit your friends and relations. They'll be glad to see you. Combine business with pleasure . . . much to learn and plenty to see. Study American business methods . . . see their factories. Send your employees . . . business will benefit."

In the twenties and thirties a feature of the town was the crowd which gathered every week at the station to see off relatives and friends. Passengers to Cork expected the lamentations of emigrants to America to be as constant a feature of train travel as the click of the rails. That was a particularly bad time. Between 1911 and 1961 forty-five per cent of the population from the area surrounding the town emigrated. It was as if the district were constantly struck by plague or waging perpetual war with a steady drain of casualties.

Skibbereen reflects the stagnation of the country around; its economic history is even more depressing than that of most Cork towns. A series of expansions when trade was good were followed in each case by hopeless regressions. For many years it was the centre of a clothing trade, with a famous weekly market; but wool and linen failed in turn. Then, during the famine, something like half the population vanished.

In the years immediately afterwards thousands of emigrants departed from all over south-west Ireland. From the port of Cork about fifteen hundred people left for North America every week. For example, in one week in April, 1851, the following ships sailed from Cork harbour: the *Dominique* for Quebec with a hundred and fifty passengers, the *Don* for New York, a hundred and sixty, the *Lockwoods* for New York, two hundred and eighty, the *Marchioness of Bute* for Quebec, a hundred and twenty, the *Sara* for Boston, a hundred and four, the *Solway* for New York, a hundred and ninety-six, the *Try Again* for Quebec, a hundred and thirty, the *Favourite* for Boston, a hundred and twenty, the *Field Marshal Rodetzsky* for New York, eighty-eight, and the *Hotspur* for New York with a hundred paupers on board from the Kenmare Union House.

The pattern was established. The geographer, T. W. Freeman, has pointed out that "within Ireland the density of population from one area to another is determined partly by the relative appeal of emigration through the years, though areas of apparent poverty do not of necessity have the greatest number of migrants".[4] Around Skibbereen emigration has been an inevitable fact of life for a hundred and thirty years.

By 1876 there were less than four thousand people living in the town. In the last years of the nineteenth century the coming of the railway brought a new short-lived era of prosperity. Small industries developed, including a brewery, distillery, iron foundry and rope factory. There was also employment in spinning, weaving, lace-making and tobacco manufacture. The town's importance as a centre of routes leading all over West Cork was enhanced by the extension of branch railway lines to Baltimore and Schull. But long before the departure of the railways, by the turn of the century, these industries were beginning to close. There seemed to be nothing left except the public houses, one to every

ninety people, according to a survey made in 1964. Their numbers
have been little affected by the fact that the first Temperance Society
in Europe was founded in Skibbereen in 1814 by a poor nailer named
Geoffrey Sedwards.

In the last few years the wilted town has shown some signs of revival.
It has been aided by the sudden importance of tourism. The new tourist
office, decorated with posters showing Ireland caught in a tropical
haze, acknowledges Skibbereen's position as "the capital of the Carberies", a centre for seeing West Cork.

The Fastnet Co-operative has been opened to provide employment
and to encourage farmers in the surrounding district to grow vegetables
for canning and freeze-drying. The processing plant employs over a
hundred people, preparing young potatoes, french beans, celery,
cabbage, carrots and parsnips as they come into season. But the co-
operative has run into difficulties in trying to persuade conservative
farmers to supply vegetables to specification and on time. Often there
are not enough to keep the factory going, and they have to be brought
in from East Cork and from as far away as Tipperary, a process that
quite defeats the object of locating the factory in West Cork.

Sciobarín means "the little boat harbour". Before the seventeenth
century there was no town here. The English settlers were the town-
builders, chosing suitable positions for their new foundations. Here was
an ideal location on the Keal and Ilen rivers with easy approach to the
sea. Originally two settlements bordered the Keal river. The land on the
east side, granted to two adventurers by Charles II, was named after
one of them and referred to in the title as "Skibbereen, to be for ever
called Stapletown". On the west side there was Bridgetown. Both
settlements joined up, reverting to the old name for the area, which
once was in the possession of the McCarthy Reaghs of Kilbrittain
Castle.

Considerable numbers of Englishmen came to West Cork throughout the seventeenth and eighteenth centuries, more so than to the
western half of Ireland generally. Like Bandon and Clonakilty, Skibbereen was a Protestant foundation. Until quite recently the majority of
businesses were owned by Protestants. Many people believe that they
held an influence quite out of proportion to their numbers. The
Skibbereen Social Survey of 1964 admits cautiously that "some
accounts suggest that Skibbereen was a town lacking in initiative and

enterprise and that its people were unduly deferential". Tom Barry, writing in his *Guerilla Days in Ireland* of the period of 1920 and 1921, was more specific. "Its inhabitants were a race apart from the sturdy people of Cork. They were different, and with few exceptions were spineless, slouching through life meek and tame, prepared to accept ruling and domination from any clique in the country, provided that they were left to vegetate in peace."[5]

This is hardly fair to a town which had earlier been an important centre for the Fenians. However, it has had difficulty in shaking off the reputation of being West British. The *Skibbereen Eagle*, for example, founded in 1857 by an Englishman named Elden Potter, was always stridently Imperial and loyalist in tone. Its rival, the *Southern Star*, established in 1889, had a much more nationalist approach to the news. The *Star* still flourishes, and I visited its offices hoping that it might know something about the old files of the *Eagle* and that I might look up the issue with the famous editorial about the *Eagle* keeping its eye on the Czar. But that particular file no longer exists.

For thirty years the *Eagle* and the *Star* took extreme opposite political opinions. During the Troubles the *Star* (in which Michael Collins had shares) became increasingly unpopular with the authorities, and it was suppressed seven times between 1919 and 1920. Then the Black and Tans raided its offices and burned the back copies and the files. In retaliation the Republicans visited the *Eagle* and did the same for that paper. A few bundles of old files of the *Eagle* somehow survived, and today they lie up in the attic of the *Star*'s offices. After the Treaty, the *Eagle* determinedly continuing its old editorial policy, was doomed as its readers evaporated. It was only a question of time before the paper went out of existence. In 1929 it was declared bankrupt and incorporated with the *Star*, which survives today, a weekly with a healthy circulation of over nineteen thousand.

Three miles west of the town, facing the Ilen, a large graveyard contains the ruins of the fourteenth-century Cistercian Abbey of Abbeystrowry. The few crumbling bits of ivy-covered walls are not what gives this place special poignancy; it is the lumpy half-acre of space beneath them. This is "the Pits", where the great open graves received the bodies of those who died near Skibbereen during the famine. Handfuls of sawdust were sprinkled over the corpses in lieu of coffins. Burials were at night, graves were packed tight and limbs broken to make room. There is a story of a boy who was found alive by the gravediggers, his legs broken by the spade. He lived, crippled, for many years.

> "I rose from the dead in the year forty-eight,
>   Though a grave in the Abbey had near been my fate."

Before the famine all the coastal parishes of West Cork had teeming populations. The onset of starvation, therefore, struck all the harder—though the notoriety of Skibbereen during these years was partly due to the fact that its distress was widely publicized. The high proportion of deaths compared to the number of the population made the Irish famine possibly the worst in recorded history. As in most famines, it was the aged and the children who suffered the most.

When Thackeray visited the district in 1842, the impression he gives is one of *crowds*. People were everywhere. His account reads strangely to anyone who knows the empty country today.

"There was no lack of population: ragged people who issued from their cabins as the coach passed. . . . Everybody seemed sitting by the wayside here. . . . All the children seemed to be on watch for the coach . . . and then hung on by the scores behind."

Of Skibbereen on a Sunday he wrote:

"The people came flocking into the place by hundreds . . . you saw their blue cloaks dotting the road . . . the women all bare legged, and many of them might be seen washing their feet in the stream before they went up to the chapel. The streets seemed to be lined on either side with blue cloaks, squatting along the doorways as is their wont."

Only five years later the blue cloaks would become shrouds; the figures in doorways would be lifeless. In the mornings shopkeepers would open up their doors gingerly for fear of bumping against those who might have died outside during the night.

It was the terrible news from Skibbereen that first told the English public of the disaster in Ireland. Mr Nicholas Cummins, a Cork magistrate, horrified at what he saw in the town and the surrounding area, wrote a report in a letter to the Duke of Wellington which was published in *The Times* on December 24th, 1847.

On the heavily congested headlands of Roaring Water Bay the
death toll was unknown; thousands died untended in their homes.
Those who had the strength flocked to the Skibbereen workhouse.
This was one of a series built around the country following the passing
of the Poor Law Relief Bill. There appeared to be need for them, since
famine was by no means unknown before 1846. In 1821 and 1822, for
example, the potato crop had failed and "distress beyond description"
was reported around Skibbereen. But the German traveller, Kohl,
who visited Ireland in the same year as Thackeray, observed that "the
Irishman would rather wander through the entire world seeking
employment than endure the discipline of a workhouse, so long as he
is in possession of his health and strength".

The workhouse in Skibbereen, built like many others in Ireland
to the specific design of an engineer called Wilkson, was described
by Thackeray as "a bastard-Gothic edifice with a profusion of cottage-
ornée roofs and pinnacles and insolent-looking stacks of chimneys".
Although it had accommodation for nine hundred inmates, he noticed
that it was half empty. In the autumn of 1846 this grotesquely in-
congruous building was totally inadequate to house the vast throngs
clamouring for entrance. "When dinner had been supplied to these
famishing creatures and the officers came to put them out, they had to
desist—such were the heartrending shrieks of the poor wretches, saying
that they would lie down and die around the walls of the house . . .
they could not drive them out into the heavy rain. . . ."

Today the workhouse has gone, burnt in 1921, although its walls
surround the modern hospital. But another memory of the famine
survives in the old steam mills alongside the river, where at Mr
Thomas H. Marmion's Store, which he had kindly offered for the
purpose, a Charity Soup House was established on October 31st,
1846.

"Gratuitous" soup served from the Skibbereen Soup House cost
the charitable three halfpence a ration. A list of rules for this establishment has survived in the possession of Mr William Kingston, who
discovered it in the lining of a hatbox. He showed me the small blue-
tinted piece of paper, as fresh and legible as the day it was printed.
Benevolence was selective, according to Rule Two: "That the distribution of the Soup be made daily upon tickets to be granted by the
subscribers." Rule Four explains the system: "That every Subscription

of One Shilling and Ninepence shall entitle the subscriber thereof to grant two tickets for each day during the month in which he shall have subscribed such sum; and that such ticket shall entitle the bearer to One Imperial Pint of Soup; or, if the ticket be a monthly one, the same quantity each day during that month."

On the back of this paper there is a handwritten list of the original subscribers. Their names are those of landowning families of the area— Townsend, Warren, Hungerford, Somerville, Donovan. The first subscriber contributed three and sixpence. This would have given four people a pint of soup a day for a month. He only arrived at this sum after some cogitation, for sevenpence, and then one shilling and ninepence have been scratched out. Of the rest, five contributors put their names down for three and sixpence, and three for one and ninepence. This was before the famine was at its worst, but it was a time when fifty per cent of the children entering the workhouse were dying of "diarrhoea acting on an exhausted constitution". A month later would come the visit of Mr Cummins, who was to shock the readers of *The Times* by describing "Scenes of frightful hunger . . . famished and ghastly skeletons . . . phantoms . . . frightful spectres . . ."

EIGHT

Roaring Water Bay

IN THE HEDGES there were puffs of whitethorn, and the sun warmed the gorse bushes so that the blossoms gave out their mothball scent. On a bicycle you catch a new smell every few yards, and along the Ilen seaweed, mud, gorse, fresh earth and manure succeeded each other.

The Ilen—*Eibhlie* or "sparkling stream"—rises west of Dunmanaway and is tidal from Skibbereen. It used to be famous for its salmon and six boats are licensed for netting. They are too efficient. "They come up by river and go down by road," people say of the fish.

Three miles from Abbeystrowry a curious brick arch stands beside the roadway. There used to be another on the far side of the road, but a lorry knocked it down some years ago. These arches were copies of the watergates at Hampton Court, built by Lord Riversdale to embellish the entrance to his estate of Newcourt. He added other decorative details, like little Gothic towers on the house, and crenellations in the outside wall that can still be seen. The house itself was pulled down to make room for a modern farmhouse; the surrounding woods were felled. Among the members of the Fleming family who lived here during the nineteenth century were my grandmother and her sisters, who waited, like characters out of Chekov, for someone to take them away. Marriage to a curate provided the best chance. Young clergymen, arriving to assist at lonely parishes in West Cork, found themselves liable to be pursued by restless Protestant spinsters. A curate was less likely to be a near relation; he was a change from cousins and second cousins and less prone, perhaps, to exhibit signs of eccentricity. If he married a lucky girl, she would be able to escape the

chilly monotony of her existence and go with him on to his next parish
—in Cork or Dublin, possibly, or even in England.

Further west Aughadown House is also in ruins, its deer park divided
up into fields. Donovan described it as "a strong castellated mansion,
entered by a drawbridge, surrounded by beautiful grounds and having a
gazebo on one of the heights behind". This gazebo was approached by
a ramp along which the quality used to drive their carriages in order
to enjoy the magnificent view out over Roaring Water Bay to the
islands and the Fastnet in the distance. I found the ramp running above
a field of winter wheat. The substantial ruins of the house lie in a hollow
behind, probably on an older site; Aughadown means the Field of the
Fortress. It was built in the early seventeenth century by a member of
the Becher family. There were Bechers all over West Cork; according
to tradition you could walk on Becher land from Castlehaven all the
way to Cork city.

The last Becher at Aughadown left the house early in the nineteenth
century in a fit of grief and remorse after he had killed his son in a
shooting accident. A monument to this young man survives in St
Matthew's, Augahdown (. . . "accomplished, friendly, intelligent,
sincere . . ."). This tablet was taken from the older church at Aughadown, now an ivy-covered shell poised on the edge of the Ilen. The
weedy graveyard, dotted with the square stone monuments to successive Bechers, is used by both Protestants and Catholics, united at last.
Such mixed burial places are described by some older people as "pre-
Patrick". Years ago a salmon fisherman returning at night took a short
cut across the graveyard. To his astonishment he heard a bell ring. A
piece of ivy, blown by the wind, was scratching against an old bell
whose existence had long been forgotten.

In 1854, Judith Fleming from Newcourt was married here, her
wedding being probably one of the last to take place before the church
fell into disuse. "I am quite mad with the girls for not having given
you a proper account, of the 14th September," she wrote later to a
friend. "Weddings are generally held to be very stupid and dismal
things, but really to judge from the merriment, laughter, words and
looks of the party assembled at mine, I should think they were decidedly
the reverse. Though of course I was (or ought to have been) in a state of
somnambulance as the bride, I preserved my faculties to observe my six
bridesmaids, Henrietta, the two little Barkers, your two girls and Lili,

blooming and floating about like ethereal clouds of muslin and lace—
then packed into carriages and setting off for the church—an empty
jingle, that had brought Elizabeth Somerville from Ross tearing away
on its own account, the jingle man being determined not to lose any
share of the fun, then arriving at the church which is rather confined,
and my standing and being married to something that had feet and
hands (I could not add anything more, except a tongue, I heard it plain
enough), and then driving home with the same members with little
boys shouting at every crossroad, and all the schoolchildren with Mrs
Young crying like anything, standing at the gate. . . ."

Unlike Newcourt and Aughadown, Whitehall survives, standing
near the edge of the little Lisheen peninsula whose rich green fields and
gorse hedges jut out into the bay beyond Aughadown. It is an elegant
white house, with a fine horseshoe staircase and tall windows dropping
down on to lawns which lead to the water's edge. Bought by Germans
some years ago, renovated, fitted out with central heating and sturdy
Teutonic furniture, it is probably in far better trim than it used to be
when it was owned by the Townsends. In the inevitable memoir, my
great-aunt recalled the long drive up to the front door, deep in mud in
which her father as a young man lost his dancing shoes. (He danced the
night through in his socks.) The white face of the idiot Townsend
relation peered down at arriving visitors from an upper window.
Another brother, a drunkard, used to hunt up his mother and sisters
about the house, waving his knife, so that they had to seek shelter
among the peaches in the greenhouse. A sister, late in life, began to
realize that there was always a man standing behind her watching
everything she did and listening to every word she said. "He was so
close behind her that no matter how quickly she turned round to see
him, she was never quick enough, nor could anyone else see him
either." They locked her in a lunatic asylum, where she seemed to be
cured, and after a time she was released. "But the moment she left the
gates, he (lying in wait outside) again followed her. So she was taken
back and lived there to a great age, long over ninety."

Until they left early this century, the Townsends at Whitehall lived in
some grandeur, entertaining elaborately in the stately dining-room, the
table laid with superb silver and Cork glass. There were endless balls and
parties and trips round the bay and out to Cape Clear in the jolly boat,
"a man from Skibbereen who could play the cornet sitting in the bows".

Cosheen copper mine near Schull

The harbour, Schull

Empty houses, Creagh

My great-aunt remembered going down to a cellar which was filled with swords used to arm the tenants during the time of the Whiteboys and also with empty stone wine jars which had carried wine smuggled in from France. From this cellar there was believed to be a passage underground leading to the O'Driscoll castle of Rincolisky, whose truncated remnants are to be found in a neighbouring field. (The missing stones were used in building the house.) An earlier Townsend sent his little negro page down the passage to see if it was clear. The boy was never seen again.

Beyond Whitehall I rode out to the point at Cunamore where the road ended at a small pier which was the nearest point to Hare Island, also known as Inishdriscoll. There was no regular ferry across, but the post boat went over several days a week, and the schoolmistress crossed daily to teach the dozen remaining children. It is a much less dramatic island than Cape or Sherkin, a low-lying slab of land with golden beaches. One road leads to a little village nicknamed Paris—probably a derivation of "pallace"—once the centre of a fleet of lobster boats. Now I listened to an old man lamenting the terrible decline.

"John has gone and Dennis has died, and we'll die too, and then the foreigners can have it all." Already half a dozen of the houses had been bought up by strangers.

One by one the smaller islands became deserted. It is a long time since they were densely populated, but until quite recently they supported a certain number of families. Only a few years ago I visited Horse Island, just opposite Ballydehob. The last people there, an elderly couple, were living all alone. It was summer, and the old man was sitting in a chair outside his house, his feet in a basin of water. His wife, behind him, fed hens. Next year they were gone. The house, still intact and comfortable, stood empty, the linoleum in place, last year's calendar on the wall. Down by the pier a plough had been thrown into the water where it looked like a gesture of despair.

Often island people do not go far away; the change to the mainland is sufficient for them. Or to another island; on Cape Clear I met a farmer's wife who had moved across from the Middle Calf, where her family had lived up to 1940. Now, like the East Calf, the Skeams, Castle Island, Coney Island and Horse Island, Middle Calf is empty.

Off Cunamore lie two of the most beautiful islands, the Skeams, uninhabited for thirty years or more. At the east end of the western

G

Skeam the forlorn ruin of a church hangs above a cliff which has eroded so that the eastern gable has tumbled into the sea. In the exposed cliff face traces of ancient burials are visible and all around other graves are extraordinarily plentiful. The burial ground has not been used for centuries, but once it must have been a place of great sanctity. Possibly a clerical community lived here. Surviving architectural features of this mysterious little church suggest that it dates back to the nineth century. Very little is known about it apart from the tradition that the name derives from St Kame, supposedly a brother of St Kieran, of Cape Clear. The brothers lived on Cape Clear with their sister. According to an old story the family had two cows, one of which was a "stripper" and gave rich milk. When Kieran was told why his weight had increased he became angry and said that the family would have to separate. He went to Ossory, his sister founded a nunnery known as the Bonavaun, and Kame came to his island.

On the mainland I crossed Lisheen peninsula through a network of lanes that skirted the edge of the sea. Some were sheltered with banks of fuchsia, others looked directly across the bay. The cottages in the area, with their lace curtains and patches of arum lilies in front, browsing hens and grinning children, made a cosy contrast to the lonely farmhouses on Hare Island. Many of them were long two-storeyed buildings, said to have been improved and rebuilt during the First World War when money was made out of the high price of horses.

Kilcoe Castle stands on a little island that can be crossed at low tide. Behind it on the next spur of land is the twelfth-century church with its graveyard overlooking the sea. (The name Kilcoe means the Sea Church.) Church and chancel were in ruins by 1615 and later it was marked as a ruin on Smith's maps. There were so many ruined churches in Co. Cork that Smith had a special symbol for them, a tiny building topped with a steeple set awry. Kilcoe church is a long low building with slitted windows that must have been dark even on a summer's day.

The castle, a landmark for miles around, is still in an excellent state of preservation. This was a McCarthy stronghold; the McCarthy's were more sophisticated soldiers than the O'Driscolls and O'Mahonys, and Kilcoe is more elaborately constructed than their gaunt fortresses. It consists of two towers, roughly square in shape, which stand corner to corner like a figure eight. The tower to the north is higher, and contains several rooms connected by staircases, including a dungeon on the lowest floor. The broad tower consists of a great hall and a gallery on a scale not to be found elsewhere along this part of the coast. Strong fortifications made this castle one of the last in West Cork to withstand the English after the battle of Kinsale. Kilcoe resisted the superior forces under Captain Roger Harvey and remained untaken for two years.

Captain Harvey is associated with many West Cork castles. A cousin of Sir George Carew, the Lord President of Munster, after Kinsale he received a commission to carry out a minor campaign against the Irish, eliminating surviving pockets of resistance by taking the minor castles in the area. In February, 1602, he accepted the surrender of Castlehaven and Baltimore, which had been garrisoned by the Spanish; and in the same month successfully besieged and subdued Dunamore on Cape Clear. After the main O'Sullivan castle of Dunboy on the Bearhaven peninsula had been sacked by Carew in June, Harvey took Dunmanus and Leamcon castles in a swift forced march. These were the last castles to fall to him. He could not capture Kilcoe, which he besieged without success. It was not until the following February, 1603, that his subordinate, Captain George Flower, succeeded in making the fortress surrender, "being a place of great strength and the only castle in Carbery holding out in rebellion", according to *Pacata Hibernia*. Harvey had died at Baltimore a few months before its capitulation, "his heart overwhelmed with sorrow" at some reprimand from Carew over his artillery. Possibly it concerned his ill-success here.

Near Kilcoe is the mouth of Roaring Water River, which gives its name to Roaring Water Bay. The Bay is an expanse of water about a hundred square miles in area bounded by Cape Clear, Sherkin, Baltimore, and, to the west, Crookhaven. "The depth of this great bay," wrote Horatio Townsend, "is proportioned to its breadth, its shores are diversified by many jutting points and headlands, on several of which are ruined castles, and its ample bosom is inlaid with a great number of verdant islands of different sizes and shapes."

The name derives from the sound made by the Roaring Water's tributary, the Mean, which joins it just at the entrance to the Bay. They are short rivers that rise in the mountains and descend by series of little waterfalls splashing over boulders into small dark pools full of trout. I saw a heron standing knee deep in front of an unfurling clump of royal fern, and upstream an otter slipped over a coarse-sanded beach. Probably these rivers have fresh-water pearls, like the Crooked River three miles west. River pearls are lodged in the swan, or fresh-water, mussel. Irish fresh-water pearls were much sought after before oriental pearls became freely available. In 1094 Gilbert, Bishop of Limerick, made a present of an Irish pearl to Anselm, Archbishop of Canterbury. At a later date the Earl of Cork purchased 140 pearls at a cost of £35 6s. for his daughter-in-law, "daughter Dungarvan". In his diary he wrote proudly that they came from "my river of Bandon", as did the "large round fair pearl" which "the poor woman who found it sold for two shillings in money and fourpence in beer and tobacco", and for which the Earl paid thirty pounds in ready money.

A few years ago I went fishing for mussels with some children in the Crooked River. Within half an hour we had collected a basket of them, for they were numerous, their long brown-black shells almost indistinguishable from the rocks on the river bottom. We boiled them; inside the shells had a pretty nacreous surface which at one time made them popular among the poor, who used them for spoons. In one we found a little grey pearl, the shape of a child's tooth. Like the pearls of Livy's description, it was "small, dim of colour and nothing orient". (He was sneering at Julius Caesar, who had been mean enough to offer a breastplate set with river pearls collected in Britain to Venus Genetrix.) In the old days it would probably have found its way to an apothecary, who would have ground it up and used it as a stomach powder to relieve indigestion among the rich.

I followed the river up to the modern Aughadown church on the main Schull road. At this time of the day traffic consisted of horses and carts, tractors and cars, all making their way to Kilcoe creamery. A twist of black smoke drifted from the tall chimney, and in front of the building farmers waited their turn to deliver their milk. But there was no obvious impatience as they sat around smoking and talking, while the churns of milk were poured into glistening steel vats, weighed and measured, and cream poured off from a tap. It has been suggested that the co-operative creamery, so often located at a cross-road, hearkens back to the fundamental needs of a Gaelic pastoral economy. Nowadays, since the decline of the fairs, it is a more important meeting ground for small farmers to exchange advice and information than any town centre. The daily social intercourse at the creamery is vitally important for the isolated farmer living apart from his neighbour on his small-holding.

The distance between Kilcoe and Ballydehob is about three miles over a boggy pastureland, dotted with small farms, with grey-brown mountains that fade out of sight. A large white horse trotted by along the road, carrying a man on his way to Ballydehob to buy his weekly provisions. He told me that he had spent twenty years in Canada, farming a four-hundred-acre farm, before coming home.

"A freer place than Ireland. Religion has this country spoiled, but in Canada it didn't matter whether you were Catholic or Protestant."

For most of the way to Ballydehob and Schull the main road runs beside the track once used by the Skibbereen and Schull Light Tramway. The Tramway was opened in 1886, not only to provide a service for people in the area, but also to transport fish and copper eastwards towards the markets of the world. For passengers, the distance between Schull and Skibbereen was fifteen miles, a journey covering six small stops and taking an hour and twenty minutes. The company had plans to extend the line to Crookhaven to collect the American mails landed there; while another branch would connect Skibbereen with Rosscarbery and Leap. But these ideas came to nothing.

Although described as a "tramway", the line carried trains. The early engines, the *Ilen*, *Marion* and *Ida*, were tin boxes with funnel stacks. They were superseded by the vastly superior *Gabriel*, which was christened by the parish priest of Schull with a bottle of champagne. The *Erin* and *Trent* followed soon afterwards. These three engines had cowbuffers in front, and drove to the accompaniment of large bells, drawing a line of pullman carriages whose seats could be reversed at the end of the journey. There was a normal day service between Skibbereen and Schull, and an extra train every Thursday for the Skibbereen market. The greatest number of passengers ever carried was a record seven hundred and fifty-two, who managed to pile themselves on board to travel to Schull regatta sometime during the nineteen thirties. On one occasion the tram was held up for an hour so that a bishop visiting Schull could enjoy his afternoon tea. During the emergency in the last war, turf was burnt instead of coal, and on the hill up from Aughadown third-class passengers were obliged to walk.

Such small local lines bind communities together. The Tramway was an important factor in the lives of people in the neighbourhood, who regarded it with a great deal of affection. But from a financial point of view, the S.&S.L.T. was a total disaster, never making money and always in debt. In 1916, for example, debts amounted to £39,200. When, in 1952, there was an announcement in some papers that the service was about to be closed down, no one was surprised. It had not run since 1947.

Coming into Ballydehob the track made a little loop around the edge of the sea before reaching the old station, now converted into a house. The river is spanned by a twelve-arched bridge which has the stately proportions of a Roman aqueduct. When the tide is in, the tourist might think that he has never seen a more beautiful place. Many a property has been sold on the merits of a full tide. Low water is quite another matter. But efforts are being made to defeat the problem of the ugliness of lowtide by building a bar to keep in the sea. At one time ships used to sail up the estuary, but now nothing comes. The name Ballydehob means the "Ford of two Mouths", and the river flowing from the village is divided into two by a delta, so entering the sea by two channels.

The day was fine and the first GB cars of the season were passing through. A mobile Bank of Ireland was trying to park between an English Land-Rover and a large vehicle marked in red letters CHIPS. The houses were being painted up for the summer in vivid colours: blue, mauve, pink, green and saffron. I rode up hill past the shops and boutiques (one called Bally Boutique) of artists who have come to live here, which displayed pewter, jewellery, Batik work, pottery, paintings and clothes. At the west end of the town I turned and made a detour into the hills.

Ballydehob was the home of the all-in wrestler, Danno O'Mahony. I rode up the mountain to Dreenlomena and the wild little cottage where he was born, high over the town looking out over sea and islands. Here Danno's brother was still living. William O'Mahony was a huge man, like the wrestler himself, over six foot high. He told me that his brother had been world champion in 1935 and 1936, and had worn the diamond-studded belt. He died in 1950 after a car accident. I told him how as a small boy I had watched the wrestling match between Danno and the equally famous Kerryman, Steve O'Casey, who came from Sneem. It had seemed a grossly unfair fight. Both wrestlers took their families along, and some of their brothers and cousins were not only spectators, but active participants in the bout. The match ended when one of the contestants was thrown out of the ring and the family of the other forcibly prevented him from climbing back until the referee had counted him out.

According to Robert Speaight, Ballydehob was once called Swantonstown after a leading family. Hilaire Belloc's grandmother was a Swanton from here.

West of the town the laneways ran into each other like the veins of a leaf. Many of them were untarred; they seemed empty, with little life except for cattle or a white horse browsing in watery fields beside them. Most seemed to end up at the sea, and each little turn had its own alignment to the bay. One looked across the islands with Kilcoe standing squat and menacing on its headland; the next inlet had a view across to Horse Island; another lane climbed a hill to where one could see the sweep from Baltimore Beacon and the Gascanane to the shattered tower of Rosbrin Castle.

Between Rosbrin and Ballydehob is the sixty-foot steeple of the Cappagh copper-mine rising above a warren of abandoned shafts and workings. Mining cottages, towers, tunnels, hillsides coated with slag are a common sight all over West Cork, and during the nineteenth century the Carbery and Beare area was surpassed, in Europe, only by Cornwall in the amount of copper produced. The Cappagh mine, opened in 1820 by Captain Hall of Glandore, was part of the Audely mines, exploited on the property of a nobleman of that name. It had a meteoric rise, was abandoned, then restarted, and finally failed utterly. There were three Audely mines, at Cappagh, at Ballycominsk and on Horse Island, all within a few miles of each other. The best veins near the surface were quickly worked out, and they went bankrupt in 1840; since worthless shares had been widely sold, West Cork copper became a byword in London for unprofitable dealing. Later, under different management, the mines flourished again, especially during the eighteen eighties when copper fetched as much as £100 a ton. But soon afterwards the rich lodes discovered in Rhodesia put an end to effective mining in the British Isles.

Mr Leary, who farms land near Cappagh, showed me the slated "Captain's House", where the mine manager used to live. A manager was always known as the "Captain", and in the heyday of Cappagh there used to be two. The copper here was supposed to be so pure, that if there had been one more per cent it would have been gold. You can still see the place where the little rail swept down the almost perpendicular slope of the hill to Audely Cove below, where trucks used to carry down the ore to waiting schooners which shipped it over to Swansea. Swansea was the centre of the copper trade, where ore collected from Ireland, Cuba and Cornwall was smelted down.

On Horse Island, after the mines were closed, a new use was found for the deep shafts there—they made excellent hiding places for brewing and storing poteen.

Ballycominsk, a couple of miles away down a corkscrew lane leading to Rosbrin harbour, was the largest of the Audely mines.

"There was a pile of men working west," Mr Leary said. "But it is hard to find any of them now." I did, however, meet Mr Patrick Collins, whose house was situated close to the Ballycominsk workings, where he had been employed as a young man until their closure in 1910. In those last years there had been little mining done, and men looked back with bitter nostalgia to the great days when six hundred and seventy-one tons had been dug out in one year.

The mine had been opened in 1814. "The pride of my grandfather's land was taken for it," Mr Collins said. "For that he didn't get a tanner." I was shown all over the heaps of grey slag, now partly overgrown with bushes, the abandoned shafts and the cement pillars of the mill. From Rosbrin the same ships that anchored off Cappagh took the ore away to Swansea. Mr Collins clearly remembered what he called "the hungry employment". He worked at "cobbing", that is, breaking up the stone with a small cobbing hammer. He still had one in his loft. Other miners used nothing but hammer and drill. Men and women would walk to the mine for work from Ballydehob six miles away. They were paid sixpence a day, and had to arrive at six o'clock even in winter; if they were even five minutes late, their wages would be cut by threepence.

Down beside a narrow inlet which empties at low tide stands Rosbrin, the most easterly of the O'Mahony castles. Like the O'Driscolls, the O'Mahonys had a passion for building castles; they built twelve, and six survive, all overlooking or right on the edge of the sea. They shared with the O'Driscolls one of the finest fishing grounds in Europe, controlling the waters and exacting dues from visiting fishing boats in much the same way. The territory and ocean they claimed was west of the O'Driscoll empire; the combined fishing grounds were considered exceptionally rich. "None of the fisheries of Munster are so well known," wrote an observer in 1688," as those of the promontory of Ivaha, whereto a great fleet of Spaniards and Portuguese go, even in the midst of winter. . . ."

The O'Mahonys were not indigenous to West Cork as the O'Driscolls were; they originated in south Tipperary. Around the twelfth and thirteenth centuries pressure from the Norman settlements along the east coast increased inter-territorial warfare among the clans of Munster. In 1254, driven out of Tipperary by attacks from the McCarthys, the O'Mahonys divided into two branches—the eastern O'Mahonys of Kinelmeaky, and the western O'Mahonys, who migrated to the "western land" and settled on Ivaha at the south-western tip of Ireland. They dispossessed the O'Driscolls of their coastline from Rosbrin up to Dunmanus, and began to build their castles there.

There were many reasons why this remote place should be desirable. In addition to the abundant fishing grounds off shore, the land itself was well wooded to provide food for their swine. Fourteen place-names on the peninsula derive from the word for oak. The sea route to the Continent was fast and direct, and there was opportunity for swift intercourse with foreign countries. Above all, this land was peaceful, far beyond the reach or control of the Normans or the warring clans to the east.

Rosbrin, constructed around 1300, was one of the most important of the O'Mahony castles, a place whose name has appeared several times in history. It was the home of the civilized scholar, Finnin O'Mahony, who, according to the *Annals of Loch Ce*, was the "general support of the hospitality and humanity of West Munster, and the most learned man of his time in Latin and Greek". Most Irish chieftains knew Latin; they used it to converse with Spaniards and Frenchmen, and their indentures and proclamations were in that language. But Finnin's erudition was widely recognized. In the *Annals of Ulster* he is described as "an intelligent, polished, erudite man, and learned in the history of the world". Donal O'Fihelly, a scholar of Oxford, dedicated his *Annals of Ireland* to him. A hundred years ago, at Rennes in Brittany, a transcript was found of Finnin's translation from English into Irish of Sir John Mandeville's *Travels in the Holy Land*.

Although Finnin's name is associated with Rosbrin, for the last seventeen years of his life he resided at nearby Ardintenant, the most important of the O'Mahony castles. Here he died a week before Christmas in 1495.

Another book emanating from Rosbrin was the *Saltair of Rosbrin*, now lost. It was probably written by the Bard to the O'Mahonys, one of the O'Daly family, and tediously consisted of the family history of the western O'Mahonys.

In 1562 Donal, the great grandson of Finnin the Scholar, chased an "English Pirate" from Rosbrin to Cobh. No doubt this ship had been sent by the English authorities to try to prevent foreign vessels from calling at Rosbrin to fish and trade. Donal landed in Cork, where he was seen within the Liberties and arrested. He was accused of piracy, attainted and hanged on September 20th, 1562. Since his lands were declared forfeit, the Cork civil authorities fitted out an expensive expedition to seize Rosbrin Castle. The expedition succeeded, and after it had yielded, the castle was made over to Cornelius O'Mahony, Donal's son and successor, who kept it for eight years and enjoyed all the profits from the fishing. In other words, the English from Cork found that it was too distant to remain within their control—they were unable to garrison it.

However, they tried again. In 1571 Sir John Perrott, the Lord President of Munster, sent a large force against Cornelius which retook Rosbrin. It was then entrusted to McSwiney Gallowglass, who was in the government's pay, but next year his garrison of mercenaries was "fined sixteen good fat cows" for rebellious behaviour. No other English garrison could be provided at the time, probably because the Desmond Rebellion had begun. The English were therefore reduced to putting Connaher O'Mahony, brother of the hanged Donal, in possession of the castle at a nominal rent.

Eight years later Donal McConnor O'Mahony, of Rosbrin, the son of Teig O'Mahony, the last chief of Rosbrin, took part in the Desmond Rebellion. With forty-five horsemen and a hundred kern, he rode to the rendezvous at Ballyhoura on August 9th, 1579, to meet the O'Mahony Chief of Kinelmeaky. The western O'Mahony chieftain, Connor Fionn the Third, did not go because he felt it necessary to protect the lands of the clan from the marauding O'Sullivan Beare, who was employing Sir James Desmond to make raids on the O'Mahonys.

Donal McConnor O'Mahony was attainted and sentenced to death following the rebellion, but since there is no record of his having been executed, he almost certainly escaped to the Continent. Meanwhile, one Oliver Lambert had been granted a lease of Rosbrin.

In 1595 McTeig O'Mahony, a son of the hanged Donal, sued to recover the castle, but was not successful. He then joined O'Neill at the Battle of Kinsale, after which he was pardoned.

Later one Teig Carthy sought to obtain a bargain from the Privy Council by offering five pounds for a half-acre called Rosbrin, hoping that no one would remember that there was a castle on the plot of land. Rosbrin was subsequently handed over by Lambert to the crown, and was leased again to a man named Morgan. He was the last owner that we know of to make use of the actual building.

One wall of the splintered tower has a crack running down the side. Another was partly blown down by a storm in 1905. If there is another great storm like that one, Rosbrin might well disappear without trace, like the O'Mahony castles at Ballydevlin, Castle Meighan and Crookhaven. It is sited in an area which is very difficult to approach from either land or sea, standing on a rock. Contrary to what may be written in Holy Scripture, buildings on rocks have little in the way of foundation, and when they fall down or are swept away there is nothing left of them except a memory.

Two miles west of Rosbrin is Ardintenant, or White Castle, the home of the chieftains of the western O'Mahonys. It is the only O'Mahony castle to be situated well back from the sea, with a farmhouse sheltering beneath its shadow. The sea is a couple of hundred yards away, reached by a lane which leads to an exposed beach looking out to the Fastnet. (On calm days during the famine, a farmer told me, coffin ships would anchor off this beach and pick up passengers for America. Unlike Rosbrin, Ardintenant, built in 1310, had a peaceful history; the O'Mahonys possessed it until 1616, when it was sold. According to Joyce's *Irish Names of Places*, the name derives from *Ard-an-tennail*, the Height of the Bonfire—recalling the old custom of lighting bonfires on the tops of hills, usually on St John's Eve.

All O'Mahony castles resemble each other in construction, and none of them could have been a comfortable habitation. Their black walls glisten with damp; not one has a fireplace, and there are very few windows of any size. As a precaution against attack their entrances are fifteen or twenty feet above ground, and they must have been reached by a wooden ladder. At Ardintenant you can scramble up to the first floor and view the little room where the lord of the castle and his family must have lived, much as the French traveller. Le Gouz de Rochefed, quoted in Donovan, observed in 1644. "The castles or houses of the nobility consist of four walls extremely high, thatched with straw; but to tell the truth they are nothing but square towers without windows, or at least, having such small apertures as to give no more light than there is in a prison. They have little furniture, and cover the rooms with rushes. Of this they make their beds in summer, and of straw in winter."

NINE

Schull and Mount Gabriel

MAY DAY IN Schull was the day for "bringing in the green". But the ancient custom is dying out. Only a few branches of green leaves were tied on doors, and a twig of fuchsia dangled from the handle of a bike. "Old pishoges," an old man muttered as he carefully arranged sycamore round a drainpipe.

At this time of year Schull was still pleasantly deserted. A few tractors were parked outside the Munster and Leinster Bank whose walls were built from the stones of the Protestant church on Cape Clear. Some locals walked up and down the main street past the coffee bar and boutique, still closed for the winter. Shopkeepers contemplated prospects for the coming season. Tourism was still an uncertain foundation for prosperity, a newly planted tree crushed easily in summer storms. There were too many reasons why visitors might stay away: a dock strike, a bank strike, a ban on dogs entering the country, an increase in hotel expenses, a poor long-range weather forecast. And trouble in the North: every stone thrown in Belfast meant a tourist less in West Cork.

Over the years, however, many tourists have stayed to become residents. Today they emerged outside into the spring sunshine to garden. Their presence increased the number of Protestants, but did not benefit the dwindling parish to any great extent.

"They are on our side, but they never go to church. One sees them digging up weeds on a Sunday . . ." Respect for Sundays lingers, perhaps in the faint memory of the punishment of the two parsons, Mr Allen of Creagh and Mr Sweetnam of Aughadown, who went out shooting on the Sabbath over half a century ago. Mr Allen shot off his right-hand finger and thumb, and Mr Sweetnam shot off two of his toes.

Schull harbour is one of the finest on the coast, and in summer it fills up with craft, small sailing boats and yachts tying up alongside the trawlers. The peak of the season is the regatta, held in August. The last two regattas that I attended took place on Sunday; both were ruined by the rain. The Sabbath was profaned. The rain poured down on the flags and fairground, and on the few blue-suited figures who remained on the end of the pier to watch the start of the Ocean Yacht Race. The appearance of St Fachtna's Silver Band from Skibbereen was not enough to draw the rest from their refuge in the bars.

Other years have been sunny and many fine regattas have been held, like that of July 18th, 1896, reported in one of the surviving files of the *Skibbereen Eagle*. ". . . Matters atmospherical were of a kindly benignant nature, and a fresh breeze tempered the extreme heat that prevailed, and made the day most favourable for sailing events. . . . The pleasure felt in watching races was made all the more agreeable because of the great beauty of the surroundings. . . ." In spite of the new bungalows, the harbour is still beautiful.

During the summer of 1969 a flotilla of American yachts that had crossed the Atlantic visited Schull. About a hundred vessels anchored one behind the other, so that the whole harbour was thick with masts. It was like old times. Nothing like it had been seen since the French mackerel fleet used to crowd into Schull in a similar fashion.

"That was in 1913, before the First War broke up everything." Postcards are still on sale which show the fleet at anchor, numerous small trawlers with high sloping funnels and a sail at the stern. The crews would come ashore dressed in canvas smocks, and go to church, where they surprised people by singing the mass. Their fine voices are still remembered. They would give away their ship's biscuits and trade supplies, brandy, wines and eau-de-Cologne. "Plenty tabac for poli," they would say. Poli meant chicken. For one chicken they would give a man enough tobacco to last for months. Some of them would climb trees up to rooks' nests and collect the eggs to eat.

The French fleet is long gone, but the mackerel are still there. In summer they come in around the pier, chasing the sprat, which boil on the surface of the water or throw themselves helplessly up on the beach. Thousands of green mackerel, striped like tigers and behaving like wolves, follow them in packs. With quick bursts of speed they dart into the packed shoals for their prey. As many as twenty undigested sprat have been found in one fish's stomach.

Before the mackerel there were pilchards, and, like Baltimore, Schull had its pilchard curing house, recalled in the name of Pallace Strand. There used to be abundant assorted fishing: at the beginning of this century it was still possible to catch lobsters around the harbour. "Fishing was the lazy easy way of making a living. A man would rather earn a pound from fishing than five pounds on the land." Now the lobsters have retreated far out to sea, and the small boat has little chance of competing with the trawlers. However, in the last few years a demand for crabs has developed. The government-built freezing plant in the harbour lay empty for a number of years when it was found to be uneconomical. Then the crab, hitherto unmolested, was discovered to be a gourmet's delight. Today the plant processes crab meat for restaurants, and crabs are hunted up and down the coast. Sharks are used for bait, their corpses dumped in fly-covered heaps all over the pier before being cut up and put into the pots. They are brought up to Schull from Kinsale, where they have been caught by sporting anglers.

At the east end of town beside the main Skibbereen road stands the prominent ivy-covered ruin of the workhouse. Up until the Troubles it survived as a hospital, but in 1921 it was burned down at the same time as the workhouses at Bandon and Skibbereen. The Republican forces considered they might be used as barracks for British soldiers; at the same time they were getting rid of a hated symbol. "You couldn't see Cosheen for the smoke." Cosheen covers a half-dozen miles of coast and hillside.

Like Skibbereen, Schull suffered terribly during the famine. Donovan described the towns as "those two famine-slain sisters of the South". At one time there were fifty deaths a day in Schull parish, which was twenty-one miles long and harboured a population of eighteen thousand people. "Frightful and fearful is the havoc around me," wrote the Reverend Robert Traill, who was to die of typhus. "The aged, who with the young, neglected perhaps, amidst the widespread destitution, are almost without exception swollen and ripening for the grave." The coastline was entirely denuded of seaweed, which had been used for food. The windowless cabins gave off a particular odour when filled with patients ill with typhus, while blood-clotted excreta surrounding them proclaimed that the inhabitants had contracted bacillary dysentery which was usually fatal.

Even in famine-stricken Ireland Schull seems to have been a place of peculiar horror. In the winter of 1846-7 Commander Caffyn, having landed a cargo of meal from H.M. Sloop *Scourge* in Schull harbour on behalf of the Society of Friends, sent a report to Charles Trevelyan, the head of the Treasury. Having described the starved and the dying, and the bodies half eaten by rats, he concluded: "Never in my life have I seen such wholesale misery." He wrote other letters which were circulated, one specifically referring to the pitiable state of many Protestants in the area. This caught the attention of a clergyman from the Midlands named the Reverend F. Trench, who wrote immediately, "If here, then, the Protestants are in the state which Captain Caffin [*sic*] describes, what must be the condition of the Roman Catholics?" Mr Trench set out for Schull at once, determined to lend assistance.

Already efforts had been made to try to relieve the district. The Quakers were there. A year earlier in 1846 they had encouraged a fishing co-operative at Cosheen begun by a mine engineer, Captain Thomas, which provided some employment. A curing house and store-house for salt were built, and boats and gear provided for the fishermen. But the venture failed. The half-starved fishermen were simply not in a fit state to convey their craft out to the fishing grounds during the storms of that bitter winter.

Mr Trench wrote a series of letters which gave a vivid impression of the misery in the area, for he was a sensitive witness with an eye for poignant detail. He noticed that not a single child played in the streets of the town, and none were to be seen outside the doors of cottages, except for a few who were obviously sick or dying. He described the frantic industry of the carpenters making coffins; the woman with a basket on her back and "the crooked corpse of a child outside it"; Mr O'Callaghan of Kilmanus using meal bags for burying the people.

In the district of Keelbronogue he gave the names of those he visited, the widow Driscoll, Matt Sullivan, widow Cunningham, Phil Regan, Paddy Ryan and their families. They told him: "We have no sickness here but the hunger." "I have within a fine young man of nineteen years of age, and *you could carry him within the palm of your hand.*"

He quoted the doctor from Schull with whom he visited another cottage. "'Look, there, sir, you cannot tell whether they are boys or

Crayfish at Crookhaven

Barley Cove

Mizen Head

girls.' Taking up a skeleton child, he said, 'Here is the way it is with them all; their legs swing and rock like the legs of a doll', and I saw that it was so in this instance. 'Sir, they have the smell of mice.' After I had seen a great number of these miserable objects, the doctor said, 'Now, sir, there is not a child you saw can live for a month; every one of them are in famine fever, a fever so sticky that it never leaves them!'"

Priest, clergyman and doctor accomplished little in the face of such starvation. "What can one physician do amongst 18,000 people in such a state (and oats for his horse so dear?)" They gave out rice milk which was strengthening, and the inevitable soup; Mr Trench set great store by his nourishing broth which cost a penny farthing a portion. Modern doctors are of the opinion that soup was worse than useless; that much of the oedema or swelling present in starving people was the result of being fed too much liquid without enough bulk. A ration of soup would contain at the most about two hundred calories, a fraction of what was necessary. Yet Mr Trench and his colleagues had a few encouraging successes. "Mr McCabe"—the curate—"has had the pleasure of seeing convalescent families and had seen that day one poor woman combing her hair and in her right mind who had been delirious in fever a few days before. . . ."

West of the town the road following the shore of Schull harbour passes brash new bungalows. A contrast to their wood and concrete is the fine Protestant rectory, with its ivy-covered wings and surrounding beech-trees. It dates from 1723, and must be one of the oldest rectories in the country. In the hall doors there are spy-holes through which the muzzle of a gun can be fitted to shoot down any unwelcome intruder. Sir John Moore is supposed to have spent his last night in Ireland here before embarking for Spain to his death at Corunna. The army, which had embarked from Cork, was blown by cross winds into Schull harbour. The field in front of the rectory known as the Camp Field is supposed to be where the soldiers pitched their tents. Whatever the truth of this story—there is no mention of it in any biography—Moore had a detailed knowledge of the area. During the ninety-eight rebellion he was given the command of Bandon, which included the coastline stretching all the way to Bantry. His duties included disarming the two Carberies and keeping a check on rebel activities. An exceptionally humane and tolerant commander, he knew enough about the evil reputation of the occupying forces of militia and yeomanry to remark:

H

"If I were an Irishman I would be a rebel." He was not above criticizing his own forces for any show of intolerance. At Skibbereen he advised a deputation complaining that rebels were cutting down trees to make pike handles, "to show a joint resolution to oppose whatever was un-lawful, but at the same time to be just themselves." A group of "Orange-boys" were put off a scheme after being told that "if it is to create distinct and separate interests for the Catholics, it is wicked and must be punished . . . Distinctions of this kind are illiberal, and for a man to boast or be proud of his religion is absurd." His success in controlling the excesses of the yeomanry contributed largely to the relative calm of West Cork during 1798.

Colla harbour and pier is the nearest point to embark for Long Island. Horse Island, Castle Island and Long Island lie in a line just outside Schull harbour. A tradition, quoted by Smith, claims that they were once all one island. "In the latter end of March, A.D. 830, Hugh Domdighe being monarch of Ireland, there happened . . . terrible shocks of thunder and lightning . . . at the same time the sea broke through the banks in a most violent manner. The island, then called Innisfadda, on the west coast of this country was forced asunder and divided into three parts. . . ."

During the thirteenth century Long Island was in the possession of a Norman adventurer, Richard de Carew; his daughter married Dermod O'Mahony and brought him the island in her dowry. In Elizabethan times Sir Peter Carew traced a bogus relationship to the original de Carew to justify his claims to large portions of West Cork.

The island passed into the possession of the Earl of Cork. A mile and a half long and two hundred yards wide, it is a featureless lump of land shaped like the back of a fish. There are no trees, no softening contours. At the west end you can see the blue scars of a copper-mine, but other-wise it seems a worthless enough piece of property to have so much significance in history.

The most prominent detail of its wind-torn slopes is the distinctive two-windowed cottages which were erected about sixty years ago by the Congested Districts Board. The Board gave generous grants to assist the struggling community; one old lady got her house for half a crown. But today the shuttered windows and surrounding weeds and nettles indicate that time has passed since Long Island was a Congested District. It is the bleakest of all the islands that are still inhabited. I talked to Mr

McCarthy, who had lived here all his life and could remember when the place had been full of fishermen all speaking a mixture of Irish and English. One by one he had watched them leave. A dozen families still remained, comprising perhaps forty people altogether. The school had shrunk year by year, to four pupils, then two—it closed after that. There was neither electricity, nor any shop—nothing to keep the young from making the short crossing over to the mainland. It would take them fifteen minutes, according to wind and weather. There they disappeared for ever. When the old ones like himself died out the place would become empty.

However, he had no regrets over a lifetime spent here. It was the grandest place to live. The air was the freshest, the food was the best. Strangers who came to Long Island with a haunted look from having lived in cities soon improved. You could see them coming on. As for company, there was no shortage of that—he still had neighbours enough. And so much to see on the mainland now. A few years ago there was only the odd light to be seen there, but now, with all the new people coming and building houses and bungalows, at night-time it glowed like a city.

Back in Schull I climbed Mount Gabriel, which rises directly behind the town. North of Bantry, the Cork and Kerry ranges have many higher mountains, but among the lower ranges of the Carbery coastline Gabriel stands out, making an impressive landmark visible for many miles. "A haunt of wolves," Bishop Downes commented in 1700. "There are no trees nor shelter, but rocks and bogs." This was one of the last places in Ireland where wolves persisted. Huge packs must have roamed over the slopes of the mountain. Wolves were plentiful in Ireland during the Middle Ages when skins were exported in large quantities. The account books of the port of Bristol, for instance, show that an average of from one hundred to three hundred Irish wolf-skins were landed each year at that one port alone. During the seventeenth century they were still common. An official order of 1652 forbade the export of wolf dogs from the country, and a bounty was offered by the Commissioners of the Revenue which could amount to six pounds for the head of a bitch. This systematic hunting, combined with the destruction of the forests, reduced their numbers dramatically, so that by 1700, the time of Bishop Downe's visit to Schull, they had become a rarity, confined to remote and mountainous regions. The last wolf in County Cork is said to have been killed near Kilcrea Castle by Bryan Townsend of Castlehaven.

On the inhospitable slopes of Gabriel neolithic men settled in considerable numbers. Ring forts protected them from wolves and weather and cattle raiders. The reason they came here was the presence of copper. From very early times Gabriel was a centre for copper-mining. Bronze axes and a mould for making bronze instruments have been discovered here. The tin would have been brought over from Cornwall to Schull harbour. The copper itself was dug out from a series of mines near the summit of the mountain. Twenty-five of these have been recognized, most of them situated west of the Barnacleve gap only a short distance from the road. The road at Barnacleve is a superb position for viewing Schull harbour and the islands; many visitors stop their cars here, unaware of the mines tucked away in a valley above them. They have only recently been discovered. There is no mention of them in any traveller's account or trace on early surveys or maps, and it is likely that they were covered by a blanket bog which only slipped away to reveal them sometime during the last hundred years. Now they are easy to find, rows of narrow shafts driven into the rock, half concealed by ferns. Some are filled with water. The method of extracting the copper was by primitive fire-setting, in which the ore was loosened by intense heat and then shattered by stone mauls.

Beside some of the shafts I came upon the dump heads taken from the mines. Here among the rocks and rubble were the mauls which miners must have thrown out and left lying two thousand years ago. Most of them were splintered halves of grey sea stones about the size and shape of ostrich eggs, which had been carried up the mountain from the coast. I found similar stones lying on a storm beach below Cosheen, and very likely they had come from there. They fitted cosily into my hand, and must have been convenient tools for hammering the ore. Marks and dents were still to be seen on them. Others were larger and had evidently been fitted with some kind of handle. In recent years the mauls have grown fewer in number since experts began climbing up to look at the mines. One was observed in Skibbereen with a sackload he had carried off.

On the north side of the mountain an elaborate stone causeway runs along its slope towards a mine that is two thousand years younger. This produced barytes, a heavy white mineral associated with copper.

There used to be a world-wide demand for barytes. Its chief characteristic was its weight, and for years it was commonly used in manufacture as an adulterant. Added to cotton sheets, it gave a fine gloss like linen which soon wore off with washing; mixed with paint or cosmetics, it produced a shine which did not last either. Just a small amount put in with a sack of sugar was undetectable, and made it quite a bit heavier than it should have been. (To be fair, barytes had some legitimate uses, and today there is still a demand for it at atomic research centres, where it is added to materials forming shields against radiation.)

The barytes deposits on Gabriel were said to have been discovered by a blind man, who picked up a heavy rock and realized that it must contain some unusual mineral. The mine, opened in 1894, reached full production after 1898 when four hundred tons were produced annually. A great deal of barytes came from Germany, so that during the First World War, when German stocks were unobtainable, the ore produced here was considered very important. Carts rumbling over the causeway carried it down to Cosheen harbour.

The mine was abandoned soon after the war. The causeway, overgrown with spongy grass and lined with rocks covered in saxifrage like a suburban garden, makes an easy walk to the two mine entrances near the summit. One of these has been opened up again recently, and some crude mining, mainly with pick and shovel, is carried on. Further down, above the deserted Glaun National School are more shafts, pale grey pickings in the heather which have been abandoned for fifty years.

From the summit most of West Cork can be seen. Near the top is the tiny Poulenine lake, a jet black circle of water contained in a hollow which is known as the Hole in the Pan. This is where the devil dug out the Fastnet and hurled it into the sea. The hollow is supposed to be so deep that it runs into an underground passage which connects with Lough Errul on Cape Clear.

Mount Gabriel was once owned by the Becher family. After the famine a Becher living near Lough Hyne went bankrupt, and his estates were sold in 1851. Part of the 120,000 acres of West Cork on offer were the seven hundred and fifty-eight acres comprising Mount Gabriel. The mining rights went for £475.

North of the mountain is the bleak Glaun valley, a wilderness of rocks and damp fields. I had read in an old journal that somewhere around here was a sweathouse, which the author of the article had visited in 1913. After much difficulty and searching, I was directed down a faint track behind an isolated farmhouse, where in a lonely place shadowed by hills I found the walls of a humble little building overgrown with furze. It could have been any age from a hundred to two thousand years old. The narrow entrance, or creep, was still discernible at the base of the circular wall, but the roof, which would have been corbelled, had collapsed. Here, perhaps not so long ago, generations of people in the valley used to cure their aches and complaints.

Up until fairly recent times men and women used sweathouses for the curing of arthritic pains, or for a clean-up, or to tone up their complexions, like the girls on Rathlin Island, who bathed before attending the annual Lammas fair at Ballycastle. Baths were generally taken in summer or early autumn. The sweathouse worked on the same principle as a sauna bath. The interior was heated for a day before it was used and then the earth floor was swept clean and strewn with green rushes. Sometimes steam was induced by pouring water over hot stones. A family or a group of men would sit and sweat with the heat for about half an hour before emerging to cool themselves with buckets of water, or probably in this case in the little stream that flowed nearby. Communal baths like these were in general use up until the nineteenth century. De Lactocnaye observed in 1798 how "wherever there are four or five cabins near each other, there is sure to be a sweathouse".

Mr and Mrs Sullivan, on whose land the sweathouse was situated, invited me into their house for a chat and a glass of whiskey. Mrs Sullivan told me that the valley was once thickly populated, and when she was a girl there had been sixty children at the school that closed last year. The way of life had gone with it. We sat in the dim kitchen with its cornerside seat and old iron stove, drinking Jameson and eating digestive biscuits while the rain battered the windows outside. Once it had been a great place to live in, her husband said. There were monthly fairs at Ballydehob and Schull, and he had walked all the way to Bantry with the cattle and all the way back again.

TEN

Leamcon to Ballydevlin

"YOU'LL GET NO punctures on our roads," the postman said, with the complacency of a man born in West Cork. I refrained from telling him that the day before I had come limping into Schull pushing the bike with its gashed tyre. But now I was ready to set off again westward along the coast road. In some fields the grass was blotted out by patches of primroses; others showed thick clumps of *euphorbia Hibernia*, the green-yellow spurge native to West Cork which Smith called *macinboy*. The sun shone on the headland where a cuckoo called persistently as if it were a sea bird. A trawler topped with gulls chugged up Long Island sound towards the open sea.

From Schull it was a short ride to Croagh Bay and Lowertown. Croagh is a winding inlet of the sea which almost dries out at low tide. Oyster-catchers and curlews skate over the mud, ignored by the heron which takes up perpetual station in the saltmarsh. In mid summer cows come down to seek relief from the heat by wallowing in the mud, and mullet swim in with the tide to nibble lazily at seaweed in the shallows.

The new bungalows are only a few miles away, but here there is the familiar silence and emptiness. Farms are deserted and boarded up. Farmers have only recently acceded to the practice of selling land and property under the pressure of the new arrivals; before the surge of tourism they would not part with an acre willingly. Each empty building is a particular case. An emigrated family will keep in careful touch with the old place. Perhaps an owner has died and the heirs are lost somewhere in America. Often there is elaborate litigation about rightful ownership. Cousin quarrels with cousin in the States and a house stands empty until its walls fall down. A typical one stands abandoned off the road, sheltering behind a line of willows, the "wild twig" once used for making baskets. There is a gaping hole in the roof and beneath the low ceilings rooms are filled with newspapers, and a lifetime's accumulation of empty bottles. Another lies up a deserted lane with its windows broken and chimney stack askew. Any short walk will lead you to half a dozen more lying empty among flowers. Primroses and violets now, later dog-rose, honeysuckle, mallow, foxglove, and banks of fuchsia, which has grown so abundantly since it was first brought over to the British Isles from South America in 1823 that country people call it "the weed". In autumn the hedges have blackberries as big as grapes; the unploughed pastures behind them are dotted with lady's tresses, whose flowers grow in a spiral and smell of almonds. Other fields are white with mushrooms. No one eats mushrooms. A man told me that this was because during the famine people had to eat all sorts of queer things, and would never willingly do so again.

South of the estuary the dirt road passed Mr Kingston's garden. Mr Kingston, retired from farming, devoted his time to filling a shelving piece of land overlooking the sea with flowers that had an exotic Caribbean appearance. Dahlias, sweet william, giant gladioli and hydrangeas, all of which flourished in the warm climate and lush soil, were racing towards their luxuriant summer growth. Bees tending them were housed in straw skips. The paths that wound through the flower beds up to the rustic seat made out of a white-painted bedstead were edged with scallop shells. Gateways to the farm were built up into domed columns of cement; white-washed and decorated with iron scrolls, they looked like Tibetan stupas.

From the farm the lane led down to the sea and a couple of little beaches beside a ring fort known as the Lover's Bed. Around them were the ruins of cottages that once housed the village of Croagh. Within Mr Kingston's lifetime the beaches had been full of fishing boats and the sound of human voices. But some cottages had been empty for a long time. One had been known as the Black Hole, where during the famine a family of eight had died and never been buried. He used to pass it in terror as a boy. In other cases he could remember who had lived in them. That one—he pointed to a nettle-filled cabin—held fourteen people before they left.

Sometime after the famine a man called Leahy emigrated to America where he did well. His son did better still, and joined the navy and became an admiral. Admiral Leahy, born in 1875, was an outstanding naval officer, whose career covered both the First and Second World Wars. A close personal friend of President Roosevelt, he had accompanied him to Yalta, and during the Second World War he participated in all major military and diplomatic decisions.

His father, the elder Leahy, did not forget the people of the village where he was born. First of all he got a good job himself, and then he found jobs for the men of Croagh. Family by family they departed, and later people followed on their own until at last no one was left here except an old woman called Kitty the Cat. She lived on until her death in the nineteen fifties, surrounded by her scores of cats.

Once the village had a bakery and there was a coastguard station to watch out for smugglers. "But the men were all in it themselves." Not long ago Mr Kingston discovered a quantity of "cutlasses" in a bed of reeds. These were probably pikes hidden at the time of the Whiteboy troubles or the Ninety-eight. Some he had given away and the rest he incorporated in the new concrete floor of his pigsty.

He still used the gardens of the deserted cottages for planting cabbages.

From Lowertown cross the road led steeply up a hill which was topped by another post-Bantry signal tower. Beneath it was the turn-off to the pier at Castlepoint and Leamcon Castle, which stands far out on the end of a narrow peninsula looking west and south. It is actually on an island, separated from the mainland by a crack in the earth less than six feet across—the "hound's leap", which is what the name Leamcon means. A shaky wooden bridge leads over the narrow gorge with the sea visible far below.

Leamcon was built around 1500 by Finnin Caol, "the Slender", alluded to in English manuscripts as "O'Mahony of Iveagh, Chief Capteyne of his Nation". Although it is two hundred years younger than Rosbrin, the builders did nothing to soften its design. There is the same narrow winding staircase, absence of fireplace, and only one proper window. Standing on its island it would appear to be impregnable, but its position had disadvantages since it was difficult to provision and there was no water immediately available. When Captain Harvey besieged it, the Irish, without gunpowder or any effective defences, yielded easily. After Dunboy fell on June 18th, 1602, he marched his forces thirty miles in four days, taking Dunmanus Castle on the way. He set up a siege at Leamcon, where the marks of the "sow", a besieging instrument that breached the west wall, are still to be seen. Both the chieftain, Conogher O'Mahony, and his men were given quarter, which indicates that they offered little resistance. On July 7th, Conogher left for Spain along with other refugees; in 1606 his name was on the list of the gentlemen pensioners of the King of Spain.

Both Leamcon and Dunanus castles were recaptured by the O'Mahonys, but they could not be held, and they were retaken by Harvey towards the end of 1602.

There is a contemporary map in the Record Office in London showing details of the taking of Dunboy and the first siege of Leamcon. In a landscape decorated with wolves and stags, the stick figures of soldiers are shown firing their arrows and cannon at the castles.

Leamcon was never forfeited, and afterwards was held as the property of the young chief, Donogh. It remained in O'Mahony hands until another Conogher O'Mahony was outlawed after the rebellion of 1641. After that it was not inhabited again.

In 1622 the land around the castle was let to a planter named Sir William Hull, who gradually took possession of most of the land in these parts, including the towns of Crookhaven and Schull. The property at Leamcon which his son inherited was described in the 1659 census of Ireland as "eleven plowlands in the parish of Scool containing eighteen English and a hundred and one Irish persons".

William Hull had come over to Ireland from Devonshire during the reign of Queen Elizabeth, and established himself in County Cork. He had land at Clonakilty where his brother, Henry, settled, becoming mayor of the town. In 1609 William Hull was appointed deputy Vice-Admiral for the Province of Munster. In 1616 he went into partnership with Richard Boyle, later the Earl of Cork, to whom he was related by marriage. They expanded existing pilchard fisheries, and under Hull's supervision fish presses were established at Crookhaven and at Ardmore, in County Waterford. In 1621 he was knighted.

One of his most profitable titles was that of Commissioner for Treating with pirates in Munster. This was an appointment which had caused much disgust among many men in authority. The reason was that Hull preferred to conciliate pirates rather than to hang them and he did not hesitate to do business with any that he happened to encounter.

The whole coast of West Cork was a haven for pirates. Not only Algerians, but Irishmen, like the men hanged at Glandore in 1675, and buccaneers from most European countries came to these quiet inlets with their booty. The coast line was virtually unpoliced during the first half of the seventeenth century and for many years the government authorities were helpless in preventing robber vessels from finding shelter in convenient little harbours and creeks like Leamcon. Here, under the protection of Sir William Hull, Continental pirates, mainly Dutchmen, brought in their spoils to dispose of them.

They began using Leamcon as their headquarters around 1610. Before that they had sold their cargoes in Devon and Cornwall, but this became too risky. They continued to come to West Cork until around 1630, after which time the British and other navies became stronger, and were able to control the seas so that a good many pirates were suppressed.

The Dutchman, Peter Easton, had a regular fleet of thirteen ships at Leamcon; he is said to have buried some treasure there. Some of his men even brought their wives and children who lived in some sort of settlement on shore. Easton had become a pirate captain in 1610 by throwing overboard the previous captain of the ship on which he was serving, who had been wounded in a raid. If he ever left any treasure near the creek, he never came back to get it; in 1616 he was surprised by a Dutch ship as he lay at anchor at Crookhaven, captured, and presumably hanged.

More famous and more successful than Easton was another Dutchman named Claus Campeon, whose ships operated down to the straits of Gibraltar where they took as prizes the rich East Indiamen heading towards their home ports. Some captured cargoes were disposed of at Salee on the Barbary Coast, while others were brought to Leamcon. At that time Salee was a picturesque little independent republic on the shores of North Africa which had become a refuge for smugglers and various shady characters who wished to pursue their illegal practices with immunity. For a time there was a sort of Leamcon–Salee axis; if the Barbary Coast was threatened, the pirates would come to Ireland, and *vice versa*.

The creek dries out at low tide, so that the pirate ships and their captures would have had to anchor at the mouth of the inlet, between the point which is still known as Gunpoint, and Coney Island, which belonged to Hull. It became the practice to land the goods somewhere here and sell them off quite openly. Purchasers came from all round the south coast to pick up bargains. Mr Joshua Boyle of Waterford bought tobacco, spices and elephant's teeth. Mr Conoway of Kenmare bought "two bed coverings with canopies which came out of a ship from the Canary Islands". Lieutenant Jaques of Cork stole from Campeon "16 lb. of massy gold, but was caught". The pirate chief, expert at interrogations, made him confess.

Both Sir William Hull and Campeon kept on good terms with the Lord Deputy, Falkland. Campeon gave the Lord Deputy a percentage of his profits. In return Falkland not only turned a blind eye to his activities, but gave him advance information about any official anti-pirate operations. When Campeon visited Dublin, Lord Falkland came to see him on board ship and spent convivial evenings with him.

Profits from pirating must have been considerable. On one occasion when Campeon took a Turkish prize to Dublin, where he sold her, a member of his crew got drunk and drowned in the Liffey. His body was weighted down with gold amounting to £684 15s. 4d. Campeon would have received at least ten times as much for a share of the prize; in modern values he must have been a millionaire several times over, even though he perpetually worried and complained about expenses. At the height of his career he took an average of a hundred ships a year. Then, when he was forty, he purchased a pardon from the Dutch government for one thousand four hundred florins. He settled down in Holland to become a respected and prosperous burgher, and to write his auto-biography. He died in 1657 at the age of seventy.

For over twenty years Sir William Hull benefited from the presence of the pirates off his land and the transactions that took place. He most probably got a commission for allowing them to take place at all. He made numerous purchases himself, on one occasion buying forty horseloads of pepper which he presumably resold. But after Campeon retired, the great buccaneering days of Leamcon were over. Pirates began to be considered a menace. Hull became law-abiding. On June 1st, 1631, he watched a number of Algerian ships, with their distinctive lateen sails, cruising just beneath his castle at Three Castle Head. They had just come from sacking Baltimore. "The ships, (Turkish pirates)," he wrote later to his partner, Boyle, "are plying off and on near Mizen Head. They have been there eight or nine days but were not known to be Turks. They took two excellent pilots with them from Baltimore. . . . If these pirates are not driven off trade will be ruined and the people will be utterly unable to pay their debts."

It is possible, however, that Hull continued his interest in piracy and smuggling well beyond the palmy days of Captain Campeon. During the rebellion of 1641 he suffered great losses, and afterwards he made a deposition to the commissioners dealing with planters who were seeking compensation. Hull claimed over eight thousand pounds, which must be multiplied by at least ten to get some idea of present-day values. He got no sympathy from the commissioners at all. In fact, one of his chief complaints was that his losses were caused, not only by the rebels, but by an Englishman, Captain Cole, who deliberately burned the town and castle of Crookhaven which were in Hull's possession, and then went on the Leamcon Castle and to Schull and burnt those as well. He may well have had orders from the Munster authorities, who were tired of Hull's varied and profitable activities. For many years newly settled Englishmen like him had proved a greater danger to the Crown than the beaten Irish. In the rebellion Hull was attacked on two sides.

In his deposition he particularly emphasized how the O'Mahonys saw an opportunity to regain their property or to extract revenge. He declared that he was "robbed and forciblye dispoyled of his goods and Chattells . . . the first robbers we the great o Mahowne al's o Mahonon Foone"—i.e. Fionn—"of the parishe of Kilmoo . . . gent . . . Dennis Roagh o Mahowne—Lord of the Castell of Donmanos and his sonn Daniell mc Donnogh o Mahowne in the parrishe of Scull gents". Seven other O'Mahonys are included in the list of his persecutors which ends with "William Candler of Schull, an Englishman and Protestant lately turned Papist with seven or eight hundred other Rebells. . . ."

The damage they inflicted was listed item by item. The list is interesting because it showed how deeply entrenched in Leamcon and Crookhaven Hull had become during the thirty years since he had first settled there. In both places he had built up an elaborate system for catching and processing pilchards. Seine nets, hogsheads, presses, fishing boats were all destroyed along with "three thousand of pickled hogsed staves for traine oyle". Other items included "spare corks for seanes", (seine nets), "sixty bucklers to press fish with", and "eight hundred barrels of new salte" for preserving the dried pilchards. In addition there must have been extensive farming around Leamcon; for Sir William claimed

damages from various tenants for whom he did work; "breaking of
rocks . . . stoninge the land five times over . . . draining the boggs and
making gutters underground whereby the boggs became good med-
dow land. . . ." On his own land he lost "eleven hundred of English
yeows in lamb", "twenty and five rams which cost tenn shillings per
ram", "twoo hundred weathers", as well as "a few cowes and mares
but knoweth not the nomber of them". With his family he had to flee
to Bandon Bridge where he continued to lose out to the rebels ". . .
one sorrel horse worth £30 . . . one black gelding £20 . . . one dun
gelding £10 . . . one grey nage £3 . . . one baye gelding stolen. . . ."

After the rebellion the Hulls returned to Leamcon. Sir William died
sometime before 1657, but his descendants continued to live in the area.
The Reverend William Hull was rector of Schull from 1675 to 1722
and gave the parish a silver chalice made by Robert Goble, master of
Cork's Goldsmith Guild, which is still preserved in the church. During
the eighteenth century the family got into straitened circumstances and
had to retire to Coney Island, where Pococke reported them to be
living. Later they were back at Leamcon, for it was a Mr Hull of
Leamcon who in 1796 caught sight of French ships sailing westwards
towards Bantry Bay and sent word to Mr White of Bantry.

The Hull house is still to be seen on a slope above the inlet. The first
house on this site was destroyed during the rebellion; Sir William
described it as "being so fortified with towers and works of defence that
it was abell to defend itself agains fower or five thousand". This is a
Georgian successor. About twenty years ago its west front, including a
ballroom, was "knocked" to avoid paying rates. Some of the newer
farms in the neighbourhood have been constructed with the aid of its
timbers. It is said that during demolition a skeleton was found in the
roof. What remains of the house is impressive, and includes a large
crenellated yard with outhouses and a building rather like a chapel
with walls made from masonry two feet thick.

The coast road west from Leamcon twists towards the wide arc of
Toomore Bay, beyond which is visible the narrow entrance to Crookhaven harbour. At a point near the sea I stopped and looked for a
cillin marked on my six-inch map. Cork is full of *cillini* designated on
maps as "children's graveyards" or "disused burial grounds". The word
is a diminutive of *cill*, which is derived from the Latin *cella*, meaning a
holy place. *Cills* were originally little huts of wood or stone associated

with some Christian purpose, being either the home of a holy man or a place of worship. As soon as they were erected, people began to bury their dead on the surrounding consecrated ground. The little building in the centre eventually fell in, or a church was built elsewhere, but burying continued to take place on the original site. The diminutive *cillini*, used to describe the "children's graveyards", suggests that these places did not have quite the same sanctity as an ordinary *cill*; so does the tradition that they were mainly used as burial places for unbaptized children. They are not hard to find, as they are usually indicated by patches of furze and briar set apart in a field. The one I tracked down near Leamcon was fairly typical, being circular, with a boundary bank surrounding it, rather like a run-down ring fort. The enclosed area inside it was divided into two parts. In each, under the bracken and grass my feet coud pick out what appeared to be large cobblestones crowded together. They were small gravestones.

Not very much is known about these burial grounds which are so numerous; there are a dozen or more around Schull alone. Two thousand years of high infant mortality would fill many such grave-yards. Probably the number of burials increased during Penal times when it was difficult to carry out baptisms regularly. In some districts there was only one mass baptism a year on St John's Day, and children who died unbaptized before or after that date were buried in *cillini*. Although the emphasis was on the interment of the unbaptized, ordin-ary burials took place in them as well. Sean O'Riordan refers to a village in Kerry where it was the custom for the first child of a family to die before reaching maturity to be buried in a *cillin*. Many of them were in use this century. Presumably in remote rural areas it was too difficult to convey a corpse ten or twelve miles to the nearest official graveyard. A good number of *cillini* are divided into two sections like this one at Leamcon, and they may mark the division between baptized and unbaptized.

Many pious people dislike the idea of an ancient practice of segre-gating countless children destined for Limbo. When I discussed *cillini* with an extremely knowledgeable parish priest, he indignantly repudiated the idea that they were for unbaptized children. It is puzzling why so many places should differ in status from ordinary church and monastic sites and carry this tradition of harbouring outcast souls. Some of them still have traces of early buildings, presumably churches or cells. Perhaps they were ancient places of worship connected with pre-Christian cults which were never properly converted, so that there was always something vaguely unsatisfactory about their position. Or they may have been used in early Christian times before ritual and doctrine were properly standardized, to foment a sort of second-class Christianity, full of traces of ancient pagan beliefs.

At Toormore, the lonely little Protestant church of Altar stands back from the road and the estuary of Toormore Bay. This church was built soon after the famine by a famous clergyman named William Fisher, who lived here in the parish of Goleen for forty years. During the nineteenth century he had a reputation among churchmen of being an earnest missionary. He made many converts during the time of the famine, and has been accused of being a souper. This reputation seems to be unfair; his success was largely due to his undoubtedly forceful personality. Also, at the time of the famine, the parish priest of Goleen was absent.

Fisher was born of Quaker parents, and in Oxford became influenced by the Oxford Movement. According to his biography, he "was on the verge of Rome when Tract 90 arrested him and shewed him that he was being led away from Christ. . . . He tied up the tracts, put them out of reach on the top of his bookcase and never more opened them." After his curacy he came to Goleen where he found a Protestant population of about eight hundred people. Some were descendants of Huguenot families settled here, whose names are still to be found in the district—Camier, Dakelow (du Clos) and Jermyn (probably Germain). Others had English ancestors, whose names, such as Roycroft, Attridge, Draper and Kingston, are familiar in West Cork. Many of their forebears had formed part of a plantation around Crookhaven founded by Sir Thomas Roper in the early part of the seventeenth century.

When Mr Fisher arrived he found a number of Protestants at work building a Methodist chapel. They were so struck by the deep piety of the new rector that they abandoned it and joined his church. The walls of the half-finished building stood for many years.

He set about converting Catholics. His enthusiasm was aided by a rough knowledge of medicine and by the fact that he could speak Irish. (The British Museum used to send him ancient Irish documents to translate.) Then, in 1847, at the time of his greatest success, there swooped down on Goleen Father John Murphy, "the Black Eagle",

Cliffs at Mizen
Head

The rose drawing room, Bantry House

Kilcrohane—daffodils and tulips in the graveyard by the sea

riding a spirited black horse and wearing a tall black hat and flowing black cape. Father Murphy had spent his early life in Northern Canada and America, before returning to Ireland. Now, at Goleen, he mounted the wall of the Protestant church every Sunday morning and berated any former Catholic parishioners whom he saw entering the building.

Whether because of the Black Eagle's efforts, or because of better times, Mr Fisher's parishioners began to return to the old faith. He made tremendous efforts to preserve his large congregation, building the church at Toormore out of his own private means and from donations used for famine relief which were paid in salary to the men who built it. He called it *Teampol-na-boct*, the poor man's church. (Today it is known as the Altar, after the big wedge-shaped prehistoric grave that stands in a nearby field.) The parish of Goleen was terribly poor, and he worked for forty years, tending the sick, and performing acts of charity which were remembered long after his death. But he could not keep his converts, and ultimately he died a disappointed man. However, his zeal and personal holiness must have been very striking. Standish O'Grady, whose father had been a curate at Goleen, wrote optimistically of him: "His memory will be preserved by tradition like that of the saintly founders of the Church of Ireland in the fifth and succeeding centuries. . . ." There is a monument to him in the church at the Altar.

The scent of gorse was almost overpowering as I rode towards Goleen between yellow banks of blossom that fell down to the edge of the road. Where the rocks jutted into a glittering silver sea there used to be an O'Mahony castle, Ballydevlin, where the last of the old O'Mahony chieftains died in 1642. Smith saw it "boldly erected on a rock hanging over the ocean", and eighty years later another writer exhorted the reader, "and westward see the bold and high Ballydevlin. It cuts the blue sky with its embattled loftiness." Today not a trace of it remains; it is quite impossible to tell exactly where it stood.

At Ballydevlin House, a Georgian cottage overlooking the sea, lived Lionel and Elizabeth Fleming during the early part of the nineteenth century. Their experiences, documented in letters and memoirs, give a clear idea of the circumscribed lives of isolated Protestant landlords.

Lionel Fleming came from Newcourt near Skibbereen, and Elizabeth was the daughter of Horatio Townsend of Derry, outside Rosscarbery. This was where Charlotte Shaw spent her unhappy childhood, but for Elizabeth Fleming, Charlotte's great-aunt, Derry was the "dear old

I

house", a paradise always to be contrasted with the bleak discomforts of Ballydevlin. Even today the area is remote; in 1819 it was entirely cut off from the rest of the world. Sir John Moore had described it as "wilder than anything I have seen out of Corsica". There were no proper roads. When Pococke had toured in 1740, he had found that the only reliable way to travel was on horseback with outriders to protect him from dangers. In 1819 there was one boggy track connecting Ballydevlin with towns to the east, and this was so bad that very few carts made the journey. When Elizabeth Fleming travelled to her new home after her marriage, she jogged along in a small open cart filled with straw and a feather bed to cushion the jolts. No carriage was narrow enough to negotiate the track.

Around Ballydevlin stretched rocky hills covered with gorse and heather, interspersed with numerous windowless cottages filled with a miserably poor Irish-speaking population. The Fleming's house, although a startling contrast to the cabins of their neighbours, was simple enough, and here the young couple settled down to live in a rough and ready way. They lived "entirely on potatoes, fowl, rabbits, fish and home-grown flour baked in a bastable". Failing cabbage, a seaweed was used as a vegetable. "Mutton fat was melted down and poured into moulds for candles. Sometimes the wicks were the pith of rushes and sometimes cotton twine. They had a nasty smell and gave poor light. . . ."

Skibbereen was the nearest post town so that post was infrequent. The long letters the Flemings wrote were delivered by courier. Peggy Jourdan jogtrotted barefoot through the mud, making the thirty-mile journey to Rosscarbery in a day. "Oh then, there's many a lifting up leg and putting down leg and bending the knee between here and Derry."

The doctor at Skibbereen was occasionally sent for in an emergency. Usually by the time he arrived the invalid was cured through some violent remedy recommended by Lionel, who tried his hand at most crafts and trades. The doctor might not even have to prescribe. "But he took his fee, of course."

There were no schools. Church was six miles away at Crookhaven. The family had to walk about six miles to Rock Island, cross in a boat and walk an extra mile to the church. At Ballydevlin their only company seems to have been Mr O'Grady, the clergyman (Standish

O'Grady's father), who joined them for musical soirées, playing Handel and Mozart on violin and 'cello. "It provided serenity in this remote place." Elizabeth, marooned in the house, rearing six children, longed to leave. But her father dissuaded her. "There are weighty considerations for remaining longer at Ballydevlin. You are doing much good there and I think it was a happy day for that country when you and Lionel went there."

He was referring to Lionel's energetic activities, for his son-in-law was not only managing his family's remote estates but most of the countryside as well. "In those days much evil-doing was prevented or put down by the powers that the landlord had over individuals . . . the evil-doer knew that he would suffer from the landlord, even in fact that he would not get a farm, or lose what he had got. . . ." This comment was written by one of Lionel's children. As magistrate in the district he discharged justice, settled quarrels before they became court cases, had a courthouse and school built as well as roads in every direction. His wife was directed to teach, to instruct in the growing of flax and to run a lending library. He acted as self-appointed coastguard, preventing wrecks along the coast from being plundered. Well meaning, officious, self-righteous, his behaviour, in the tradition of benevolent colonialism, made him enemies. Elizabeth's unhappiness was compounded by the threat of boycott. At one time there was the prospect of a duel with a man whom Lionel accused of meddling with public money. And years later, long after the family had left Ballydevlin and returned to civilization at Skibbereen and Rosscarbery, he earned the enmity of O'Donovan Rossa. The family story was that in his capacity as magistrate he once convicted the patriot for poaching. Whatever the case, in his reminiscences Rossa, writing of the famine, mentions that Lionel was Chairman of the Poor Law Board at Skibbereen, and further depicts him as a monster. "The faster the men, women and children in the poorhouse would die . . . the oftener would Liney thank the Lord. . . . If the number one week would be less than the number last week, his remark would be 'too bad, too bad. Last week was a better week than this. . . .'"

In fact during the famine the Flemings acted no differently from others in their position, no better, no worse. "One day I saw a poor woman sitting on the footpath surrounded by her starving children. I at once ran back to the house and brought a jug of soup and tin mugs.

But she was dead when I returned. I laid her on the footpath, fed the poor children and sent them in a cart to the workhouse." "Everyone diminished their house expense to provide food. We gave up two horses, retaining one, and a donkey. Dogs were also killed, and many persons gave up having wine or any stimulant. Our teachers, governesses, butler and other dependents were parted with, and the house was reduced to a very low ebb in every way. Indian meal became a common food, and many persons made it their breakfast."

How did the gentry of West Cork act during those terrible years? We know in particular of the clergymen who joined with priests and doctors to bring relief, visiting the fever-stricken cabins day after day, month after month. Dr Traill of Schull, one of the first private persons in Ireland to establish a soup kitchen, died of typhus; so did Mr Townsend, the clergyman in Skibbereen. There were private acts of charity and bravery like that of the ladies of Ballydehob who toured the area around the town at a time when typhus was raging, distributing food and clothing. Before the Soup Kitchen Act the cauldron of soup rapidly became a standard piece of equipment in most households, and some families beggared themselves to keep it filled. At the same time, all over the area the admirable Quakers worked among the suffering to emerge here as elsewhere in Ireland with their reputation intact.

However, "few classes of men have had so much abuse heaped on them," Cecil Woodham Smith wrote of the Irish landlord, ". . . and with justification."[6] She qualifies this statement by listing numerous exceptions. But in West Cork many landlords undoubtedly behaved disgracefully, shipping off boatloads of destitute people to ports in England and Wales, or declining to provide their tenants with seed in order to discourage them from staying on the land. There was also the vexed question of "souping" by clergymen.

Sir Randolph Routh, the Commissary General for Ireland during the famine, blamed the distress in Skibbereen entirely on the landlords and the high rents they collected. This was unjust, but it was true that Lord Carbery, Sir William Wrexham-Becher and others, numbering a dozen altogether, gathered an annual income of £50,000 from the impoverished area. When Mr Townsend was buried in Skibbereen he had a long funeral, for both Catholic and Protestant turned out to mourn him for the devoted work he had done to relieve suffering. But previously he had drawn eight thousand pounds a year in rents.

ELEVEN

Crookhaven

FROM GOLEEN THE old road wound high over a ridge before dropping down to Crookhaven. Almost all the land was rocky around Knocknamaddree; the quilted shadows of clouds passed along the high ground over to the sea. At Daslough, above a circular lake banked by reeds, were two gallery graves which had partially collapsed. I walked along the ridge with the Fastnet and Crookhaven below me on one side, and Barley Cove on the other. A little way along I found a small stone circle with one of the stones marked with a cross. There is a tradition that St Kieran's mother was buried in this circle. It used to be one of the objectives of a pattern, along with a nearby well famous for its cures, but today no one makes the pilgrimage.

Crookhaven, the last town in Ireland, is a little port built on the far side of a long bony spit of land which runs eastward for a couple of miles, enclosing a fine harbour. On the south-eastern end of this tongue of land is the lighthouse at Streek Head, which has now become automatic, its buildings converted to flats for tourists. The heights above are dominated by two Gothic towers that were once lookouts for smugglers. There used to be four of these towers; the Coughlan Tower, which old charts show as standing a hundred and five feet above the harbour, was used as a fix for entering ships. It survived until 1965, when it was pulled down so that a bungalow could be built on the site.

There was also an O'Mahony castle on either side of the harbour. Very little is known about them. Castle Meighan on the north side was built around 1450. Crookhaven Castle on the south side was inhabited by Finin O'Mahony of Crookhaven around the year 1570. His sister, Johanna, married an O'Driscoll and became the mother of the famous

Sir Fineen O'Driscoll. Later, when Bishop Downes visited Crookhaven in 1700 he noted that this castle was being used by the English authorities as a prison. Both fortresses have vanished without trace.

The north bank of the harbour is dominated by the rough buildings and rubble of the abandoned stone quarry that gave employment to more than a hundred men before the last war. West of it lie the ruins of the pilchard pallace owned in vigorous partnership by the Earl of Cork and Sir William Hull. Crookhaven pilchards were exported as far as Marseilles. In 1641 this pallace, along with the town across the water, was destroyed. Some walls remain, enclosing square holes chiselled out of the rock for taking beams. Another building stood on the site at a later date, probably a corn store. A farmer told me that during the famine this was known as the meal or gruel house. The lane leading down to it was always thick with people waiting to be fed.

Not only was the town—named after the developer of Baltimore, Thomas Crooke—a centre for fishing, but its position as the most westerly harbour on the coast gave it a strategic importance in the days of sailing ships. Smith noted that it was "one of the best outlets in Europe for vessels to sail to any place whatsoever". During the eighteenth century the deep and protected anchorage was used by the West Indian and Jamaican fleets to weather out storms or await more favourable winds. In the Napoleonic wars a provisioning depot was established, where ships were supplied with wheat, oats, corn and butter. In the mid-nineteenth century American mails were collected from here.

Early in this century the mackerel fleet from the Isle of Man called regularly. Manx boats anchored here by the score, each with its crew of six men and a boy. "They would arrive in March and leave for the Shetlands in June after the herrings." Other vessels crowded in. Mr Jim O'Driscoll, who is over eighty, can remember when "you couldn't drag your feet for sailors". On one occasion he had seen four windjammers, grain ships from Australia, sheltering in the harbour with their masts rising over the hills. Ships like these made a wonderful spectacle as their canvas billowed while they luffed up into a westerly wind and waited for the pilot boat to bring them in. From Crookhaven the masters would telephone to their head offices for instructions. To which port in the British Isles should they take their cargoes? In order to provision such visitors, butchers would be sent out all over the countryside to slaughter and dress meat, a practice that made local prices sky high. "If it blew from the east they would remain outside the harbour. We would row out to them in whalers and give them newspapers—that way they would catch up." Recently skin divers exploring the harbour bottom found it covered with empty bottles, most of them rum-bottles.

The decline of fishing and the vanishing of the sailing ship hit this port very hard. Other coastal towns could still serve as focal points for farming communities. But Crookhaven, out on its peninsula, is too isolated for contact with the land. Until recently it presented an extremely dilapidated appearance, its houses empty and falling down, the pier deserted and the population gone. But during the past decade many empty houses have been renovated. Yachts and sailing ships anchor in fair numbers during the summer, although it is nothing like the old days when the inlet was so packed with ships that a man could walk from one side to the other across their decks.

At the Welcome Inn I met the proprietor, Mr Nottage, an Englishman, who as a young man trained to be a telegraphist for the Ely railway. Afterwards he transferred to the Marconi Wireless and Telegraph Company. Marconi, who had already experimented successfully in transmitting radio waves from Cornwall, planned to set up a transmitting station at Crookhaven. In 1902 he travelled down to Schull by train with his Irish wife and family, and then westward to McCarthy's Hotel in Crookhaven, which has long been a ruin. "A small thin fellow who could speak good English." He stayed for about five weeks, during which time the first radio mast was erected opposite the church at what is now called Marconi House. Local people blamed it for the bad weather they had that year. Its range proved to be too limited, and afterwards Marconi obtained permission to use the station at Brow Head from which Lloyd's operated a telegraph service. Lloyd's welcomed Marconi, since they had considerable trouble in contacting their ships. Although they had dropped a cable out to the Fastnet, it had broken twice. The wide range of Marconi's radio waves reached far into the Atlantic. Lloyds used Marconi's company for a number of years—the rupture came eventually because he was charging them sixpence a word for his services.

Mr Nottage was the second radio operator to be sent to Crookhaven. He showed me the log book which he kept in a drawer in the bar. The first entry, written in spidery red ink, stated: "Took over Marconi Wireless Station Saturday 10 p.m. December 17th, 1904." He worked for eighteen months at Brow Head before the station was transferred to Valentia, mostly sending and receiving messages from White Star or Cunard liners. There was also a radio receiver on the Fastnet with which he kept in contact. After the station closed down, he settled in Crookhaven, marrying a local girl. He had lived here without regrets for sixty-five years.

The little Protestant church a half-mile west of the town was built on the site of an earlier church. It is the only place of worship, and there is very little use for it. Catholics must walk or motor seven miles to the church in Goleen. In Baltimore and Castletownshend the situation is similar; Catholics allowed to build churches during the mid-nineteenth century were encouraged to do so a good step outside the town. They are not so difficult to reach now that so many people have cars, but for decades their situation meant a cruel wet Sunday walk. From Crookhaven the Catholic population first rowed across the inlet and then trudged for miles over rock and mud, viewing, behind them the pale light filtering through fog and drizzle from the diamond-latticed windows of the Protestant church.

At either end of the Crookhaven peninsula are the ruins of copper-mines. The oldest, which has been closed for almost a century, is east of the town under Streek Head. A shaft filled with water is used as a well by a farmer living beside it. Above the heaps of rubble stand two round powder magazines looking like turrets of a buried castle, each fancifully painted with the outline of eight Gothic windows.

The other mine is situated two miles south-west of Crookhaven on the massive crag of Brow Head, the most south-westerly point of Ireland. The magnificent cliff-head with its stupendous views is cluttered up with deserted buildings where the shambles of ruined mining cottages seems to suggest that some disaster convulsed the cliff top. Overlooking them is the shell of the usual post 1798 signal tower, linked with neighbouring towers at Leamcon and Mizen Head, and beside it lie the ruins of the old Lloyd's station. One of the few constructions that have not yet fallen into decay is the new radio beacon with a range of three hundred miles to help hydrographic ships working in the Atlantic.

Most of the mine shafts lie right down at the foot of the cliffs at water level. From their entrance beneath seagulls' nests, they were driven in right under the sea. The ore was brought out and lifted to the top of the Head by cable. A man who worked in the mine fifty years ago told me that in spite of their position these shafts never leaked. "Down under the water you wouldn't feel a puff of wind, even a gale." For illumination miners were supplied with boxes of candles from the Welcome Inn.

On Rock Island, at the entrance to Crookhaven harbour, stand the shell of the coastguard station and a line of houses belonging to the Irish Lighthouse Service. In 1881 several new buildings were constructed which included a large barracks for the workmen who were being mobilized to build a second lighthouse on the Fastnet Rock.

The Fastnet stands four-and-a-half miles out in the Atlantic, equidistant from the west end of Cape Clear and from Crookhaven. It is actually two rocks, the larger towering a hundred and forty-seven feet above the sea and separated by a narrow cleft from the smaller Little Fastnet. Together they have been known as Paddy's Milestone and the Teardrop of Ireland, since they were the very last bit of the old country that an emigrant could see before the waves rose up and hid it as his ship sailed westward.

When after a series of tragic shipwrecks, the original lighthouse on Cape Clear proved to be inadequate it was decided to erect a tower on the Fastnet. This first tower, completed in 1854, was made of metal, like so many Victorian engineering masterpieces. But it proved unable to stand up to the fierce pounding of the waves, and in 1881 it collapsed, fortunately without loss of life. The second tower, the one we see today, was located on a different part of the rock and built out of specially cut blocks of granite shipped over from Cornwall. It was completed in 1903 at the cost of £70,000, a fraction of what would be required today. With its distinctive shape and double balcony the Fastnet was considered one of the most beautiful lighthouses in the world. Sir Robert Ball, the scientific adviser to the Commissioners for the Irish Lights, set out enthusiastically from Crookhaven to visit the new structure. . . . "As to the beams of the Fastnet, during all the time of our return to harbour I can only describe them as magnificent. At ten miles distant the great revolving spokes of light succeeding each other at intervals of five seconds, gave the most distinctive character possible . . . each great flash as it swept past lighted up the ship and the rigging like a search-light."[7]

Because of the heavy swell there are very few days in the year when ships can berth beside the rock. Until very recently supplies and relief were landed by breeches buoy, but this task has been taken over by a helicopter.

Certain banana boats used to keep so rigidly to their schedule, passing the Fastnet every Friday, that the keepers used to check their clocks by them.

In the two world wars the lighthouse was used as a mark for convoys. Many ships were torpedoed within sweep of its light, such as the *Hazelside*, whose survivors were picked up by boats from Cape Clear during the last war.

Under the shadow of the old coastguard station on Rock Island is the lobster fishery which was started in the nineteen-twenties by a Breton named Trehiou. Realizing that the French had eaten most of their own lobsters, he found a new untapped source of crustacea around Irish coastal waters. Pococke had noted that at Crookhaven "lobsters, cray-fish and crabs sell for pence a piece and are very good". Up until quite recently they were abundant; it was possible for farmers to make a good second living by potting lobsters from small boats around the shores and inlets near their homes. Today they have to be gathered far out to sea. They have been overfished, and fishermen have failed to observe the 83-millimetre minimum or to throw back coralled female lobsters.

I talked to the manager of the company, who was deeply pessimistic about the future of the Irish lobster. He estimated that within the next decade his plant at Crookhaven would have to close down for lack of supplies. Not only were the lobsters and crayfish disappearing; the periwinkles, scallops, clams and prawns which were shipped to the omnivorous Frenchmen were rapidly dwindling in numbers and in size. The shoreline is inexorably scraped clean of shellfish.

He showed me the tanks covering three-quarters of an acre of tidal sea water where the lobsters and crayfish were stored, protected from sun by slotted wooden awnings. Only a few years ago it would have been crowded with green and red crustaceans gliding noiselessly through the water. Today there were far fewer. The tide was out and the sea had ebbed away, so that the sad bewhiskered creatures were stranded helplessly creaking their tails.

Their future would be a royal captivity, ending in sumptuous sacrifice. They would be carried over to Brittany by boat, and from there loaded on to lorries bound for Paris and their expensive deaths. The ultimate destination of a crayfish caught off Mizen Head would probably be a silver dish in front of a group of banqueting Parisians.

TWELVE

Dunmanus

ROARING WATER BAY was a light green, fringed with white breakers. Every headland, every rock had its own white spout that rose and fell rhythmically as the waves came crashing in. Across the pale green a dark leaden band fell over the water. In Crookhaven, the *Rosko*, the Breton trawler on its fortnightly trip to pick up lobsters, rode out at anchor beside a couple of miserable yachts. Near Barley Cove groups of swans lay huddled against the rushes that bordered the lake.

I stayed at Barley Cove in the wooden hotel overlooking the beach. The building, flanked by lines of chalets, was built in 1967 amid controversy. Before that the beach was wild and empty. But tourists are important, and their needs are considered first. Even the farmers who live nearby have found that their ancient privilege of taking sand for the land has been called into question. They come from as far away as Dunmanway to collect it, for it is supposed to have special properties. But there is fear that they may deplete the only substantial beach for thirty miles, and deprive children of material for their buckets and spades.

In the bar I met a tourist who was driving out to Mizen Head to see the full fury of the storm. Mizen, which Edith Somerville described as "a giant spoke of a headland that sticks up like a boar's tusk above the rugged lip of the Irish coast", is a few miles west of Barley Cove. There were lines of cars parked at the end of the road with tourists inside gazing out at Ireland's Land's End through windscreens misted by spray rising from waves exploding like bombs hundreds of feet below. The foam drifted lazily upwards in thick yellow suds. The sea pushed and heaved in a series of silver scythes slicing the rocks away. Beyond was a raging expanse of grey and white ocean.

It was barely possible to walk down the path to the lighthouse. (In really bad storms men have to move on their hands and knees.) The lighthouse, or, as it is correctly called, the Fog Signal Station, stands on an island of rock separated from the Head. Steps lead down to the bridge slung across the narrow divide from where, in better weather, one can look down a drop of a hundred and fifty feet and a perspective of jagged rocks. Seals are supposed to shelter among them during storm; I wondered if any were there now. From inside the station, the rock was scarcely visible and the atmosphere was just like that of a ship. After reading the permission I had obtained from the Commissioners of the Irish Lights, a keeper showed me round the engines and generators and the transmitter for the radio beacon, which has a range of two hundred miles. All instruments are duplicated in case of any breakdown. Even the library is like a ship's library, with its meagre assortment of obscure titles, including *The Expulsion of the Jews from Spain* and an unnecessary *Elementary Gardening*.

I returned to the hotel, which was immensely comfortable. From inside I could not see the ribbon of rain-soaked wooden huts, but looked out instead over the sweep of sand flanked by walls of cliffs and boulders which formed one of the most superb beaches in the country.

Next morning the wind had died and the sun shone. The only remnants of the storm were the curling lines of breakers which had an hypnotic effect, viewed through the plate glass. Outside larks sang above the dunes covered with small yellow pansies. Behind Barley Lake the swans were again dipping in the water. A portion of the dunes behind the beach had been groomed and planted with grass for a golf course. Somewhere in the sand are supposed to lie the bones of Frenchmen who were washed up here in 1796, when their ship foundered after the invasion of Bantry.

On the slopes leading to Mizen Head are ruins which indicate another community almost wiped out by emigration. The people who remain sell land to tourists. A man whom I encountered surveying the empty scene told me that a nearby farm had been sold to an Englishman for ten thousand pounds.

"That was a big place. But the little places do nicely. How much do you think that was worth?" He pointed to a cottage.

"A thousand?" I guessed.

"You can double that and add another five hundred more," he said happily. "I sold it to the man myself."

"What's happened to the people who used to live in these places?"

"There's no coming back from where they've gone. All of them are dead!"

He asked me where I had come from and I mentioned that I had been at the hotel. He looked at my bicycle and shabby windcheater dubiously.

"The guests there are the biggest of the big." I tried to persuade him that not only millionaires stayed there, but he remained unconvinced.

I cycled along the road which leads to Dunlough Bay, another rent in the coast with lines of cliffs and the sea roaring in. In scenery of great breadth and scale stands the most isolated of the O'Mahony castles. It is still difficult to reach, far from any road, standing right at the end of the headland. Not many people make the long approach, possibly deterred by the notice which a farmer has put up in recent years:

"Take notice. Visitors to three castles admission 2/6 and pay 1/6 at farmhouse. Caution. Anybody that doesn't abide by this stay out. No dogs allowed." And added in pencil: "No cats."

Visitors tend to remain around the slipway in front of this directive where the rocks beside the pier have become a favourite place for fishing. But it is worth leaving the dog behind, paying the money, and walking the miles over the heather to Three Castle Head. The three castles are in fact one castle made up of a tower and two flankers. As you approach over rough pathless ground, Dunlough Castle appears suddenly in view, situated on the edge of a lake in a shallow depression on the cliff top. A couple of hundred feet away the cliffs fall down in a deep chasm pounded by waves. To an invading army, the cliff's edge, the defensive wall, the lake and the sternly inaccessible approach would have made the castle appear impregnable. But although its defences were so elaborate, there is no record that they were ever put to use.

According to the *Annals of Innisfallen*, Dunlough was built in 1217, and is therefore the oldest of the O'Mahony castles. The O'Mahonys considered it their main property, along with Ardintenant, and one of their chieftains, Dermot of Dunlough, lived in it for a time before he became chief in 1535. Its ultimate prosaic fate was to fall into the hands of the Earl of Cork along with 1869 acres of forfeited lands.

Here I planned to spend the night. After the luxury of Barley Cove, bedding down was a cold contrast. The little orange tent that I pitched beside the lake rattled with the wind, and the slightest movement disturbed the equilibrium of the interior that I had created. I ate a can of porridge heated up over a fire, and then walked around the black stretch of lake, which is haunted by a lady, "to see whom is to die". At the northern end the ground fell away among some great splinters of rock down to Dunmanus, overlooking the restless waters of Dunmanus Bay far below. Around me there were no birds, or living creatures, and the only movement was from the wind making waves on the dark surface of the water. It seemed that the evening light might fall on a hand and a sword rising from its depths. Coming back around the neck of land I stumbled on a souterrain filled with lichen-covered bones. Were they human? Nervously I took a couple and placed them in a plastic bag some yards away from the tent—they were afterwards identified as belonging to long deceased cattle.

I spent an uncomfortable night, disturbed by heavy showers of rain and the flapping of the tent. Weak and jittery, I emerged into a cold wind to try and cook more porridge. Clouds were low and the bright colours of the day before had turned into a uniform grey, as I trudged back over the heather carrying my tent and my bag of bones.

I cycled along the road to Barley Cove once again, and from there turned northwards across the hills to the southern slopes of Dunmanus Bay. Tractors with churn-laden trailers passed me going to the cream-ery. A man herded cows on his motorbike, his dogs running behind, and a woman cleaned out her cottage, whose interior was painted bright pink, matching the thrift that grew outside.

Dunmanus is the most southerly of the inlets that splice the south-west coast, which are drowned valleys or *rias*. Bantry Bay, the Kenmare River and Dingle Bay are the others. The south side of Dunmanus is rocky and unproductive, the land falling steeply into a sea patrolled by gannets. The only signs of a former prosperity are the remains of the Durode copper-mines overlooking a line of cliffs opposite Bird Island. The geologist, Francis Lisabe, wrote of Durode in 1861 that "the amphi-theatre-like appearance of the mine reminds us of its rich neighbour, Bearhaven, and the late rich discoveries made induce the belief that in a short time the present spirited proprietors will be amply rewarded for their perseverance and energy".

Such hopes were in vain, in spite of Durode's promise. "There was the devil's nature in copper there," a man called Patrick McCarthy told me. He claimed that because of the copper in the soil, he had no need to spray potatoes against the blight.

The lonely coast road looped up and down beside the sea, its edges lined with reeds and dark lily pools. Rabbits squatted peaceably on the tarmac. I rode through Dunkelly, where the empty houses contained a hundred people thirty years ago. Only three families lived there now, one of them consisting of English holiday-makers who came in the summer. A lane led down to Ghurtdove, a harbour so narrow that it was almost dark with the cliffs rising above it. More abandoned houses and a pier which had been built by the Congested Districts Board. It was a deft piece of engineering, a series of piers arranged around a natural cleft in the cliff's face. But there were no boats left to use the slipway or to be secured by the iron rings. A few old men were left in the village to recall the days when people were plentiful and not wiped out like now, and when Ghurtdove, Canty's Cove and Dunmanus were famous for fishing, with twelve boats and seventy-two men regularly working. Dunmanus was the home of the mackerel, and in the season the men would be busy all night catching the fish with seine nets, while the women salted them during the day. Every summer a steamship belonging to the Limerick Steam Company would pick up the barrels and bring them to Liverpool from where they would be exported to America. It was the decline of the fishing that had started the emigration. The speaker himself had gone across and spent a number of years in Canada on the Great Lakes before returning here. But not to the same way of life. In the old days they had lived mainly on a diet of mackerel and milk, and also they made their own mountain dew. It was easy then to square off officials with a few bottles. People had enjoyed themselves before. Today on this side of Dunmanus Bay there was no bus service, and for supplies they had only one shop to go to between Goleen and Durrus, a distance of twenty miles. And that only opened on Friday. On Sunday they banded together to hire a car to go to mass at Goleen.

Ghurtdove was succeeded by Canty's Cove, and then Dunmanus harbour with its castle standing above it on a ledge of rock. Dunmanus, the largest and best preserved of the O'Mahony castles, was built around 1465 by Donagh, later chieftain of the sept. Being near to the Bantry area, it was subject to raids by the O'Sullivans, and in the course of time it acquired walls, a moat and six flanking towers, as we know from a description written in 1750. However, these extras have disappeared. After the Battle of Kinsale, Dunmanus, together with Leamcon, was considered worth defending by the O'Mahonys. During the six months that followed, a number of people sought to capture it. First it was raided by the O'Briens and O'Sullivans. Donogh O'Brien, Earl of Thomond, was sent into O'Mahony territory "to burn the corn, to take the cows and to use all possible persecution". Then, while he concentrated on Dunboy, which he was besieging during March, he dispatched a foraging party to Dunmanus, which captured "three scores and six cows and other things". In June, while Dunboy was in the final stages of its siege, a body of soldiers led by Owen O'Sullivan, renegade relative of the unfortunate O'Sullivan Beare, finally captured Dunmanus by surprise, possibly when its defenders were out foraging or hunting. In 1603 Captain Harvey formally took it over during his campaign. Later, the ubiquitous William Hull lived here for a while.

Behind the harbour and castle loomed a conspicuous ring fort, one of scores in the area. Ring forts are durable signs of ancient dwelling places which survive in great numbers; there are more than forty thousand of them all over Ireland. In aerial photographs they can be seen as green craters on hill slopes. Already I had passed dozens on my journey; they were common as pubs.

The elaborate ramparts around ring forts are not always of military significance. In many cases they were protective rather than defensive, to keep out wind and wolves as well as to discourage cattle-raiders. Inside them were not only dwelling places, but monastic cells and huts which housed small industries. At Garranes near Bandon a fort was found to contain implements used for the manufacture of metal and glass objects. Earthworks are of various types; they may have more than one bank or ditch, and may be built of stone and earth or hard-packed earth only. Most of those which I had seen would have contained farmsteads. The other enclosure was the *rath*; the interior was the *lios*, and within the *lios* there would once have been a wood or wattle dwelling, now long perished. This was known as a *teach*. There might be several dwellings within one ring, and perhaps a souterrain or two.

It is difficult to date ring forts since they were occupied over so long a period—some have been recorded as being inhabited through medieval

K

times right up to the seventeenth century. But generally they are
associated with the distant past, and here at Dunmanus many ages
seemed to converge at the small harbour which offered one of the few
natural places of shelter in the open bay. The fort, the castle, the moor-
ings for the vanished fishing fleet, the half-filled school bus suggested
two thousand years of struggle against an unfriendly environment.

When he learned that I wished to spend the night in Dunmanus
Ring, the farmer on whose land it stood warned me about fairies. But
settling down in the midst of the surrounding earth embankment and
the weed-filled fosse, I shared some of the security that they must have
brought to the original inhabitants of the ring. Most likely they would
have been farmers driving their cattle inside in the evenings. Dr Fahy
has noted that eighty-five per cent of West Cork rings are situated on
grade A boulder soil. This would indicate that the men who constructed them were less worried about defence than about having the
best land available for their livestock. In this case they may also have
been fishermen, since the harbour was beneath them, and the bay
provided an immediate rich fishing ground. Within their snug huts
under the protection of the earthen wall they could listen safely to the
howling of marauding wolf packs or to westerly gales. Possibly the nettles
beside which I had pitched my tent were relics of their habitation.

The ramparts of the earthwork were a perfect lookout from which
to watch a gilded sunset spreading across the bay and observe the last
rays of light sinking behind Sheep's Head until there was nothing left
but the silver reflection of the sea.

During the night I discovered that a ring is not quite a perfect shelter.
A surprising amount of wind began to shake the tent about, and by
dawn a gentle rain was falling. I departed hastily, and rode into the
countryside behind Dunmanus harbour, which opened up into a
pocket of level land squeezed between Mount Gabriel and the bay. At
Lissacaha I passed a particularly fine ring fort, with double earthen walls
twenty feet high and a deep earthen fosse between them choked with
willows and briars. Guarding the gap of the outer wall were two
boulders, thrown down there, said the farmer who owned this immense
earthwork, from the top of Mount Gabriel by Finn McCool who
wished to frighten the fairies.

Near the head of Dunmanus Bay were traces of two isolated gentlemen's estates. The house known as Prairie Cottage had gone, but a few

trees survived to show where it had stood. It was once a shooting lodge won over a game of cards by an ancestor of mine from Lord Riversdale. The slate ruin of neighbouring Rock Cottage is far more substantial. This small Georgian house was hidden in a wood, whose fine beeches and chestnut-trees appeared as out of place in their surroundings as if they were date palms. The house was still in one piece, although every year the darkened rooms, filled with litter behind the beautiful doorway and fanlight, decayed a little more. It had the reputation of being haunted by one of the previous owners, a man who lived alone, and shared his dinner with the rats with whom he was on speaking terms. Since I saw its gloom the house has been bought up by a Dublin man for renovation.

From Rock Cottage the road went inland past an abandoned National School and the ruin of the fourteenth-century church of Killangel. Then it joined the sea again, near a wafer-like edge of wall standing on the water so that the spray washed over it, all that remains of the O'Mahony castle of Dunbeacon. This is another location associated with human habitation over many centuries, for nearby is the outline of a promontory fort.

I made a detour inland up the mountains above Durrus to where there is nothing but rocks and gorse and distant views northward to the Slieve Miskish and Hungry Hill. This untarred bog road looped over the side of Mount Corin before descending again to Durrus. The ride, or rather walk, uphill took me past the abandoned barytes mine of Bereenmolane, which, according to the man who still lived beside it, was one of the most important in the country. He had a pile of white barytes outside his door, for he still did a little mining on the side. In the old days the ore used to be taken by overhead cable to Durrus where, because of its weight, it was used as ballast by the sailing ships that called there.

The road down which I freewheeled must have followed the sweep of the vanished cable. Pursued by a couple of yapping dogs I rushed down through hawthorn bushes, past a cottage, then lonely Dunbeacon circle glimpsed on a far hill and a pair of standing stones side by side in a field of mangels. A man working on the road told me that about twenty years ago there were four others which were removed to clear the ground. Similar stones must have been shifted from their position all over the country, and many must have vanished.

At Durrus, five roads converged on the main street. One came from Bantry, another from Schull and Mizen Head, a third from Kilcrohane, the other two from elsewhere. Each seemed to bring a wind with it. Durrus derives from *durus*, meaning a door or gate, and the name suggests cross roads. I stayed in a pub where the dark misty little bar filled up early with drinkers. Among them was an out-of-work labourer who a few years ago had made sixty pounds a week on Whiddy Island while the oil storage tanks were being built there. A man with bushy side-whiskers played the mouth organ. "It's all done by the tongue," he said, spitting out. Most of the evening there were tunes picked from a thin sound that could penetrate any conversation. Sometimes men gave up drinking and hummed a chorus. Once or twice I sidled out of the bar into the landlady's kitchen, or out for a turn around the rain-washed village before returning to the smoke and songs and frothy pints.

Next morning I took the road that leads to Sheep's Head, at the west end of the Kilcrohane peninsula, which stretches along the north side of Dunmanus Bay. I biked down an empty road beside the Durrus river, dyed a milky blue from the effluent of the creamery, past a massive three-storey corn store on the far shore. This building had a doubly sinister reputation during the famine, for not only was it naturally associated with the export of grain away from the starving populace, but later it was used as one of the notorious "auxiliary workhouses". In December, 1847, governing boards throughout the country were instructed to reserve the workhouses exclusively for able-bodied men and their families. Further accommodation for the destitute was to be provided by any means that presented itself. In the middle of winter disused buildings of every sort, mainly distilleries and warehouses, all without heating or sanitation, were commandeered and filled with what were known as the "indigent poor". These were generally the old and infirm, widows and children, turned out of the workhouses, with nowhere to go. The corn store at Durrus was filled with children.

Now and again among the sedgy fields a startling new holiday house looked out at the foam-flecked waters of the bay. I turned up a road to see the extensive ruins of Durrus Court, a smaller edition of Coppinger's Court with three high chimneys and massive gable ends. Early seventeenth-century buildings on this scale are rare in Ireland and with one or two exceptions are in ruins. Durrus only lost its roof this century. Built for the McCarthy Muclagh, probably after the Battle of Kinsale, it was designed in a spirit of optimism, when a period of peace was expected and Irishmen who had managed to stay out of trouble could construct residences in the manner of Elizabethan gentlemen. The McCarthy Muclagh held Durrus for almost a century, until they joined the Jacobites during the Williamite wars.

At Ahakista the slopes surrounding a pink Regency house gave off the first whiff of the moist luxuriance which reaches its peak in the gardens of Glengarriff and Parknasilla. In sunshine after rain the glossy leaves of dripping rhododendrons steamed like a rain forest. A stretch of woodland along the barren road glittered with magnolia and clumps of azalea and rhododendron in parrot colours. Then beyond the pocket of trees the familiar landscape of rock and small reedy fields was resumed.

Down on the sea stood the curious tower built by Lord Bandon to match Dunmanus, which stood directly opposite on the other side of the bay. Lord Bandon did not copy the O'Mahony style of architecture, for his folly has large windows, a parapeted step and three superfluous medieval chimneys. From a distance, however, it perfectly balances the castle on the southern shore.

Near Kilcrohane is a bit of O'Daly's Bardic School. The O'Dalys were a sept especially privileged because of their poetic gifts, and chieftains would grant them land in recognition of their importance. (This did not prevent Carew from employing an O'Daly, Angus-na-n-Aor (of the Satires), to compose lampoons of ancient families, a betrayal for which he was stabbed to death by the chief of the O'Meighers.) The places chosen by the O'Dalys to build their schools were always remote, where the rigours of bardic composition, the fasting and solitary confinement, might be practised far away from the usual haunts of mankind. At Kilcrohane their school stands in a little farmyard filled with sheepdogs, hens and manure. There is not much to see. A corner of a henhouse has a stronger wall than usual laid with a careful dry-stone technique, surrounding a slit window.

Kilcrohane was in the usual Sunday-morning mood, alternating between crowds and silence. One minute the shops were selling newspapers to jostling men who had come in from the surrounding country, and the next there were nothing but lines of empty cars and the murmur of voices from the church. At such a time, during Mass, the little village, the only one on the peninsula between Durrus and Sheep's Head, presented an austerely neat appearance. Between the creamery and the hotel ran the one and only street, from which a track went down to the deserted pier. Here were the remains of an older church. Like the castles, all the medieval churches along the coast are beside the sea or overlooking it, as near as possible to the water's edge. A pair of standing stones kept guard over fields of wilted daffodils. They were first planted here in 1962, and since that time Kilcrohane has become a centre for commercially grown spring flowers. Daffodils bloom by 20th January; an acre can bring in six hundred pounds. Later tulips and irises are harvested, then gladioli for the florists of Dublin and Cork.

Westward beyond Kilcrohane the land became very wild and empty. A closed National School, then a harbour with rusting bollards and the lap of sea against the piers. The road began to climb the headland, crowned with its signal tower. In a reedy pool a heron was reflected with mirror sharpness in the black water. There were stacks of turf piled by the road and a few farmhouses with shelter belts of sycamore and holly.

Sheep's Head cleft the waves like the bow of a ship, its edges white with foam. From the summit I got my first view of Bantry Bay with Bear Island and the far-off chain of the Slieve Miskish mountains. Shadows and sunshine danced across the water. Almost at the end of the head stood four inhabited farmhouses surrounded by neat little fields that fell down steeply to the sea. Beyond them a new automatic beacon guided the tankers round the coast into the Bay and their anchorage at Whiddy Island. After the struggle up hill, it was an anti-climax to find at the end of the wild road two GB cars whose occupants were reading the Sunday papers.

Next morning I set out from Kilcrohane in bright sunshine. As I cycled over the pass to Bantry the sky changed, and in Edith Somerville's words, "the glory had departed from the weather and an ugly wall of cloud was rising out of the west to meet the sun. The hills had darkened and lost colour, and the white bog cotton shivered in a cold wind that smelt of rain". The ceaseless battle between clouds and sun, the strokes of light on mountains and sea followed by swollen black clouds with their bellyful of rain, must have a conditioning effect on environment.

I cycled up the Goat's Path, climbing the side of Mount Sefin to the summit, crowned unexpectedly with a gleaming white marble copy of Michelangelo's Pietà. Then there was Bantry Bay once more, "the noblest Bay in the world and capable of containing all the navies of Europe". It was almost invisible in the rain which stung my face as the bike rattled downhill. The downpour became heavier, hard and relentless. With one hand holding my umbrella over my head, the other grasping the handle of the bike, I cycled on into the town.

THIRTEEN

Bantry

IT SEEMS TO rain a lot in Bantry. It had rained steadily last time I had visited the town to see the official opening of the oil terminal at Whiddy Island, a much publicized event. BANTRY IS WAITING, the headline in the *Southern Star* had proclaimed. A new coating of tarmac was laid on the pier, and lines of trees appeared overnight. "The quickest wood I've ever seen grown." The oil company also decorated the lamp posts with blue pennants and provided the lines of black Austin Princesses and Mercedes with orange stickers marked Gulf Oil. Tubs of flowers were placed in the old horse-trough in the main square, and crackly music was relayed through loudspeakers, which St Brendan the Navigator could not hear because he had a hood pulled over his head which would not be removed until the following day. He was another gift to the town from the company.

There had been an unusual air of festivity, as the presence of the P. & O. liner, *Orsova*, with the Taoiseach and other important guests aboard, livened up Bantry's usual deadly gloom. Except that it rained. Garda reinforcements patrolling the streets put on their waterproof capes. As the first guests disembarked from the ferry, they were pelted with a heavy shower while attendants rushed forward with armfuls of umbrellas. Mr Lynch and his party, the senior officials of Gulf Oil and their party, stood under the downpour making lengthy speeches until at last the statue of St Brendan was unveiled. He stood in a tiny boat with arms upraised, two monkish companions crouching behind him.

"She's a bit awkward with all them crowded together in the stern!"

Heads bent, the dignitaries departed rapidly to a banquet on board the *Orsova*, and soon the square was empty except for two lorries

marked CHIPS and a queue of schoolgirls from the nearby convent buying ninepenny bags. In the pubs men were remarking that the festivi-
ties must have cost a lot of money. "Sure it's nothing to that lot. They
make a million on each ship—that's a million pounds to invest."

Gulf Oil had chosen Bantry for its new oil terminal after an ex-
haustive search around the coasts of Europe. It was the first large company to realize the advantages that the Bay afforded: a deep safe harbour
and a government bending over backwards to entice it to settle in this
depressed part of West Cork.

The company was tactful and generous, exhibiting an understanding
of the dangers of polluting and disfiguring one of the best known tourist
areas in Ireland. "Gulf is Oil and an Attitude towards Mountains", ran
its advertisements, published in many newspapers. "We are fully
conscious of the wonderful scenery here," Mr E. D. Broderick, the
chairman of Gulf had said. "It is our intention to preserve as fully as
possible, while still accomplishing the purpose of our project." An
artificial hill was raised to screen the unsightly lines of tanks like over-
blown mushrooms, and the tankers themselves, whose size appeared to
cleave the Bay in two.

For two years almost a thousand workmen of eight different
nationalities worked on the storage terminal, and an estimated £30,000
a week flowed into the town. The dichotomy between tourism and
industrial development had apparently been settled satisfactorily.
However, today many people have doubts about the government's
wisdom in encouraging this vast development. Was it possible that
mistakes were made, and that Gulf Oil benefits more from the terminal
than does West Cork? The company does not pay harbour dues, only
an annual £25,000 a year for the rent of Whiddy. It is estimated that
Ireland loses a million pounds a year because the government did not
insist on having a harbour authority in Bantry which would collect
dues from each tanker anchoring at the terminal. Moreover, the
automated terminal, once built, needs no more than a skeleton staff to
run it. Hopes that unemployment would be relieved by Gulf's presence
have proved to be chimeric.

"Bantry, tucked up into the crotch of two peninsulas, is as warm as
the Scillies," wrote a recent travel writer. But not when it rains. I took
the liberty boat from the pier out to Whiddy to visit one of the six
tankers that call in there. Also on board were some new members of the

crew who had flown in the day before from New York. They were West Indian, and oblivious to the steady drenching drizzle, they wore butterfly colours, pink, orange, and bright blue, or white frilled shirts. They all had cowboy boots.

Through the mist we could make out the vast shape of the tanker rising out of the waves and behind it lines of grey-green tanks. A series of metal ladders led up to the terminal pier and the only visible building—a public telephone box, its door flapping open in the wind. Dragging their suitcases—there were no formalities—the new crew were swallowed up, so many Jonahs devoured by the biggest whale ever. On board, everything about the tanker was spotless and impersonal. I went past lines of grey doors over red lino floors up a lift between several decks to the control room. Innumerable coloured lights glowed from the instrument panels against the walls. One man was sufficient to control the discharge of oil from the ship, an estimated two-and-a-half million barrels. In smaller tankers, which weigh only fifty to a hundred thousand tons, this discharge is done manually. But I was aboard the *Universe Kuwait*, three hundred and twenty-six thousand tons, and figures about her tended to become meaningless. On the bridge you could comfortably play games of tennis; the twin grey funnels seemed as high as the surrounding mountains, the deck, crossed with black pipes, wide as the Arabian desert. The voyage to Kuwait averaged thirty days, and then back to Bantry. For such a large vessel, the crew was incredibly small—about sixty men of varying nationalities. German and Dutch officers, a few Americans and many Japanese and West Indians. The pay was good, but the run was particularly monotonous, shuffling back and forth between two dismally contrasting terminals, with a minimum of entertainment at each end. In Kuwait, where crews were not allowed to land, there had been no rain for two years.

On the first Friday of the month which was Fair Day, it was raining. Fair Days are usually wet, they say, as a consequence of the profanities spoken. Not so long ago this day marked a social occasion, and from all around the neighbourhood farmers would come to sell and buy cattle and to enjoy Bantry Fair, which used to be the best in Munster.

"It was like going to Mass on Sunday—like a holiday," recalled a farmer who had been attending for fifty years. But fairs are slowly dying out, as the co-operative selling of cattle takes over. Although the

standard of cattle sold is raised, the smaller farmer finds it more difficult
to sell his inferior animals in the impersonal atmosphere of the marts.
However, the change is inevitable.

"The marts have the Fair best!"

Instead of hundreds of animals offered for sale, only a few stood
patiently in the downpour as buyers huddled in the shelter of doorways
or under dripping trees. Later, while tourists took refuge in the tea-
shops, the farmers gathered in pubs to do what little business there was.
The bleak scene of dung-filled streets taken over by shivering beasts
will sooner or later cease to exist. It is the end of a very old tradition.
For hundreds of years, long before Bantry came into existence as a
town, cattle were bartered at this spot. Professor Estyn Evans has
written:

"Anyone who has watched a small town on Fair Day must get the
impression that he is looking at something which has been going on
through the ages . . . he is in the presence of a force older and more
fundamental than the town which has given it hospitality."

"The chief support of the town is fish and a clandestine import of
French brandy," wrote Pococke. Twenty years before his arrival
Bantry, like other coastal towns, had a flourishing pilchard trade, which
was already dying out. But there were still other varieties of fish to be
caught in Bantry Bay. Mr James Young caught and cured 482,000
herrings and 231 barrels of sprat in one year. Even up until recent times
fish were plentiful.

"You could fall off the pier and they would support your back."

Now there is little to be caught near the shore and local boats have
moved down to Bearhaven.

Around the main square were many of the curing houses and fish
cellars where the pilchards were smoked and train oil extracted. There
is a tradition that one of the stores of G. W. Biggs and Co. was used
for the purpose, and if anyone could confirm it, it is the present proprietor, Paddy O'Keefe. Mr O'Keefe is perhaps the best informed of all
West Cork's sages. His knowledge of the area appears to be limitless.
One has only to mention a subject—any early church west of Bandon,
any castle, an intricate relationship between branches of some local
family, and immediately he will give you the relevant information.

He referred me to the many travellers who have visited Bantry in
the past three hundred years. The town has never had a very good press.

In the late seventeenth century an English Jacobite described it as "a miserable place where good water was scarce and little accommodation was to be found". He had to lie on "a little dirty straw in a cabin no better than a hogstye".

"If you wish to seek out the poor, go to Bantry," Father Mathew told an American missionary just six years before the famine. Asenath Nicholson, dressed in her polka dot coat, her portmanteau full of bibles for distribution, took his advice. "I . . . went to Bantry and there found a wild dirty seaport with cabins built on the rocks and hills, having the most antiquated and forlorn appearance of any town I had seen; and the people in rags and tatters such as no country but Ireland could hang out."

Thackerary, commenting on the magnificent scenery, considered that "it looked like a seaport scene at a theatre, gay, cheerful and picturesque". He recorded "some smart houses on the quays", "a handsome courthouse as usual", and "a large grave Roman Catholic chapel". But with the exception of the main street, "thronged with the blue cloaks carrying on their eager trade of buttermilk and green apples and such cheap wares", it was a town of cabins. "The wretchedness of some of them is quite curious . . . I declare I believe a Hottentot kraal has more comforts in it; even to write of the place makes one unhappy and the words move slow. . . ." Mrs Nicholson also compared a cabin to an African kraal; the only building of any consequence that she noticed was "a lofty well-finished poor-house".

Bantry was a focal point for the poor and for the dispossessed throughout the region. In 1845, just before the famine, a correspondent of the London *Times*, Foster. T. Campbell, who was writing a series of articles on "the condition of the People of Ireland", made a careful analysis of the town. He noted that there were eight hundred and eighty-one families comprising four thousand and eighty-two people (twice as many as there are now). Of the heads of families some 250 were supported by fishing and curing, largely sprats and herrings; 50 were shopkeepers, 20 nailers, 50 pig jobbers, hide-buyers or butchers, 50 gentry, doctors, police or craftsmen, and 50 labourers in constant employment. Of the remaining 400 heads of families, about 50 lived by begging, and the rest subsisted off their little gardens and their pig, or from the proceeds of collecting coral, sand and seaweed from the Bay, which they sold. Many of them were ejected tenants who had come to town to seek some sort of a dwelling place and to try to find work; they had settled as squatters in hovels such as Thackerary described.

The terrible cabins and evidence of long-term stress and poverty have been changed for a subdued prosperity based on tourism. (However, no tourism, or development of small industries, or introduction of oil companies has been able to stop emigration.) But although the muddy streets are now tarred and filled with cars, Bantry still manages to retain a nineteenth-century air. In the huddle of streets behind the main square the shops are largely unchanged. A Trade Emporium with a long varnished counter is situated near a grocer whose copper scales hang from the ceiling. Boarded windows conceal ancient pubs with worn wooden floors. Vickery's Hotel, once the stop for coaches with Bianconi cars, is implacably Victorian. The harbour presents a view of mountains and bay framing the side of Whiddy Island which is empty of oil tanks. An enterprising house agent had displayed Spenser's verse about it in his window:

> "Hail Bantry's noble harbour deep
> Where Britain's fleet may ride
> And mighty ships in safety keep
> May in and outward glide."

There used to be a Franciscan abbey here, but it was levelled to the ground in 1602 to prevent it falling into the hands of the English. Only a large graveyard remains, overlooking the harbour and Whiddy Island. Whiddy, once a deer park belonging to the White family, became a naval base after the scare of the French invasion. As late as 1845 it was still heavily fortified. Now Gulf controls it.

A few French or Spanish trawlers call. Sometimes a member of the crew is sick, or emergency supplies are needed. But mostly they have no need to come into harbour, for they are pretty well self-supporting. Many of them come from the north-west coast of Spain and spend up to twenty-six days at sea before returning to their home ports. Each voyage entails hardship and danger, and from time to time a trawler is lost in winter storms. The food eaten on board is rudimentary.

"Hake is their god. Nothing wasted. Even the heads are used for boiling down to soup."

Outside the east end of the town, in a muddy field surrounded by some wildly irregular pieces of wire fencing which protect it from cattle, stands the finely carved Kilnaruane pillar. Once the shaft of a cross, it is a thin edge of rock so worn that the carving with which it was covered has worn away so that it is only a shadow. The stone itself has become weathered and groined like a piece of board.

The pillar overlooks the demesne and mansion of the Earls of Bantry. Bantry House, built early in the nineteenth century stands in a setting of lush decay, largely falling to pieces. Untenanted wings full of mould and soggy plaster look over the box garden. The crumbling stable-yards, with domed gateways and carved sandstone heads of horses, lead to an overgrown Italian garden with steep flights of steps and terraces planted out with conifers and rhododendrons run wild. A circular trellis glittering with wistaria drips into a weed-choked pool. Then, on the west side of the mansion, all this melancholy claustro-phobia is shattered by a wide terrace overlooking a view that might have been composed by Claude Lorraine, Whiddy Island in mid-distance, and then the length of the Bay.

The house, which is open to the public, is crammed with magnificent French furniture. The second earl was a passionate collector who had the good luck to be in Paris when the contents of the French royal palaces were being auctioned off. He brought back shiploads of acquisi-tions to Bantry. The walls of the main drawing-room are covered with rose-coloured tapestries said to have been ordered by Louis XV for Marie Antoinette on her marriage to the Dauphin. Other panels formed part of the royal *Garde Meuble* of the Tuileries. There is a Napoleonic fireplace flanked by eagles, a few odd little tables and desks said to have been used by Marie Antoinette, and some faded Aubusson carpets. The walls, where they are not tapestried, are heaped with gilt mirrors. Pink and gold and marble blend beneath the dim woven scenes on the tapestries. It is very different from the usual chilly good taste of Irish country houses. It was too much for succeeding members of the White family. The gods and goddesses on the Guardi ceiling panels were removed, rolled up, stored away in the stables, and then inadvertently sold to passing dealers at a fraction of their value.

Even more theatrical than the rose drawing-room is the dark damp-stained dining-room with its blue walls and cold ceiling, Spanish leather screens and copies of Alan Ramsay's full-length portraits of George III and his queen. I preferred the hall, which offered an eccentric display of bric-à-brac, including an Arab chest, a Flemish clock, a Russian iconotasis, some dark portraits, a photograph of a sultan of Zanzibar, and a copy of the Cave Canem mosaic at Pompeii.

"Do you like old things?" asked the attendant who showed me around. "I think it's a lot of old rubbish."

The White family, which had settled on Whiddy Island during the seventeenth century, moved to this situation dominating Bantry in 1746. Most of its initial wealth came from pilchard-fishing and iron-smelting, and by the time they made their change of residence, the Whites had become important landlords, whose property included large parts of Glengarriff and the Beare peninsula. Ennoblement followed when Richard White was, in the words of his monument in the Protestant church, "elevated to the peerage by his majesty George IIIrd in recognition of his spirited conduct and important services when a hostile French fleet anchored in Bantry Bay, 24th December, 1796". (The wall monuments to the Bantry family in this church are unusually attractive examples of nineteenth-century stonework).

Richard White, having received warning from Mr Hull of Leamcon, is believed to have been the first to send news of the invasion to the authorities in Cork. His warning coincided with a message from the British sloop, *Kangaroo*, which had sighted the French fleet before it rounded Mizen Head and landed an officer at Crookhaven to forward the news. White mustered his volunteers, commanded important outposts, and altogether expended a great deal of energy. His activities were to prove unnecessary, since the French never landed, but his loyalty was considered to be worthy of reward.

The French invasion was inspired by Wolfe Tone, who was staying in Paris and bombarding the Directoire with his convictions that Ireland was ready to be liberated. Persuaded by his crusading zeal and his persistence, the French government allowed itself to be dazzled with the proposition of crushing Britain's naval superiority. The expedition was commanded by General Hoche, a brilliant thirty-two-year-old officer who achieved success at a time when the policy of the Revolutionary government was to employ young men in high positions. He pressed his superiors to provide fourteen thousand soldiers who would be transferred to a point on the south-west coast of Ireland and then disembarked. From there Cork would be invaded. The presence of the

French, it was argued, would arouse Irishmen to overthrow the tyranny that oppressed them.

The large force was assembled at Brest during the summer and autumn of 1796. But the fleet that was to transport it to Ireland was in a very poor way at that particular moment. Morale in the French navy was low because it had been defeated so often. In 1796, only a few years after the Revolution, the old officers, who were previously selected from aristocratic families, had been dismissed the service and replaced by men from the lower deck who lacked the experience of command. The sullen sailors gathered to man the ships consisted largely of felons and impressed men. There was a scarcity of provisions and equipment which caused long delays throughout the autumn, so that the fleet was not ready to sail until late in November. It consisted of sixteen ships of the line, thirteen frigates, six corvettes, seven transports and one powder ship. The vessels were all over-crowded, each line ship carrying about six hundred soldiers, and the frigates up to two hundred and fifty apiece, besides stores, artillery and ammunition.

The four admirals in charge and General Hoche sailed in frigates, a tactical error. In unsettled conditions these lighter craft would tend to be separated from the main body of the fleet. Wolfe Tone, who accompanied the expedition, also sailed in one of these frigates, the *Indomptable*, with Admiral Bédout. The fleet set out on the night of December 16th, 1796. The British were blockading Brest, and in order to evade them the French fleet divided into two parts at the outset. Eighteen vessels were in one group and twenty-six in the other. At this point one of the battleships, the *Séduisant*, ran on to a sunken rock and sank with the loss of five hundred men. This was the first of the disasters.

On the way to Ireland the bulk of the main fleet became reunited. But unfortunately the little frigate, the *Fraternité*, carrying General Hoche and Admiral Morade de Galles with all the money and plans for the invasion, disappeared from sight, not to appear again throughout the entire expedition. Bouvet, on board the *Immortalité* (another frigate), found himself in charge and proceeded to the rendezvous at Mizen Head. At last Ireland was sighted, probably at a point off Crook-haven. Tone wrote in his diary: "We are under easy sail within three leagues of the coast, so that I can discover here and there patches of snow on the mountains."

New Street, Bantry, *circa* 1900

Bantry Fair, *circa* 1900

Glengarriff

Bouvet now made the mistake of sailing too far westward in his efforts to avoid the British fleet under Admiral Colpoys. He only altered course to the north on the noon of December 18th, and when he sighted land again he discovered that he had come too far north to Dursey Island instead of Mizen Head. In the face of a persistent east wind the fleet was sent drifting westwards. For over thirty hours it tacked helplessly to and fro, trying without success to enter Bantry Bay. Finally, on December 22nd, eight ships of the line and seven other craft, including the *Indomptable* carrying Wolfe Tone, and the *Immortalité* carrying Bouvet, succeeded in reaching Beare Island. Their progress had been painful. "These delays are dreadful to my patience," wrote Tone. "I am now so near the shore that I can see distinctly two old castles, yet I am utterly uncertain whether I shall ever set foot on it. . . . Two o'clock: we have been tacking ever since eight this morning, and I am sure we have not gained one hundred yards. . . ."

Twenty other ships remained outside, rendered helpless by their inefficient crews and divided command in the face of the inexorable easterly gale. During the night of the 23rd there was a storm which covered the mountains with snow and dispersed all those ships which had not entered the Bay and achieved the inhospitable shelter of the south side of Bear Island where Bouvet had nervously dropped anchor. He made no attempt to enter the sound on the far side of the island. All the time he was conscious of his naval inferiority and terrified at the prospect of joining battle or, even worse, being trapped in the Bay with the British fleet waiting for him at the mouth. He wanted to give up and return to Brest. He and his military advisers dithered whether to land or not. They were not to know how easily they could have defeated the inadequate forces on shore. Mr White was wasting no time in regarding the extraordinary sight, before his residence, of French ships beating up towards him. He took charge of the available yeomanry and established a chain of outposts from his house to Sheep's Head. But if the French had been properly led, had they effected a landing they would have found such defences easy enough to overcome.

On December 26th the pusillanimous Bouvet found that the anchor of the *Immortalité* was dragging and that he was drifting towards Bearhaven. He decided that he had had enough. He headed for the open sea, first firing two cannon as a signal for the remainder of the vessels to quit the Bay. Before he left, he also hailed Bédout, his second in command, to put to sea instantly, but Bédout misunderstood and stayed where he was. The *Immortalité* was soon out of the Bay and Bouvet, finding himself short of provisions, deserted his fleet and returned to Brest. The other ships continued to tack to and fro in front of Beare Island; they had no orders, no rendezvous, no leaders. One by one they departed; the *Indomptable*, the last to leave, abandoned its station on December 29th after riding out a violent storm. Most of the ships got safely back to Brest without even seeing a British man-of-war. But there were casualties, nearly all a result of the terrible weather. The ship of the line, *Droits de l'Homme*, sank with all hands, and three frigates, the *Scévola*, the *Impatient* and the *Surveillant*, also foundered. A fourth frigate, the *Tortue*, together with four transports, was captured by the British.

The expedition had utterly failed in its objective. However, for over a fortnight French ships had been converging on Bantry unmolested by any part of the British fleet. The authorities were justifiably alarmed. They knew how unlucky the French had been. Wolfe Tone summed up the disaster of the invasion, writing shakily on board the tossing *Indomptable* on December 26th:

"Notwithstanding all our blunders, it is the most dreadful stormy weather and easterly winds which have been blowing furiously and without intermission since we made Bantry Bay that have ruined us. Well, England has not made such an escape since the Spanish Armada, and that expedition, like ours, was defeated by the weather."

Those who struck the medal given to volunteers who had held isolated stations along the craggy Kilcrohane peninsula thought similarly. In the field of the medal were shown ships dismasted and driven before a storm. The motto, *Affavit Deus et Dissipater*, had been used two hundred years before on medals celebrating the destruction of the Armada.

Even if the French had made a successful landing, it is doubtful whether their forces would have achieved much success in arousing the country as Tone had predicted. The majority of Irishmen were apathetic to the idea of liberty imposed by Frenchmen, while the revolutionary ideal was anathema to the clergy. Dr Moylan, the Catholic Bishop of Cork, was not the only churchman to stress the desirability of maintaining the established order. "At a moment of such general alarm

and consternation it is a duty I owe to you, my beloved flock, to recall
to your minds the sacred principles of loyalty, allegiance and good
order." He meant allegiance to George III.

The Mayor of Bantry was knighted and Richard White received a
baronetcy. (Later he became a viscount, and finally, at the Act of Union,
he was graciously offered an earldom.) On September 21st, 1797, the
town celebrated its deliverance by illumination and a special perform-
ance at the theatre in the presence of the Lord Lieutenant.

In the hall of Bantry House hangs a portrait of the first earl proudly
wearing his ermine, while nearby stands the faded silk flag of his
volunteers, the Bantry Cavalry. At one time there was also the sloop
in which Lieutenant Proteau and eight men, setting out from one of
the French ships on an exploratory expedition, became the only
Frenchmen to land on the shores of Bantry Bay, when their boat was
driven on shore. They were captured by Mr White's militia and
brought in triumph as prisoners to Bantry House.

Occasionally a trawler will find in its nets a piece of copper sheeting
from the keel of a French ship, and a few years ago a heavy sixteen-
hundredweight anchor was recovered. It now stands on display beside
the main Cork road just outside the town.

FOURTEEN

Glengarriff and Hungry Hill

I LEFT THE DESERTED main square of Bantry where St Brendan's companions were peering out of their bronze boat at the downpour, which the saint himself, his arms outstretched, appeared to be enjoying. It was another grey-black day, with bursts of rain and mountains covered in mist. On the Glengarriff road a mean little street of old houses tapered off, and was quickly transformed into an avenue of garish modern houses. An empty factory had a FOR SALE notice hanging from its gate and nearby stood the first motel. Then began the ten-mile stretch of hotels and bungalows that divides Bantry from Glengarriff. The bungalows were enlarged versions of those that children build with Minibricks, the colours of their roofs and windows bright and unreal. Even the flowers in their trim gardens appeared artificial, the pastel-blue hydrangeas set against pink and marmalade-tinted roses before lawns cut out from lengths of felt. I cycled past the Falls of Donemark which had struck Pococke with their wild beauty; a plastic gnome stood guard over a money-box for donations.

At Ballylickey, just beyond the black waters of the Ouvane river, was the dignified shell of Reenadisert Court. The bungalows threatened to overwhelm it, like a lot of Yorkshire terriers surrounding a stag. But still it survived, a Jacobean fortified house fallen into decay, and unlike Durrus or Coppinger's Court it still had a roof, though barely so, for there was a large hole in it. Inside a huge hearth took up one side of the kitchen. Some clothes hung from a line and an old spinet stood against a wall lined with calendars. There was no electricity nor running water, the floors were liable to collapse, the plaster was sagging and the rain poured through the hole in the roof. But even so, the small dark rooms with their four-foot thick walls and pieces of carved panelling retained the atmosphere of a dwelling house rather than a ruin.

Reenadisert was probably built by the immediate heirs of Sir Owen O'Sullivan at the beginning of the seventeenth century. Sir Owen was uncle to Donal Cam O'Sullivan, the famous chieftain of Beare who undertook the great march from Glengarriff to Leitrim after the fall of Dunboy Castle. This uncle was a renegade who, after accepting a knighthood from Queen Elizabeth, fought on the side of the English against his nephew following a family row. He attacked other Irish chieftains who rebelled, the O'Mahonys among them. It was his son who went with a party to capture Dunmanus castle after the Battle of Kinsale. This branch of the O'Sullivan family was afterwards known as *gallda*—the word means "foreigner", and therefore quisling. However, since Sir Owen had been on the winning side, he retained much of the traditional O'Sullivan property after the downfall of his nephew. He owned Whiddy Island and most of the northern shore of Bantry Bay. A castle of his, Carriganass, stands a few miles from Reenadisert up the Ouvane. Perhaps only a hundred years separate the construction of the two buildings, but they represent two different concepts of civilization. One is spaciously designed and gabled like an Elizabethan manor, although it retains features of defence, like having thick stubborn walls, few windows and two protruding fortified corbels in the corners of the upstairs rooms. The other is built on the older pattern of a simplified Norman castle. Very little remains of the older structure; a couple of ivy-covered walls that overlook the river and show every sign of collapsing soon.

When Bantry House was enlarged over a century ago, cut stone from Carriganass was used in part of the structure. Robbing old castles of stone used to be a common enough practice. Ardea on the Kenmare river, Rosbrin and Castle Island Castle outside Schull are all partly incorporated in surrounding farm buildings. The castle on Whiddy Island stood intact except for the roof until about seventy years ago, but island farmers have steadily demolished it for building material, so that there is scarcely anything left. Most of Rincolisky was pulled down to build Whitehall House. A number of vanished castles may have disappeared in this way, or their stones may even have been used for roadmaking.

The route to Glengarriff follows the curve of the sea, looking over the discreetly camouflaged storage tanks on Whiddy and the puffed-up shapes of mountains. Just as I reached a house called Atlantic View, my bike gave a lurch, and inspection showed that a front spindle had broken. The rain came down harder as I trudged on. I had a short respite sheltering in the tiny Snave church, which is built on to the end of a cottage. An unsatisfactory pause in the minute Gothic interior, as my clothes dripped water and I looked out on to soaked rhododendron bushes and a rock on which a passing evangelist had painted: BE SURE YOUR SINS WILL FIND YOU OUT. Then the walk down to Glengarriff, passing the guesthouses one by one . . . St Anthony's, Bay View, Sea View, Arbutus House, Woodlands, Mountain View, The Hollies.

Since early Victorian times Glengarriff has appealed to the romantic-minded traveller. "What sends picturesque tourists to the Rhine and Saxon Switzerland?" Thackeray asked. "Within five miles around the pretty inn of Glengarriff there is a country of the magnificence of which no pen can give an idea." He preferred this part of the coast to any place he visited in Ireland. During the twentieth century countless tourists have travelled here to admire the views. Fifty years ago there used to be weekend excursions from London at a cost of thirty shillings. The route was still known as the Prince of Wales Route after the visit of the young prince in 1858. The Cork–Bantry train (now disappeared) would drop passengers at Bantry pier, where a steamer (also long gone), waited to transport them to Glengarriff.

One of the best known hotels was Roches.

"By cars and coaches we came to Roches
We found the tariff as fair as Glengarriff . . ."

And then there was Eccles, Thackeray's "pretty inn", of which the locals used to say: "The village of Glengarriff is near Eccles Hotel." Eccles still survives, as comfortable as ever. Shaw is supposed to have written St Joan there, inspired perhaps by the set of steel engravings in the dark panelled hall, illustrating scenes from Shakespeare's plays.

My own guesthouse was a sad contrast to Eccles's snug opulence. A bar-cum-shop, and upstairs little rooms with peeling rose-patterned wall-paper. In the bathroom old copies of The Irish Messenger of the Sacred Heart. I had breakfast in the bar under a kipper-coloured ceiling

surrounded by bottles of Camp coffee, and packets of soup, all impregnated with smells of old beer. The fry had slices of thick salty bacon
burned to a frizzle, and a grey broken-yolked egg looking like fungus
from a diseased tree. I hurriedly threw it into the fire before my landlady returned from the kitchen with enquiries as to how I had enjoyed
my breakfast. The tourist season only lasts three months: it is an economic mystery how so many similar establishments can survive year
after year and actually expand—they seem to be for ever adding on
extensions with extra bedrooms.

I have never liked Glengarriff and its lines of shops, guesthouses and
hotels. "A mean place—blast it!" one local man agreed with me. I
watched Americans descending from a bus on to the souvenir shops.
Old ladies in white boots jingling charm bracelets, their costume
jewellery visible through clear plastic raincoats. Clean-smelling young
girls with a repoussé of spots beaten on their cheeks. Two red-faced
heart-diseased old men in mushroom-coloured stetsons. All with their
arms full of Foxford rugs, musical cottages and dishtowels decorated
with leprechauns.

Visitors can go over to Garnish Island. Indeed they are almost forced
to by the tough touting ferrymen who try to stop passing cars for
custom. Sixty years ago Garnish Island was little more than an outcrop
of rock and heather surmounted by a Martello tower. Mr Annan
Bryce, the Belfast business man who bought it in 1910, was among a
series of enthusiasts who created gardens in the mild sheltered conditions of the south-western bays. In the neighbouring Kenmare river
the Earl of Dunraven planted out the similarly named Garnish Island,
which in his lifetime had grown up into a carefully tended jungle.
Many years later my own parents did much the same with a smaller
island, and as a child I watched the phenomenal growth rate that can be
achieved with careful planting. Shelter belts of pine and fir grow visibly
bigger year by year, while tree ferns, species rhododendron, camellias,
and other shrubs which love the warmth and damp and take root easily
in the peaty soil, are suddenly thirty feet high.

The island garden of Glengarriff is planned more carefully than the
effect of controlled luxuriance achieved by other gardens in the area.
Bryce hired Harold Pinto, the well-known architect and gardener, to
plan the whole project, giving him unlimited financial scope. From
1911 to 1914 a hundred men were constantly engaged in bringing over

soil, planting and building pavilions, walled enclosures, a lily pond and a clock tower. Unfortunately the outbreak of the First World War put an end to the construction of the main house to which the garden would have been linked. This has resulted in an unevenness of design. It has been called a garden in search of a house.

Bryce died in 1925 and the work of completing the garden was carried on by his son, Roland Bryce, who bequeathed it to the Irish government in 1953. As a result tourists and gardeners from all over the world can wander among the Burmese statues, down the loggia, past the lily pond, gazing at the sodden flowers. The garden was in full bloom as I walked through the careful landscaping that led up to spectacular vistas of the Bay and the Sugarloaf mountains. Perhaps it should be visited in the early morning so that the right Arcadian impression might be received. Instead of bird song there was a gabble of tourist voices and five hundred pairs of feet tramped the path at one time. Sweet papers were dropped and raincoats brushed against dripping bushes sounded as loud as machinery.

Behind Glengarriff is the state forest which was acquired from the Bantry estate in 1954. An area of about a thousand acres is situated in a bowl of the Caha mountains through which the black coil of the Glengarriff river runs among the trees. These consist partly of giant oaks and ash furred over in moss, a remnant of the indigenous forest. Most of it was destroyed by Mr White's ironworks, at a time when the ancestor of the first earl was laying the foundations of his fortune. Today much of the forest has been replanted with conifers, but the effect is not wholly ugly as the edges of the plantations have been softened with birch and other deciduous trees. The long U-shaped valley behind the tiny village of Croster West, has escaped the invasion of fir-trees; there are a few bones of the old forest to be seen in whitened stumps standing out of bog. An hour's stiff climb brought me to Barley Lake, a lovely triangular piece of water surrounded on all sides by the rise and fall of hills.

West of Glengarriff the road divides. One fork goes to Killarney, thirty-seven miles away, and the other follows the coastline along the Beare peninsula to the town of Castletown Bearhaven. Just outside the town is the so-called Cromwell's Bridge. In fact, Cromwell never reached this part of West Cork, nor travelled further west than Bandon. There is a tradition that the bridge was built in twenty-four hours.

Down at Adrigole a swan had built its nest beside the pier, and sat looking imperiously across the water to the few shops, the new bungalow development and the remains of a stone circle. Except for scattered new buildings like this, there were far fewer signs of tourism.

I explored the maze of little lanes running up and down the sides of the Caha mountains. At Mass Mount I found the remains of an old church site, and nearby two standing stones and two early house sites. A couple of ring forts stood out clearly, their circles emphasized by the blue-green willow that filled their ditches. Ahead of me the sun shone on the knuckle of Hungry Hill. But mist whirled around the summit as I came to climb it.

"That place is awfully cross," a man in a horse-drawn cart advised me. "More often than not the weather up there is bad."

I walked up the eastern shoulder, avoiding the formidable western face that rises out of the valley. It was a long sloping route from ridge to ridge over boggy ground vibrant with moths and butterflies hovering over sedge. Then the summit, covered with a smooth skin of bog and grass perpetually dabbed with mist. I reached a little concrete obelisk from where the climber can sometimes see a view that comprises the Killarney ranges to the north and the Fastnet and Cape Clear to the south. Hungry Hill stands by itself between two mountain ranges, the Caha and the Slieve Miskish, which run across the whole peninsula, forming a natural barrier between Cork and Kerry. I waited for a while in the damp, hoping the mist would clear; finally I gave up and descended to the sunshine, only a few hundred yards below. If I could not look northwards, at least I had the sweep of Bantry Bay at my feet.

The south-east slope of the mountain is splattered with a waterfall, long thin streams of water tumbling down a blackened face of rock. Local people call it the Mare's Tail, and Pococke, always a good observer, compared it to a "vein of sparr" on seeing it from a distance.

The valley leading up to Hungry Hill is called Coumgira. It used to be quite densely populated. "There were fifty men at every cross-road," I was told by a farmer whose two brothers had settled in America. At Dree sixty families had lived where there were six today. Most crossed the Atlantic; the few left behind envied them. "My God, it's like a cemetery here in winter," a woman in a shop at Curyglass told me as it

poured rain outside. Later at Adrigole I met two elderly priests who
were arguing that the Irish should never have been farmers.

"They can't stand the loneliness and monotony. The reasons they
leave are not wholly economic. It's just that the Irishman is happier in a
crowd. That's the reason that one day or another he'll just bolt his door
and walk away!"

Down in Bank Harbour about five miles from Adrigole the Sod Fort
might be another ancient dateless relic. But ruins catch up with each
other pretty quickly and the scanty remains of the Sod Fort look back a
mere two hundred years to a time when they witnessed the dramatic
struggle of an unusual settler family which elected to come and live at
this lonely place. The quiet inlet with its two harbours, peaceful today,
with only the occasional boat bringing in sand, is where James Fontaine
tried to establish his little community and his pilchard fisheries.

Jacques de la Fontaine was a French Huguenot parson who arrived in
Cork in 1694 with his family. An excitable quarrelsome refugee, he
survived the upheavals and disasters that marked his life with a degree
of self-confidence and resourcefulness that was evenly matched by the
sterling qualities of his wife.

After coming to Ireland, he first of all lived in Cork city, where in
1695, he was appointed pastor of the Huguenot families living there.
However, when they proved too poor to support him, he turned to
trade. He started by manufacturing broadcloth in the city, a venture
which soon failed. Then he observed that the catching and exporting
of fish was a very profitable undertaking around the west coast. He
travelled out to Beare, where he proceeded to set up his own fishery
at Bank Harbour.

The Beare peninsula was still wild and remote, with few English
settlers. Travellers shunned it long after other parts of the country had
been subdued. When the Bishop of Cork set out from Bantry to visit
his flock at Bearhaven, he preferred to go by boat rather than risk the
dangers of the pathways west of Glengarriff. The coastline was a refuge
for pirates, outlaws and privateers. The nearest armed force on the side
of the law was the garrison at Bantry.

Undaunted, Fontaine settled at Bank Harbour with a community
consisting of his own family and thirteen destitute Huguenot families
recently arrived in Cork. His stone house overlooking the harbour was
provided with towers and a high wall to protect it from corsairs. His

fishery began to prosper and by May, 1700, he had collected a fleet of six ships together with a total crew of forty-five men. Although the first season was poor, during the following year the fish were abundant. So many herring were caught that he complained that "every place was piled up with them, even to the very door of the chamber in which my wife was confined". His total catch was impressive. "Two hundred thousand herrings pressed enough to fill 200 hogsheads, also 200 barrels of pickled herrings. Also had 12 tiercas of salmon, 700 or 800 dried codfish, 3,000 flukes . . . ." Unfortunately, through what he described as the deceitfulness of his partners, the fish were never collected. They choked up his little settlement and gradually rotted away. Business was ruined for that year. Most of his settlers departed.

Worse followed three years later in June, 1704, when he was attacked by a French privateer with eighty-six men aboard. He had been given an official appointment as an anti-smuggling officer, and carried out his duties too zealously. His unpopularity was probably intensified by the fact that he was a Huguenot. Moreover, he seemed to have a knack of creating enemies. There had been some trouble among his parishioners in Cork. Relationships with his fellow settlers at Bank had plainly been uneasy, and on reading his biography one gathers the general impression that he was a difficult person. Certainly the French captain found help from a contingent of local men who felt strongly about the fishing magnate in their midst. Many members of the crew of the privateer were Irishmen who had taken service with the French. The ship was guided into the inlet by four local fishermen.

Fontaine made a spirited defence of his fort, in spite of having only half the number of men. A gallery of his Irish neighbours watched the battle from the safety of a neighbouring hill. The enemy landed and set up gun emplacements, but the cannon-balls only scratched the walls "as if they were so many apples". His wife, acting as his aide-de-camp as well as medical officer to the garrison, helped him to carry up ammunition to the walls of the fort. After three Frenchmen among the enemy were killed and seven wounded, the rest retired in confusion. For this exploit Fontaine received a letter from the government complimenting him on his conduct and granting him a pension of five shillings a day. He was also made a Justice of the Peace.

Four years later, in October, 1708, another French privateer sailed into Bearhaven under English colours. From there a party of troops led by two Irish lieutenants succeeded in surrounding the fort once more. By this time Fontaine's settlement had been reduced to a pitiful handful of defenders. A breach was made in the walls, Fontaine was wounded and taken back to the ship as a hostage. When he was brought on board he was greeted by jeering sailors, who shouted: "*Vive le roi!*" According to his own account, he was not in the least put out by his reception.

"Gentlemen," he addressed them, "how long is it since victories have been so rare in France that you are glad to avail yourself of such an occasion as this to sing in triumph? Eighty men accustomed to warfare have actually been so successful as to compel one poor minister, four cowherds and five children to surrender on terms."

The remarkable Madame Fontaine, having seen her house destroyed and her husband carried away, set out at once to rescue him. First she went to the parish priest for help, but none was forthcoming from him. Then she followed the privateer with her husband on board, walking down the coastline, which in those days must have lacked all but the most rudimentary tracks and paths. From time to time, coming down to the shore from the forest, she caught sight of the vessel tacking at so slow a pace that she was able to catch up with it just at the narrow entrance to the Dursey Sound. Here she managed to signal across, using her apron, tied to the end of a stick. A boat was dispatched, and after protracted negotiations the captain agreed to ransom Fontaine for a hundred pounds. She returned to Bearheaven, where she went round from neighbour to distant neighbour until she managed to borrow thirty pounds. This sum the Captain only agreed to take if one of her sons was held as hostage instead of her husband until the remainder of the money was paid.

After he was set free, Fontaine gave up his colony and fishery, and retired to Dublin with the remainder of his family to try to raise money for his son's release. Months later the boy was returned unharmed. Fontaine then turned from fishing to teaching languages. After his death the family emigrated to America.

A few years ago an American clergyman was seen poking around the ruins of Sod Fort. He turned out to be the Reverend Fontaine on a visit to Ireland, come to view the scene of his ancestor's adventures. But there is little to see now, only a piece of wall overlooking Bank Harbour which is all that remains of the fort and fish cellars. Sometimes cannonballs are dug up out of the nearby fields.

FIFTEEN

Castletown Bearhaven

CASTLETOWN BEARHAVEN (also called Castletownbere) had not changed a lot in the thirty years since I last visited it, and the images of childhood were safe. In the market square a Celtic cross commemorated the men of the Bearhaven battalion that fought from 1916 to 1923. At one end of the town Brandy Hall Bridge retained ancient memories of smuggling; at the other a standing stone rose elegantly from a field. Between them were the blue-painted Bearhaven Hotel, and all the shops with their old-fashioned fronts and long windows . . . Warner's Cash Warehouse, the Woollen Hall, Central Bar, Bearhaven Bakery. . .

At the beginning of the nineteenth century there had been no town here at all, merely a small settlement and a castle, now vanished, for which the place was named Castledermot. The early nineteenth century proved to be a time of prosperity when Bearhaven benefited from the development of the copper deposits discovered on the peninsula, which were the richest in West Cork. In addition the town had a fishing fleet and four fairs a year for cattle, sheep, pigs and pedlar's goods. The fishing changed from time to time much as it did in other ports. The pilchards came, the pilchards went, the herrings came and the herrings went. Herring and sprat vanished by 1815 and there was little fishing for several decades, a period that coincided tragically with the famine. It had already lapsed as a means of livelihood when the potato failed in 1846; the winter that followed was particularly stormy and the currachs could not venture out to the open sea where the fish were to be found. The fishing station founded at that time, like the one in Schull, by the Quakers was unsuccessful and closed down in 1852.

In 1890 the mackerel came and the fishing picked up again with the introduction of larger boats. Some prosperity also resulted from the presence of the naval station on nearby Bear Island. But emigration in the area from the time of the famine right up to the present day has equalled that of the rest of West Cork.

Today Bearhaven has become the centre of the south-western trawler fleet. Down at the harbour I found many changes and the little pier which I remembered had been swallowed up in a massive concrete apron. There was a new freezing plant, and the fishmeal factory scheduled to be built on nearby Dinish Island would cost nearly half a million pounds.

On the outskirts of the town stands The Glebe, a solid Georgian house which was the birthplace of Standish O'Grady, author of such forgotten works as *The Chain of Gold* and *In the Wake of King James*. Much of his material was taken from the violent history of the Beare peninsula which he had learned in his childhood. Here, too, he learned Irish from the people around him, and he is better remembered as a brilliant Irish scholar, whose translations of medieval Irish poetry and sagas were read by Yeats and Lady Gregory, bringing them into initial contact with Gaelic literature.

My uncle, a rector of Bearhaven, lived at The Glebe for twenty years. Every Sunday, dressed in full canonicals, he used to be taken out by motor launch to hold services in the camp church on Bear Island and on whichever British destroyer happened to be taking station in the sound. The destroyers departed in 1938, but all these years after his death I found his own little boat, the *Heather*, lying in the harbour, still in use.

A few miles west of the town, facing the sound to Bear Island, is the site of the O'Sullivan stronghold of Dunboy Castle, the scene of the siege and massacre that crushed Donal O'Sullivan Beare and sent him on his epic march to Leitrim. Some broken walls and pieces of fortification stand on a knoll surrounded by evergreen oaks.

The O'Sullivans, like the O'Mahonys, were not indigenous to West Cork, and the year 1192 is usually given as the date when they migrated to the Beare peninsula from Tipperary. Beara was the legendary daughter of a king of Castile who was supposed to have married an Irishman. In time the name became associated with the main branch of the O'Sullivan family, whose chieftains called themselves chiefs of Beare. They became wealthy, having found here the same advantages that the O'Mahonys discovered on Ivaha: access to the Continent, freedom from the military pressures in central Ireland, and, above all, profitable fishing. Carew wrote later: "When Dunboy was unruined, it commanded this spacious and goodly haven, which afforded no small profit to O'Sullivan Beare while his castle was standing; for the castle yields such abundance of seafish as few places in Christiandom. . . ."

For three centuries the O'Sullivans controlled the waters around Beare. Those who interfered with their rights courted disaster, like the English sea captain hanged at Bearhaven in 1331 by Dermot O'Sullivan, for having captured a Spanish fishing vessel which had paid its dues to the Prince of Beare. Not until 1543 were the English strong enough to get some way towards enforcing the law that no ship was to fish along the Irish coast until it had been duly entered in the Customs books. It did little to deprive the O'Sullivans of their income: foreign fishermen still paid them their taxes.

The end came for them as it did for so many with the aftermath of Kinsale. If the O'Sullivans went out with more éclat than others, it was because of the siege, which historians consider the hardest-fought affair of its kind in Ireland during the reign of Elizabeth. It was a far fiercer fight than Kinsale, which ended as a rout. The siege came about partly because the castle Dunboy was too remote for the English to seize quickly and easily, and partly because there were stocks of gunpowder there left by the Spaniards. The Spaniards at Dunboy had no time to surrender formally to the English as their compatriots had done at Castlehaven and Baltimore; the castle had been retaken by Donal O'Sullivan Beare, who, in anticipation of a siege, began adding to the existing fortifications by facing the barbican walls with sods to a depth of eighteen feet as a defence against artillery. He sent the Spanish garrison to Baltimore, keeping in his hands the captain and four of the gunners who he hoped would take part in the defence. He wrote to the King of Spain explaining his action of February 20th.

Kinsale had taken place on December 24th, 1601. Dunboy remained untaken for six months, and became a major objective of the English. Late in February Captain Flower had sailed for Bearhaven, but was driven back by contrary winds, and lost no less than fifty men from seasickness.

Then Sir George Carew, the Lord President of Munster, took over the subjection of the castle. Carew was an astute politician and an ambitious, able soldier, who shared the obsession of his deceased cousin that the family was heir to immense estates in Ireland granted by Henry II to a remote ancestor, Robert Fitz-Stephen. George Carew managed his long campaign in Munster largely by setting the Irish against themselves, encouraging them by a system of rewards and punishments to attack their kinsmen and countrymen. (Sir Owen O'Sullivan, uncle of Donal O'Sullivan, was one of those who had come within the orbit of his influence.) Now he directed the Earl of Thomond to march through Carbery with twelve hundred foot to burn the corn, take the cattle, and reconnoitre Dunboy. Thomond reported back on Donal O'Sullivan's efforts to fortify the castle.

On April 29th, 1602, Carew set out from Cork with a large force of men, reaching Bantry at the beginning of May. Here he was joined by Sir Charles Wilmot who had come from Kerry, and their combined forces numbered four thousand men. Throughout the last days of May this army was kept in camp by bad weather, much to the disgust of Carew, who wrote to Mountjoy that "the country of Bere was full of witches".

On May 31st the fine weather returned. To avoid the rough terrain of the Beare mountains, Carew marched instead along the Sheep's Head peninsula on the southern side of Bantry Bay. From Sheep's Head a portion of his troops crossed by boat to a point opposite Bear Island. Thomond's regiment crossed the next day and the remainder followed. The Constable of Dunboy Castle, Richard MacGeoghegan, came across and had an indecisive interview with Thomond. Subsequently Carew ordered the work of entrenchment and building of platforms for guns to be trained upon the castle. His ships patrolled the sound between the castle and Bear Island so that no one could escape. At the same time a force of a hundred and fifty foot, including some Irishmen, were dispatched to capture Dursey Island where O'Sullivan Beare had intended to make his last stand if Dunboy was taken. The castle on Dursey was crowded with refugees who were all killed.

The trapped defenders of Dunboy, numbering a hundred and forty-three men, were under the command of Richard MacGeoghegan and Thomas Taylor, a renegade Englishman who had married into the family of Richard Tyrell, Donal O'Sullivan's Companion at Arms. Tyrell had lately been defeated by Wilmot in Kerry. The first men to die were two spies sent out from the castle to reconnoitre the enemy's

Glengarriff

Paulgorm, Glengarriff

"The village of Glengarriff is near Eccles Hotel"
Shopfront, Castletown Bearhaven

position, who were captured and hanged. After holding out for eleven days the garrison tried to surrender, but they were not permitted to do so and their messenger who tried to negotiate an honourable defeat was also hanged. After that the besieged knew what was in store for them. On June 16th the English guns were set in place. About dawn the next day a demi-cannon, two culverns and a demi-culvern opened fire on the castle. Within an hour a turret had collapsed. Carew's forces endeavoured to take the castle by assault, but were repulsed in a fierce hand-to-hand engagement in which twenty-three of the defenders died. About forty more endeavoured to escape by swimming the sound but were either drowned or killed.

The remaining seventy-seven members of the garrison retired within the cellars of the castle which they stubbornly defended against attack. "The fighting was long and protracted there," wrote Phillip O'Sullivan, Donal Cam's cousin and historian of the eclipse of his family and race. "Many fell under wounds of both sides. There lay a great heap of bodies and arms and the whole hall ran streams of blood. For the greater part of the defenders fell, especially the Captain, Richard, whose high spirit was defending the chieftaincy with the valour of his race." MacGeoghegan was killed as he attempted to blow up the castle. Following this, Thomas Taylor and those defenders who had not already laid down their arms surrendered to Carew and were taken prisoner. Fifty-eight were hanged at the Market Place (the site of the modern town) on June 18th, and a further twelve were executed on June 22nd. Taylor was taken to Cork to be hanged there and a priest named Brother Dominic Collins suffered in his native Youghal.

Thus the defenders of Dunboy all perished. But Donal Cam, the O'Sullivan Beare, was not at the siege at all, and so survived. On June 5th, the day before the English brought up their cannon to set against the castle, a Spanish ship was reported to have arrived in Ardea on the Kenmare side of the Bearhaven peninsula. It contained munitions and several thousand pounds of gold, and in addition carried a priest named Owen MacEagan, described as the Vicar Apostolic, with messages from Spain. Donal Cam set out from Dunboy with a small party to meet it. Some of his detractors have hinted that he was glad to do so; in fact that he abandoned his men at Dunboy in order to save his own life. Whatever the truth may be, after the siege was over he was in a desperate position. The countryside was laid waste, his castles were captured, his relatives had sided with the enemy, crops were destroyed and winter had come. He set out from Glengarriff on December 31st, 1602, leading four hundred fighting men and six hundred non-combatants, including a number of women. His dreadful march took him through bleak and hostile country, across mountain ranges, over the Shannon and up to Leitrim, where he sought sanctuary with O'Rourke of Breffni. At the end of a fortnight of battles, snow and hunger, the survivors who staggered into O'Rourke's castle numbered thirty-five—eighteen soldiers, sixteen horseboys and one woman. After a few days' rest Donal Cam continued to the slopes of Lough Neagh where he hoped to make contact with O'Neill. But O'Neill had already surrendered and departed for Spain. Donal Cam followed him there to an exile's death.

The English made no attempt to establish a firm hold over such a distant outpost, but left the peninsula under the control of Sir Owen O'Sullivan. After the siege Dunboy itself was blown up with gunpowder and the fortifications were destroyed. But it was too important a military position to be abandoned, and the site was used fifty years later. Recent excavations there have revealed the walls of a typical Cromwellian star-pattern fort.

Behind the ruins of the old castle with its heroic memories the vulgar remains of the newer Dunboy spread out amidst a wilderness of rhododendron. This was a mansion designed in a blend of styles: French chateaux, Italian villa and Elizabethan house all contributed their influence and were blended together with some vaguely defined castellation. Most of it was built late in the nineteenth century. But it is much nicer now that it is a ruin. The mullioned windows look across the water towards Hungry Hill and the great hallway with its ribbed Gothic roof and bunches of red-and-black marble columns is open to the sky.

A description of the mansion as it used to be has been left by an English butler, Albert Thomas, who wrote an autobiography entitled *Wait and See*. He was employed here just before the place was burned. "It was a noble building, very tall chimneys, turrets as in the olden days, and in fact everything that a castle should be."[8]

It belonged to the Puxley family, the local landowners upon whose vast estates deposits of copper had been found in the early nineteenth century. Royalties from copper had subsidized the construction of this pseudo-castle, which had taken over thirty years, and even then it had still been only half completed. The main hall lacked a staircase, while most of the statues and other ornaments brought over from Italy had never been unpacked. Workmen had also been imported from Italy, but they left suddenly because of local resentment over their employment. Only the older part of the building was finished, and was used by the family when it came over to Ireland from Cornwall for holidays. It included the drawing-room: "the largest I ever saw. Panelled in really lovely black oak with blue tapestry, it looked truly beautiful when the candles were lit."

Alas for the butler's feeling for grandeur! He and his wife were engaged at an inopportune time and arrived at Dunboy in 1921. The I.R.A. were using the grounds for training their men and after various scares they burned the house down. A few days before the fire Albert Thomas and his wife had been taken to the safety of the British garrison on Bear Island.

"One night I was called up and was shown a very large glow in the sky overlooking the castle about a mile away. The rebels had burned the castle down as they said they would. I was very sorry, sorry for all the lovely old silver, the beautiful glass and splendid linen all being burnt, all those gorgeous statues and pictures, the wonderful drawing-room all burning for what? One can sometimes understand war with all its horrors, but this seemed to me a very wanton thing to do."

The I.R.A. had few regrets. They said officially that they feared the castle would be used as a garrison for British soldiers. But the mansion belonged to the Puxleys, and even today few good words are said about the family.

"They were tough landlords. It was as much as a person dared to sneak into their estates."

The Puxleys were a Welsh family, originally settled in Galway; two brothers, John and Henry Puxley, moved down to Beare in 1730. This was a very late date for settlers, but the area was inhospitable. A plantation under Cromwellian soldiers in 1652 had made little headway; others, like the Fontaines, who had endeavoured to make their homes in Beare had found life very difficult and departed. As a result the Whites and the Puxleys, who persisted in staying, eventually divided up a good deal of the land between them.

The activities of the Puxleys inspired two works of popular fiction, one Victorian, one modern, both widely read in their time. Daphne du Maurier's *Hungry Hill* is an account of the rise of the family's prosperity as a result of the opening of copper-mines during the nineteenth century. Froude's *Two Chiefs of Dunboy* is about events which took place a century earlier. His narrative, which tends to be highly coloured and inaccurate, describes the long-standing feud between Henry Puxley, the first member of his family to settle on Beare, and Murty Og O'Sullivan, a descendant of the O'Sullivans, the previous masters of the peninsula.

The background to the dispute was smuggling. We have seen how smuggling became a recognized way of life throughout Munster in remote areas where authority was impotent. The people were poor, and regular farming was discouraged by their inability to lease land for more than a year. They found that there were easier ways of earning a living. The coastline, with its indented harbours, was ideal for landing illegal cargoes, so that heavily taxed silk, laces and wine found a regular market among the leisured classes in their lonely homes. The law struggled to combat these activities, and there were regular affrays between its officers and the smugglers. At first the authorities made little headway, but gradually they moved westward, clearing out harbours like Glandore, Clonakilty and Leamcon, which used to be favourite landing places for smugglers. More remote locations still were needed by those who wished to continue the import of contraband cargoes. Kilmakilloge and Sneem on the Kenmare river were popular rendezvous, and Bearhaven, equally wild and unsettled, several days away from Cork, was also ideally placed.

About the year 1730, the government attempted to bring the Beare peninsula under control by appointing a Customs officer named Richard Tonson. He had to contend with innumerable difficulties. Writing to the Lord Lieutenant, he complained of being the only representative of the law in "about sixty miles of coast, extending through a wild and barbarous country, mostly inhabited by Papists, and in the most distant part of the kingdom in which there are many harbours and creeks, to which your Memorialist is very often obliged to resort personally to the great hazard of his life, and at vast expense in carrying a number of servants to defend him . . ."

His position was invidious, because he had to contend with Protestants, as well as with the local people. The Puxleys, like many other settlers on the Munster coast, indulged freely in smuggling with their Catholic neighbours. Together with Murty Og O'Sullivan and his followers, they conspired to defeat the efforts of the unfortunate Tonson. In 1723, for example, when Tonson seized a ship owned by Murttogh McOwen O'Sullivan which was carrying a contraband cargo, John and Henry Puxley invited him to the local clergyman's home for refreshment. While he was absent, the O'Sullivans recaptured the ship and murdered the prize crew. During the following years, in spite of government proclamations and Tonson's efforts, the smuggling continued with the Puxleys and O'Sullivans playing a leading part. At the same time a friendship developed between Henry Puxley and Murty Og O'Sullivan.

Murty Og was a prominent member of the family, which continued to live in the area after the sack of Dunboy. (In 1699 Bishop Downe had seen the last chieftain living "in a cabin at the foot of the hill".) He was born in a house a little to the west of the village of Eyeries on the Kenmare side of the peninsula. Like so many Irish Catholics of the time, he looked for employment abroad. Continental ports like Nantes, Bordeaux and Cadiz all had their Irish merchants, while Irish priests were educated in Spain and France. Any Irishman landing in Spain automatically acquired Spanish citizenship. So fast and efficient was communication between the Continent and Ireland, that Murty Og could follow an extraordinary double career. Sometimes he was a mercenary soldier, and sometimes a smuggler, sailing to and fro from France to his home on Beare.

As a soldier he fought in most of the wars of the time. In 1742 he distinguished himself in the army of Queen Maria Theresa in the war of the Austrian Succession, and received a sword from her in recognition of his bravery. He fought at Fontenoy in May, 1745, and in April, 1746, was at Cullodon with Prince Charles. In 1747, back at Beare, he married an O'Sullivan of Roscowan and took a house in the townland of Coulagh near Eyeries. (He is reputed to have kept several other ladies, one at Bearhaven, others on the Continent.) Together with the Puxleys, he continued to oppose Tonson and profit from smuggling. But at the same time he had become a recruiting agent for the Irish Brigades in Europe, an activity which brought him the enmity of Henry Puxley, who was naturally enough a loyal subject of King George.

Large numbers of Irishmen went as soldiers to France during the eighteenth century. Some estimates have been as high as sixty thousand. Many were recruited from Munster, where French privateers, cruising off the coast, could easily pick them up and transport them to France, using the smuggling routes. A two-day traffic was established, brandy and silks going one way, potential soldiers the other. "I am credibly informed," wrote a Mr John Moore in 1751, "that since last Michael-mas they have sent out of Carbery, Muskery and Kerry about 400 recruits and from other parts 2,000."

But the Irish who found themselves on the battlefields of Europe did not always go voluntarily. Although officers might expect glittering rewards for their services, the foot soldiers could only find the hardships of mercenary life. Patriotism and hatred for the conqueror did not always inspire the peasants of Cork and Kerry to enlist for Continental armies. Numbers had to be supplemented by impressment.

Impressment is a system of recruiting usually associated with the British navy, who used it as a regular means of finding sailors, since no one in his right mind would volunteer for the terrible life aboard His Majesty's ships. But although the British exploited the system to its utmost during the wars against France, they did not invent it. Along the shores of Beare, cottages and farms were seldom built directly on the water, but in little valleys behind, from where men could escape easily at the sight of an unfamiliar sail. French privateers would muster press gangs from their crews, since kidnapped men made good ballast for ships returning empty after landing smuggled cargoes. And for years Murty Og's small vessel busily carried his countrymen over to France, how many by force it is now impossible to say.

A prolonged quarrel developed between him and the Puxley brothers. The brothers might connive at smuggling and profit from it, but not at a practice that might call into account their loyalty to the Crown. Henry Puxley's opinions were reinforced by his appointment as Commissioner of the Peace, with a special task to stop foreign recruitment. He was given a frigate and a body of soldiers to help him in his opposition to Murty Og.

In 1741 an O'Sullivan had been killed in a brawl involving the two families. After that, the feud dragged on for thirteen years until the day that Henry Puxley was shot on his way to church. He had built a conventicle for the small group of dissenters who had settled in the district, and there he used to conduct the service himself. On Sunday morning, March 10th, 1757, he was ambushed by Murty Og, who waited for him with two henchmen, little John O'Sullivan and Daniel O'Connell, outside the ruins of Darby Harrington's forge. Traditionally this forge is said to have been outside the gate of Dunboy, but it is more likely to have been at Eskenacaten (which means "the low place of the forge"), half-way between Dunboy and Castledermot.

Pococke, who visited the area only four years later, when the murder was still a recent incident in people's minds, wrote the following account:

"On the second I set out on horseback from Bearhaven to cross the head of land Northwards. In the way to the church we passed a narrow defile between rocks, over which are the ruins of a Smith's forge, from which Murty Og O'Sullivan shot Mr Puxley, he first saw blood on his hands when he was wounded and thought his own pistols had gone off. The second volley came to him as soon as he had passed the rock and twenty balls were found in him. As soon as it was over Murty Og and his two bravoes went and stood behind the rocks near in sight of everybody and drank a bottle of brandy, he then went to Mass and said if anyone was sorry for Puxley's death they might go and cry over him, concerning which I am thus particular, because it was the most villainous, audacious and extraordinary act that probably ever was committed. . . ."

The fact that Puxley went armed, even to church, indicates that he was expecting trouble.

Murty Og, now on the run, fled to France. But the call of Beare was too strong, and he returned to see his family. His presence at home was betrayed, it is said, by a servant named Scully, and two ships were sent round from Cork to capture him. A party of soldiers crept up to his place of refuge but one of them, apparently his friend, let off his musket to give the alarm. For this he was executed.

Murty Og escaped that time, but before leaving for France he paid a final visit to his family at Eyeries. Here the soldiers suprised him again, and the house was surrounded. The thatch roof was set on fire, as one by one members of the family rushed out into the mob of soldiers, who allowed them to go free. They were waiting for one man only. At last only Murty Og lingered in the burning house. Suddenly he burst from the door, carrying his carbine, which he called The Pretender. He had a cocked pistol in his belt, and in his pocket a short Spanish dagger. He aimed his carbine at two of the soldiers, but it missed fire, and his last chance was in flight. Of the muskets aimed at him as he fled, only one went off, but the bullet from that hit him full in the back and came out through his left breast as he fell dead.

His body was slung on horseback and carried down to Dunboy, where it was buried in the courtyard. After four days they dug it up and lashed it to the stern of the government frigate which was returning to Cork with his captured companions at arms, O'Connell and O'Sullivan. In Cork it was beheaded and the head was stuck on a spike of the railings of the South Jail. O'Connell and O'Sullivan were executed. On the night before he died, O'Connell composed a lament for his dead friend.

A century later the Clonakilty poet, Jeremiah Callanan, wrote:

"A curse, blessed ocean, is on the green water
From the haven of Cork to Iveragh of slaughter,
Since the billows were dyed with the red wounds of fear
Of Murteagh Oge, our O'Sullivan Beare."

SIXTEEN

Bear Island

IN THE GUESTHOUSE I met a retired Irish-American, who had emigrated from Bearhaven in 1915. Like so many men born on the peninsula with its history of copper-mining, Vince had taken the trade with him, and worked the mines at Butte in Montana during the nineteen twenties. Although most of his life had been spent away, he could remember with particular vividness the Bearhaven of his boyhood, when life had been more lively than it was now. There had been *Princess Beara*, the passenger ship which went to Bantry every morning to meet the train, returning in the evening. He recalled town characters like the porter, nicknamed "Crabtrees", and the woman who sold trinkets along the quay and had a reputation for being as companionable as a tombstone. The sergeant of police at Ardgroom had honoured his girl friend, who lived on Dursey Island, with a poem which Vince could still recite. He spoke of his father, who had handed down memories of more distant times still, when people had crowded into town on fair days to drink whiskey in the taprooms at sixpence a pint. Shaking his head at the thought, he refilled my glass, before embarking on a series of anecdotes about the pioneer conditions of the Montana mines.

I had a hangover the following morning, and the tractors, bulldozers and Ruston Bucyrus crane which had begun work on the new extensions of the pier were already making earth-shaking noises by nine o'clock. A yellow school bus crossed the main square, and at the same time the small ferry, *Morning Star*, was arriving from Bear Island, bringing the few children who lived there over to school.

I made the return trip to the island. Bear measures roughly seven miles long by three wide, and from the mainland appears to be rather well-named—it does seem like a crouching bear guarding the sound. This is the deep passage of water where the British fleet could be anchored safely. It narrows at either end where the island closes in on the mainland. On these points forts and gun emplacements guarded the ships from potential enemies; in addition, the high points of the island are covered with a signal tower and two Martello fortifications look over its southern flanks.

Since the English first arrived, Bear Island was always associated with some sort of military or naval activity. Carew used it as a stepping stone for shipping his soldiers to Dunboy. The *Indomptable* with Wolfe Tone on board anchored for a time in the sound, "so near the shore, that I can in a manner touch the sides of Bantry Bay with my right and left hand". Later, when the naval base was established, the island's position became one of increasing importance. During the First World War the Channel Fleet regularly used the sound. Admiral Beatty brought the whole lot in here, just prior to the Battle of Jutland. The Allied Fleet assembled before Bearhaven; people can remember the names of the lines of anchored ships: the British battleships, like the *Lion*, *Agamemnon*, *Hercules*, and *Superb*; the dreadnoughts, *London* and *Dublin*; American ships, the *Oklahoma*, *Nevada*, *Utah*. "Terrible bloody things, altogether, man. The crockery would dance on the dresser with the noise of their guns."

One of the conditions of the treaty of 1921 was that the British should continue to maintain a garrison on Bear Island and post a destroyer in Bantry Bay. This arrangement lapsed in April, 1938, when both Lough Swilly and Bearhaven were handed over to the Irish government. Although there was no agreement to the effect, the British felt that they could resume use of them in an emergency. When the emergency came about with the outbreak of war seventeen months later, Churchill—then first Lord of the Admiralty—felt strongly that if the Irish government would not permit England to make use of these ports then they would have to be seized by force. He had never agreed to their ceding, and almost alone had protested to the House of Commons. Later he wrote: "I never saw the House more completely misled."

In October 1939 U-boats were cruising off the Irish coast. The first German air-raids of the war had been carried out over Scapa Flow and Rosyth. At a cabinet meeting of October 17th Churchill emphasized the importance of the Irish ports, so much further away from Germany, in a position outside the reach of German planes. The time had come to make it clear to the Irish government that Britain must have the use of these harbours and intended to use them in any case.

Sir John Maffey, British special envoy in Dublin, was instructed to approach De Valera and put Britain's case. The 90-minute interview took place on October 21st, when Maffey had the unpleasant task of trying to put pressure on the implacable Taoiseach. De Valera's mind was already made up. He had no intention whatsoever of handing over the ports. He told Maffey that if Britain had paved the way to Irish unity, Ireland "might" have been able to help. His sympathies were with the Allies, and he would greatly regret a German victory, but the public mood in Ireland would react violently to any threats on the part of the British government. Maffey urged him that when the ports has been handed over eighteen months before, "the path of generosity had been followed as an act of faith and in the belief that in the hour of need the hand of friendship would be extended". De Valera replied that the British had no right to gain advantage from what was not theirs.

Two days later, when the results of this meeting, which Sir Anthony Eden described as "the rigid and unsatisfactory attitude adopted by Mr De Valera", were disclosed to the British Cabinet, there was a heated argument as to whether Bearhaven and Lough Swilly were worth a passage of arms. Eden was against seizing them by force. He feared that not only would the Irish be alienated by such an action, but also many people in the Dominions and the United States. In addition, De Valera might decide to grant facilities to the Germans.

Churchill totally disagreed. He wished the Cabinet to authorize seizure of the ports under any pretext. He suggested that Britain should challenge the compatibility of the Irish Free State's neutrality with her position under the Crown. Unlike the Dominions, which were far away, Ireland was an integral part of the British Empire. He felt that action need not come immediately; it would be as well to wait until the United States Neutrality Act had been repealed, when it would be too late for Ireland to appeal to American public opinion.

The moderating voice at this meeting was finally Chamberlain's. He postponed any decision by declaring that force should be used only if seizure of the ports became a matter of life or death. The question was therefore left open. Very fortunately, a month later the Cabinet considered that Britain had obtained "control over the U-boat menace in the Western Approaches and it could not be said that in present circumstances the use of Bearhaven constituted a vital interest. . . ." Ireland was saved from invasion. U-boat casualties were not considered a matter of urgency at that time, and Churchill's attention was diverted to the prospects of curbing the activities of enemy submarines by means of magnetic mines.

De Valera refused to change his mind, even at the proposal of a deal— the end of partition after the war in exchange for the use of the bases throughout its duration. Churchill continued to feel strongly about this insistence on neutrality, as he revealed in a bitter speech at the end of the war.

Bearhaven rode out the Second World War in unnatural calm, when for six years of global conflict Ireland remained in the eye of the storm. Since that time Bear Island, like so many others, has steadily lost its men and women until today its population stands at about two hundred and fifty. Perhaps because of the vigour of those military activities of long ago, there is something particularly mournful about the abandoned farms and general air of pessimism. Few of the ageing islanders see much prospect for the future.

"Yerra, we have only our own government to blame. Talk, talk of saving the islands, but nothing is done. The place is finished unless they build a bridge to the mainland."

"What about tourism?"

"Tourists! One or two in summer, and then it's batten down for the long winter ahead!"

Most of the population lives on the northern slopes of the island which is patched with small farms looking across the sound towards the flat ridge of the Slieve Miskish and the dome of Hungry Hill. I travelled along the road which skirts the sound, passing by the large house, once Hotel Cross, where officers and their wives used to stay. Below was the inlet and pier from where boats crossed to Pontoon on the mainland. Near the settlement of houses was the small blue-painted church of St Michael, full of pamphlets about emigration and the Bishop of Kerry's Marriage Introduction Bureau. Rerrin, the main village, was in the next bay, one street of houses dominated by the two blank iron eyes of pill-boxes. Most of the shops were closed and boarded up.

During the First World War Rerrin was given an electricity supply—
the first place to have it along the whole coastline—and all around the
village hundreds of soldiers were trained for the bloody campaigns in
the trenches. The deserted harbour was once filled with liberty boats
from the destroyers and battleships anchored out in the sound. Sailors
thronged the street; because of bad relations between the Americans and
English, only one nationality was allowed ashore at a time. On the flat
piece of land behind the harbour, local teams used to play football
against the troops.

In the main camp situated behind Rerrin, the lines of huts are still
kept up by the Irish army. This eastern end of Bear Island abounds in
military remains. There are a firing range, the old garrison church and
the hospital to which the wounded used to be ferried back from France.
At the Rerrin battery eight-inch guns once guarded the astern entrance
to the sound. The ramp and the concrete embankments are overgrown
with gorse, while the metal fittings have rusted away. However,
another fort is still fitted with six-inch guns and newly painted bright
green. When the Irish army has manœuvres these guns are actually
fired. The inhabitants of neighbouring houses are warned to keep all
windows open because of the danger of shock.

"Why do they bother at all?" asked a man who was cleaning up one
of the paths leading to the embankment. "Is it likely nowadays that a
foreign ship would come up and attack Ireland?"

He thought that the barracks should be turned into a holiday camp.
"If only we had the beaches, we could get the blondes!" he said wist-
fully.

There are no longer any guesthouses or hotels on the island, and I was
lucky to get accommodation at a remote little farmhouse at the western
end. The cottage was owned by a native of Bear who had spent the last
twenty years in the States. Every summer she came back to the island as
regularly as clockwork and there she casually switched into the role of
an Irish housewife.

I collapsed in a chair, exhausted at having pushed my battered
bicycle up the unsurfaced lane. On the wall Jesus wearing thorns was
flanked by two Currier and Ives prints. A further hint of America was
provided by the pile of glossy magazines and the landlady's cheerful
voice calling out to her niece: "Fetch the cookies, Norah!" Perhaps I
might get American-style food? But no, the supper was orthodox Irish,

a heavy fry dominated by thick home-cured bacon, with black pudding, steamed fish and a pot of tea to wash it down.

From the house it was only a few yards to the southern flank of the island, which is almost entirely deserted. The fields turned into gorse and rocks ending in the line of cliffs reaching out to Doonbeg Head. Cut off from the north side by the ridge that runs the whole east-west length of Bear, the long slopes, lacking any sort of road or track, were left to sea birds and hares. To return to the civilized northern side meant a climb up past the ruins of the signal tower which marked the highest point on the island; from there I looked down once more through the mist over Castletownbere and towards the battlements of Dunboy in their cluster of trees. Down the northern slope the gradual transition to cultivated land was marked by small signs . . . a fuchsia hedge, some reeds, an iron fence with a bedhead filling a gap. Some empty cottages overlooked three more abandoned batteries that guarded battleships anchored in the sound. In one of the concrete embrasures a faded notice was still legible; countless gunners must have sat and pondered it during the long boredom of sentry duty. *All Visible Water is Within Effective Limit of Auto-Sight Range Guns 23 Feet Seven Inches Above MSL.*

In the evening I got a drink in the pub in Rerrin, not without difficulty. Although the day was Saturday, the place was quite empty and the back door had to be unlocked for me. On other Saturday nights, half a century ago, the dark little bar must have been crowded.

It was difficult to leave the island. When did the next boat leave? No one knew. Not today, anyway, try tomorrow. We have no regular service here, but tomorrow there'll be a few going over. So I spent another night at the cottage, marred by the collapse of my American pine bed, which forced me to sleep at a tilt of forty-five degrees. I hurried down early next morning eager to cross and get away. It was sadder here than on any of the other dying islands. The air was full of old echoes. If ghosts were to exist they would be those of soldiers and sailors.

SEVENTEEN

Allihies to Dursey Island

The Bearhaven Fair had been a good one. It was because of the Common Market, farmers thought. The dealers were already gambling on its provenance. The "wranglers" were in full force, prodding animals with their sticks and waiting for the man from the Department to inspect for warble fly. Among the cattle a speckled grey stallion trotted briskly up and down, its owner advertising for service and making appointments for mares. Cows were sold and resold throughout the morning, each time with a further edge of profit. Most of the buying stopped by midday; the pubs, already full, become fuller and remained so.

I met the driver of a Volkswagen bus which had come in from Allihies specially for the occasion. Yes, I could return with him as far as Cahermore if I didn't mind a crush nor waiting until five o'clock. His people, who were in drinking along with the happy lads who had made their money, would not be ready for some time.

At five the bus began driving up the main street gathering in passengers.

"Don't wait for Jimmy. Good luck to him, he'll stay with the pubs till the morning."

"It's a grand day at the graveyard . . . we best enjoy the time we have now."

Finally we set out filled to more than capacity. "There's twice the number we had this morning," grumbled the woman wedged beside me, as mud from the roots of her ill-tied parcel of cabbage plants scattered in the crush. Outside the rain had ceased, and for once it was a proper summer evening. "The weather has been very bad this year.

After the Scabareen it usually settles." Scabareen time is in the spring, the last two weeks in April and the first two of May, when the cattle are put out in the fields and the lobster fishing, such as it is, traditionally begins.

The road followed the line of the sea across bogs and reedy fields where cattle grazed under the late afternoon sky. I got out and collected my bike at Cahermore, a few miles west of the bleak Gour Gap. Two piers on the harbour were small protection from the Atlantic rollers that piled up in a scud of foam against the rocks. Above me was a row of mainly deserted houses where coastguards used to live, and a church, the only one between Bearhaven and Allihies. At one time it was thatched, and in the autumn the men who worshipped there each brought a sheaf of oats for the thatching. Today it is filled with gifts from emigrants who did not forget the little church beside the sea. Beside the emigration and marriage bureau notices there is a list of names and donations.

"Set of purple Gothic vestments: Mary Healy, New York. Station of the Cross: Cornelius Sullivan, New York. Golden Ciborium: Miss Kitty Sullivan, New York."

Between Blackball Head with its tower, another empty soundbox for the wind, and the long neck of Crow Head, the deserted country is bordered by cliffs towering over the sea. The restless water fills the air with a shifting light, never constant for a moment but perpetually flecked with different blues and greens. Then from the top of Barnes Gap and the turn-off for Dursey Island, the traveller becomes aware that he is approaching the end of the Beare peninsula; the sea is on both sides of him, with Ballydonegan Bay to the north and the widening mouth of the Kenmare river. The pockets of fields north of the Miskish range, which seem exquisitely rich and green, were once known as the Fields of a Thousand Cattle. Beyond them, on the far side of a shallow valley, is Allihies, with a roofless Protestant church and many empty houses. The small harbour used to be a centre for seine fishing, when, during the mackerel season, the pier was crowded out with women standing at trestle tables, salting and casking fish. But the place was more important for the copper-mines around it.

Of all the mines in West Cork, those at Allihies were the most consistently productive. The lodes at the Caminche and at the Mountain, which stands five hundred and fifty feet above sea level, had ore

The Square, Castletown Bearhaven, 1900

Hungry Hill capped in mist

Beara coastline

with a copper content of ten to fifteen per cent. The strand which faces the rolling waters of Ballydonegan Bay is an entirely artificial creation of sediment washed down from the slag heaps by the river. Above the village, entrances to the abandoned pumping houses and the stacks which mark the locations of the Mountain and the Caminche stand out like medieval fortresses.

These are the mines that Daphne du Maurier wrote about in her novel, *Hungry Hill*. They were owned by the Puxleys. Nearly a century after Henry Puxley's feud with Murty Og O'Sullivan, enough copper was found on Puxley land to bring the family wealth enough to build their own castle beside the ruins of Dunboy. Daphne du Maurier gathered the material for her novel from the Puxley family papers. Those who have lived in the area have testified to the accuracy of the events she describes—the mining accidents, the flooding of the mine, the financial ups and downs and the final blaze at the castle are all faithfully depicted. Names in the novel can easily be transposed into their real equivalents—"Mundy" is Bantry, "Doonhaven", Bear-haven, and so on. Only the mountain itself has kept its own name, and the biggest departure from the truth is locating the mines actually on the slopes of Hungry Hill. The characters, too, are supposed to be founded on real people, and every member of the "Broderick" family can be identified as a Puxley. The "Reverend Tom Callaghan", friend of "Copper John", was in real life the Reverend John Hallahan, rector of Castletown Bearhaven from 1862 to 1919, surely a record span, even in a long-lived occupation. It is said locally that his wife objected to *Hungry Hill* because of the way the author portrayed her.

"She has a description of me churning butter . . . as if I ever churned butter in my life!"

The copper at Allihies was discovered by the enterprising Colonel Hall of Glandore, who, having discovered the ore outside his own home, strove tirelessly to locate it in other parts of West Cork. The mines yielded most of their wealth between 1812 and 1842, when altogether 88,636 tons of copper were brought to the surface. Lady Chatterton, who visited Allihies in 1838, noted that "the work employs a thousand people. Girls who attend to the washing get $3\frac{1}{2}d$. a day, boys 6*d*., men from one shilling to one and four pence." At the end of every month tools were weighed and the value of the metal which had been worn away was deducted from these earnings. There were four

N

hundred actual miners, and six hundred workers, supervised by four mine captains. As water power was lacking, apart from that supplied by the little stream that descends to the bay, steam engines were used to crush and dress the ore. During the summer it was carried over to Swansea by schooners which departed from the pier at Allihies, but this was too exposed for winter launchings, and in winter months the operation was transferred to Bearhaven.

Like other West Cork mines, Allihies proved to be a disappointment, losing money because of various speculations and episodes involving litigation. In the good years there had been a yearly average of around three thousand tons of ore, but this fell to a hundred tons in 1883 and gradually sank to nothing.

Sporadic attempts have been made to reopen Allihies, for there are still large quantities of copper at levels lower than the old shafts. Rising copper prices might make it worth while bringing the old workings into operation. At present they are leased to a Canadian company. I found outside the old Doneen mine a notice warning visitors not to throw stones down the mine shafts. Geologists had been exploring the shafts taking rock samples. Earlier in the year they used to emerge as regularly as prairie dogs, and dump their cores outside the entrances to the workings. But then holiday makers had found them and senselessly destroyed them, throwing about and destroying thousands of dollars' worth of exploration. The old rough history of mining at Allihies seemed to continue.

The distance between the Mountain and the Caminche mines is about a mile. Hidden in a little valley between them, the ruins of the "Cornish village" face out to sea across the Bull and the Calf towards the distant Skelligs. In these cottages, now broken walls faced with banks of fuchsia, there once lived a community of Cornish miners and their families. When the mines first opened, it was considered that the experience of men who had worked in Cornwall would be necessary. No sooner had they arrived than the local people, resentful of their presence, boycotted them, and they were unable to buy food or fuel from the shopkeepers. They had to be fed by the ships coming over from Wales, which brought them supplies before taking away the ore. Up on the hillside their wives and children spent cloistered lives, seldom venturing below, and continuing to be segregated from their Irish neighbours. John Lavellin Puxley, the original "Copper John", built them their own chapel, for they were non-conformists. There is a tradition that Cornish miners like these first brought the fuchsia to Ireland after its introduction into England.

A book like *Hungry Hill*, which supposedly describes life on Beare during the nineteenth century and makes no mention of the famine, must be considered a work of the imagination. But there is some reason to believe that starvation was not so widespread in the immediate neighbourhood of the mines as it was in other places. My friend, Dan O'Brien, who lives in nearby Eyeries, had a conversation some years ago with a ninety-year-old man whose grandmother had lived through the famine near Allihies. His principal memory of her was her great concern with food and the care with which she would save the crumbs from the table. She had told him that although they were always hungry, they were never actually starving. It seems probable that the copper gave regular employment to most people living near them, and possibly the ore ships, already accustomed to bringing in supplies for the Cornishmen, carried in a certain amount of food to those who worked in the mines.

One lone descendant of the Cornish miners still lives in Allihies, a farmer named Hodges. He told me that he and his family were the only surviving Protestants in the area. As the sole parishioner, he had been given the job of dismantling the church and taking the roof off. "Fine quality. Man, you wouldn't ever see pitch-pine like that today!" Most of the wood he had been able to save went into the new barn he built himself.

Next morning I set out for Dursey Island, pushing uphill towards Barnes Gap. After the overnight rain slugs shone in the grass on either side of the road. Milk-carts rattled on their way to the creamery. I stopped one on which a farmer balanced precariously at the edge of the board, almost pushed off on to his horse's back by the volume of the churns behind him. Did he know "if the post boat went to Dursey today?"

"I suppose she do," he looked down at me from where he stood, reins in hand, above the cart. "Ye can only try. It will depend on the weather."

The turn-off for Dursey tilted down to the sea past the occasional small farmhouse, which often had an outhouse roofed over with the tarred hulk of a boat. Today the light from the sea was opaline. Outside a National School some pairs of children walked from scattered places. There seemed to be countless stretches of low barren hills. Then I realized that the fields ahead were separated by a narrow channel. This was Dursey Sound, and across the narrow water was Dursey Island, three hills strung one behind the other and edged with cliffs.

Every small inhabited island develops its own particular atmosphere compounded from the personality of its community, the harshness of the environment and the degree of isolation. Dursey has one or two bushy trees, but no real place of shelter which the wind cannot reach. A few wet fields with some shivering cattle are located on top of steep cliffs. The island is so close to the mainland that it seems a strong arm could throw a stone across the dividing channel, which is two hundred and twenty yards across at its narrowest point. But although the post boat is scheduled to cross daily, and many Dursey people are fishermen possessing their own boats, the treacherous nature of the sound cuts them off for long periods, mainly during winter months. An exceptionally dangerous tidal race rushes back and forth through the channel, often making the water boil with white foam, like a river over rapids. "The least gale of wind raises such billows as it is very dangerous for any boat to come near the shore," Smith wrote, and this has always been the case. Over the years the isolated islanders have developed into a gruff idiosyncratic community, self reliant, difficult to approach and having little time for those who do not share their hardships.

Just as I arrived to visit Dursey, I found that at last it was being linked to the mainland. Two English engineers, aided by a squad of workmen, were pegging out the site for a cable car. Their company, British Chairlifts Ltd., had experience of building cable cars all over the world; one of their more recent assignments had been in the Himalayas, where a cable now linked Sikkim with the Tibetan frontier. Compared to that, the small swing over to Dursey offered few problems; two metal trestles on either side of the channel would carry the cable seventy-five feet over high-water level, which would allow room for ships passing underneath. Passengers would be conveyed across by a hand-operated winching gear, and in case the mechanism broke down, a klaxon was being installed which they could hoot to attract attention while the car swung helplessly over the water.

But these refinements lay in the future. Meanwhile I found that the only method of crossing was still by boat. I had missed the post boat, and my visit depended on whether someone was on this side with a desire to ferry me over. I had been warned that Dursey boatmen had a reputation for scorching the stranger. They might even extort large sums from their own people, if they were in the mood or the weather was bad. I had heard of seven pounds being charged for the short return trip. So in a way I was lucky that there was a boat available to the engineers and that it was a calm day. The grumpy boatman charged me a pound for the crossing which his Seagull engine made in under four minutes.

On the other side there were six lobster boats pulled up on the hard beneath the ruins of a church, lashed down with ropes to prevent them being swept away in a sudden storm. An old woman waited beside the pier, standing by a donkey loaded with turf crammed into creches made of beer crates. She watched my arrival closely and as I stepped off she advanced, shouting to know if I were the English engineer. When I told her I was not, her indignant voice became a little mollified.

"Those sneaky men of the mainland want everything for themselves. It is only right that islanders should be given the work for building the new construction." All Dursey's isolation has not preserved the Irish language, and its people have their own sharp English idiom. It is only with the past two generations that Irish has died away, for in 1925 Beare and Dursey were both declared Gaeltacht areas.

I followed her and her donkey across the hump of the first hill to the small cluster of houses which is called Ballynacallagh. The sight of an old man leaning against a wall roused her to another outburst.

"There are eight men working in the east, and you sleeping in your bed."

He showed little interest at the news; a thousand men might be building a pyramid for all he cared. While the dame continued to abuse him, her shrill voice was counterpointed by vigorous barking as three dogs came running towards me, showing their teeth. Their fur was the mottled grey, white and black lizard-skin mixture of many West Cork dogs, and three out of their six eyes were blue, showing their inbreeding. Behind them was their owner, a saturnine man, his face blurred with days of dark beard. He said that he farmed on the east side, looking back towards the sound and the budding cable car. I went back with him to his land, where he pointed out a field in which I could camp, which he said had a good supply of water.

"Ye can pour away the stuff in your bottle." It was as well that I did not, for most of his water was hidden under irises and cowpats. He was known, he said as The Pirate.

"Late this evening I'll be down to you for a talk." He produced a bottle of whiskey from his pocket, insisting, "Keep it safe till I come. You're not worried that I'll return and kill ye?"

He wandered off, leaving the bottle as a pledge. I put it beneath the tent and then went back to the church with its graveyard overlooking the pier where I had landed. Among the gravestones which surrounded the few remaining walls, one recalled Timothy Harrington, who had died in 1919 aged a hundred and four years. A large stepped-up monument to the O'Sullivan Beares stood over a vault filled with coffins. I had been told that there were still two remaining members of the family living on the island who could trace their ancestry back to the O'Sullivan Beare, and who hoped in due course to top the pile.

Down on the water at the south entrance to the sound was the jutting headland of Ilanebeg, which once had a castle on it. Nothing remains of it, although as recently as 1846 it was marked on maps. Ilanebeg is actually an island, and at that time it was connected with Dursey by a drawbridge. But today it can only be reached when the tide is low and a journey is made over jagged seaweed-covered rocks. The castle, along with the church, was brought to ruin in 1602, a fortnight before the capitulation of Dunboy. After Ilanebeg was captured every person found on it was slaughtered.

This bloody incident was described in detail by the historian, Don Phillip O'Sullivan, who was born on Dursey. A cousin of Donal Cam, he was one of a family of seventeen children, of whom thirteen are said to have perished in the wars. As a boy he was shipped to Spain after the Battle of Kinsale to receive a Spanish education, while his parents remained behind to take part in the march to Leitrim. In Spain he tried his hand at various careers—he was a soldier and a sailor, and eventually died fighting against the Turks on Spain's behalf. (Earlier in 1618, he had been involved in the brawl in which his cousin, Donal Cam, was fatally wounded.) He was also a writer, and his main claim to fame rests with his most important work, the *Catholic History of Ireland*. *Historiae Catholicae Iberniae Compendium* was written in Latin, the universal language. Part of it described the final wars that drove his family from Ireland, and might be described as the Irish answer to

Pacata Hibernia, which was written by Carew's nephew, Thomas Stafford. It was dedicated to Philip III of Spain. "You are ever a barrier to the pestilence of hellish heresy. You are the refuge of Catholics; Ireland turns to you as to an asylum. . . ."

In his history Phillip describes how in June, 1602, this castle of Ilanebeg was packed with people, islanders and dependants of O'Sullivan Beare who had come over from Dunboy and its neighbourhood as refugees. It was here that Donal Cam planned to make a last stand. Carew claimed that the small fort had three pieces of Spanish ordnance, but Phillip, perhaps on the word of exiles he had questioned, declared that it was unarmed. A party of Englishmen was detached from the siege of Dunboy and sent over here; it was led by a man called John Broderick, and included Sir Owen O'Sullivan. Before the castle and church were burnt to the ground, "the English, after their wonted manner, committed a crime far more notable for its cruelty than their honour. The garrison was put to the sword. Some ran their swords up to the hilt through the babe and mother who was carrying it to her breast, others paraded before their comrades little children writhing and convulsed on their spears, and finally, binding all the survivors, they threw them into the sea over jagged and sharp rocks, showering on them shots and stones. In this way perished three hundred Catholics." Five hundred cattle were taken away as spoils, ten times the number of animals that there are on the island today.

As I made my way westward again, I overtook a young couple walking together, who told me they were brother and sister. He worked the lobster pots by hand—a tough operation on such a dangerous coast. She informed me with great satisfaction that she was the only marriageable girl on the island. The others had gone.

Kilmichael was a scattered village where most of the houses were built with blocks of stone, with tiny windows tunnelled through walls thick as a man's arm. Black smoke puffed out of their chimneys and streaks of rusty water ran down from their thatched roofs. On the mainland, nearly all houses of this type have gone to ruin or to shelter for cows, but it was difficult to bring concrete blocks and cement across the sound to the island, and few people had made the effort to modernize their homes. It seemed that little had changed for centuries. There were no cars or tractors, and no electricity supply; the only signs of modern life were a few yellow gas bombs and, once, the sound of a radio. The children, just out of school, followed me about with the shy curiosity of children unused to strangers. They giggled, grinned and shied away like Arab urchins in desert settlements.

About three-quarters of the houses were empty, their windows boarded up, the pathways to their doors blocked with wooden barriers and with nettles. Nearly all were overshadowed by their surrounding hedges of New Zealand flax, one of the few plants to flourish here. One little ruined building had belonged to the O'Sullivan Beares. Near the pump a piece of wall and a heap of stones remained of an early church of St Michael the Archangel.

In the post office a tattered poster, recalling a nationwide campaign about television licences, warned: "T.V. Spongers Beware!" I tried to buy cigarettes, but unfortunately the place was quite out of supplies for that moment. All that it could offer for sale was matches. Nothing else, certainly no drink. My friend with the whiskey must have been on a trip to the mainland.

West of Kilmichael the only road followed the southern shore to reach Tillickfinna overlooking the Atlantic. Here just three houses were lived in by two families, one of which consisted of a single man named Mick Leary, whom I encountered riding along above the cliff on his white horse. His neighbour, who had lived for forty years in the shuttered house beside him, had left for America two years ago, and nothing had been heard of him since.

To the south was Crow Head, long and deserted, tipped with its little island; Murty Og O'Sullivan is reputed to have sailed his ship through the narrow passage between them. Sheep's Head, Three Castle Head and the far-off Mizen dug into the ocean like the prongs of a fork. To the north the Kerry mountains spanned the horizon, and ahead of me stretched the silver dimpled Atlantic. Past some men cutting scalps of turf on the last headland above the sea, I came to Dursey Head itself beyond faint boundaries of abandoned fields and stone walls. Out on the cliffs among the gulls' nests were the remains of the old lighthouse, superseded by the Bull lighthouse on the Bull Rock, which stands formidably off Dursey, attended by the Cow and the Calf. The precipitous cone of the Bull, six hundred feet in diameter, rises three hundred feet above sea level, a full stop punctuating this barren point of Europe.

Returning to the east side, I settled in my tent to await the dusk and the coming of the Pirate to share his whiskey. He looked less alarming

in the dim light, and was briskly sociable as we took it in turn to drink
from my tin cup. He talked about the cable car; it would make farming
easier, he said. At present the cows had to be swum over, and there were
times when they would be lost. But it had come ten years too late.
There were fifty people left now. Twelve were children at the school.
But Ballynacallagh, Kilmichael and Tillickfinna were filled with empty
cottages still waiting for people who said they would return. Still, at least
the car would end the old winter isolation which could last for weeks.
Several times election papers had been sent over by breeches buoy. A
priest might have to give his blessing for an island funeral standing on
the shore of the mainland, making the sign of the cross over the water.

"What about doctors?"

"God helps those who live in simple places." Timothy Harrington
had lived for over a century without the aid of a doctor, and the rest of
the islanders managed without as well.

He talked angrily about the O'Sullivan Beares. No later overlord had
troubled the gloomy peace of Dursey, and he was indignant about very
old wrongs. Of Donal Cam in particular, he had no good word to say.
A whoremaster who took first crack at all the women around—even if
they were married. He was as indignant as if his own wife had suffered
at the hands of the hero. For good measure Donal Cam also impressed
many of the local people for foreign armies on the continent. "A right
bastard!" I remembered a friend of mine coming to Dursey some years
ago, and having a violent argument with an old islander who insisted
that Bonnie Prince Charlie spent a night here on his voyage back
after escaping from Culloden. Of course, it is just possible that he did.

The Pirate ducked out of the tent, called up his dogs and strode off,
his boots squelching over the soft mud of his field. The rain thumping
above me soon seeped through the canvas and dripped over my head.
At dawn I struggled with making tea, shaking out of the cup a slug
which had come in to drink the dregs. When the rain eased, I walked
over the wet turf through Kilmichael, which was silent, every house
that still had inhabitants heavily curtained. I climbed the far hummock
of the island where the bog and heather were lifted out of the mist, and
above me twenty or thirty larks were singing, their voices punctuated
by the mournful fog signal from the Bull. At the top was a hollow signal
tower, its presence on such a difficult site emphasizing the panic that
must have followed the invasion of Bantry Bay.

The rain came on again, and it was with difficulty that I found a man willing to make the short expensive journey back to the mainland.

Months later I returned to Dursey after the car had been completed. The fat little green cabin was designed to take six passengers, or a man and a cow. I climbed inside along with three nurses from Bantry hospital who also hoped to make the trip across. We shut the door and contemplated three buttons in black, yellow and red, "Hooter", "Call Cabin" and "Send Cabin". The idea of a hand-operated winch had been abandoned: although it would undoubtedly have made the cable car less expensive to build, it would have inflicted an intolerable strain on some of the older members of the community.

We pressed all three buttons, but nothing happened. The current had been turned off. The islanders were not going to risk their new cable in the hands of irresponsible strangers.

Two cars, packed with people returning from church, drove up and waited with us; it was a new luxury to be able to go across so easily and make their way in hired cars to Cahermore. At last, well after noon, there arrived the man who worked the cable, also back from Mass. As we prepared to climb into the cabin once again, he stopped us.

"There'll only be the one trip across." On that day, as on most days of the week, the movement of the cabin was rationed to a single journey; it would sail over and stay on the other side until its return the following morning. I had not brought my tent, and the girls from Bantry, who had planned the trip for weeks, had to be back that evening. Clearly it would be some time before Dursey was affected by tourism.

EIGHTEEN

Eyeries to the Tim Healy Pass

ACROSS THE BROAD sweep of the Kenmare river, the Kerry mountains presented a jumble of peaks capped with cloud, Himalayas to the
Alps of Beare. I cycled through barren stretches of hillside on which a
few fertile fields were scattered, picked out in dazzling green from the
brown wastes of rock and bog. The number of these increased, until I
came down to Eyeries, a trim little village set beside the sea in a crescent
of rich pasture as bright as rice paddies.

Through Eyeries the road led towards Ballycrovane Bay, bounded
by the peninsula of Kilcatherine. Past the ruins of a coastguard station
stood the Eyeries pillar stone, seventeen feet high. It was no larger than
a young ash-tree, but it dominated sea and mountains, defying the eye
to believe that it was not on the same scale. In its beautiful setting it has
a grandeur that makes it one of the most marvellous of neolithic monuments. The Ogham on its side looks like an old feather; scratch marks
run slantwise or perpendicular off a centre line, or *fleasc*, to make a
simple code. "The grave of the son of Decceda and grandson of Tor-
ani". The stone was quarried from the side of a hill about a mile away,
and near the place in the rock from which it was hewn there lies another
pillar stone on its side, never moved or erected.

I visited Dan O'Brien in his small house outside the village which
overlooks Pallace Strand near the place where Murty Og O'Sullivan
was tracked down and killed. (Eyeries was Murty Og's home port, and
to reach it from France he would round Dursey or cut through the
sound before sailing up the Kenmare river.) A retired bank manager,
Dan had settled at Eyeries to indulge in amateur archaeology. He
had infected his neighbours with his enthusiasm so that farmers and

school-children joined him in searching the fields and mountains for house sites, kernstones and kileens.

The Beare peninsula is particularly rich in traces of Bronze-Age man. As elsewhere in West Cork, there does not seem to have been a classical Iron-Age settlement, and the Bronze-Age cult appears to have continued into early Christian times without a trace of a true iron age. During the early Christian period there was a sharp increase in population, but Beare never became really crowded. Traces of ancient settlements are found everywhere; in the Journal of the Cork Archaeological Society, Dan has produced a massive list of sites which he has noted, west of Glengarriff—a hundred and fifty in all. No guide points out these places in any detail, and many of them are not even marked on the six-inch map. They are all unexcavated; up until 1970 the only site which had been properly investigated by archaeologists was the relatively uninteresting remains of the fortifications of Dunboy.

Dan took me on a swift tour of the local ruins and relics. We went to Caheravart near the Bearhaven–Eyeries road, where there was a fine *cillin*, an early Christian religious settlement, in which a collapsed cell or small church was surrounded by gravestones, many of them the small graves of unbaptized children. The burial ground would have been used a great deal during penal times, when priests were scarce and baptisms infrequent, but the site was much older, probably with a long period of pre-Christian associations. A battered old cross stood among the graves, worn away as if it had been melted, and the whole was surrounded by an earthen ring. The fields round about were studded with house sites, and below them were the traces of an ancient water mill, where an opening had been cut in the rock through which water was conducted to drive the horizontal wheel, now long vanished. Dan was on the lookout for it, and had asked neighbouring farmers to bring him any piece of wood they might dig up. But it was probably long destroyed.

From the settlement, which was situated on a hillside, two standing stones were visible across the valley. On Beare every sixth or seventh field seemed to have the white smudge of a standing stone, sometimes a hefty memorial to the dead or a cult symbol, sometimes a smaller boundary mark, perhaps indicating the division of land. We travelled from Caheravart in a radius of perhaps five miles, viewing a number of these stones, a portal dolmen, a boulder dolmen, a pair of stones that

had heeled over in the ground, the ring of an early house, a circle, and
a little pile of rocks in the middle of a bog which neither Dan nor any
visiting archaeologist cared to commit themselves in identifying.

"It's not a court cairn. At least, it isn't allowed to be one. There are
not supposed to be any in the Beare area."

He hopped from site to site with the enthusiasm of an early Egypto-
logist journeying up the Nile. He had discovered many of the remains
himself, for he had the right sort of eye, and could pick them out, like
boys who can find birds' nests. Moreover, this was virgin territory and
the six-inch map was by no means inexhaustible, although it was just
as necessary to his search as his binoculars. He also required infinite
caution to temper his energy. Care was needed before a name was put
to a pile of stones on a hillside. It might be something interesting, or a
platform for drying turf. A couple of large, oddly angled boulders
were perhaps a collapsed dolmen, or merely what the experts termed a
"glacial erratic". Rough patches of land covered with gorse were
perhaps house sites, but they could be the efforts of a farmer to clear his
fields. A souterrain could turn out to be a henhouse, and a standing
stone might have been erected in the last ten years as a scratching post for
cattle.

We climbed a mountain to examine a neolithic copper-mine which
Dan had found above Eyeries. It seemed obvious that there should
be prehistoric mines in the area, but this was the first indication that
copper had been exploited thousands of years ago. The climb was long
and steep, and halfway up I left Dan sitting in what he called "the
fiddler's field" to tackle the last part of the mountain by myself. The
mines were similar to those I had seen on Mount Gabriel, small man-
made caves scooped out of the rock. Dan had found a few mauls, the
same type of rounded sea stones that I saw lying about on Mount
Gabriel. He had wondered where the miners lived, and had been looking for some trace of a house site or ring fort near the mines. When I
reached the fiddler's field once more, I found him jubilant; as he rested
and waited for my return, he had noticed that the bank beside him had
a curve to it, and through the layout of boulders it was possible to
distinguish the shape of a large circle smothered in heather and bracken.
An obvious place for neolithic miners to have their huts.

I stayed the night in Dan's cottage and set out next morning. At nine
o'clock the only inhabitants of Eyeries to be seen were two sad dogs

that had stretched out across the road, feeling secure that there would be no danger from passing traffic. Outside the village whirls of mist rose gently from the surrounding hills, but the Kilcatherine peninsula gleamed in the early morning sun. The road curved upwards from Bally-crovane harbour towards Kilcatherine Point and a high place with distant views, which is called Ard Na Cailleach, or the Height of the Hag. In a field below, looking towards the south-west, is the *Cailleach Beara* herself. A slender jagged piece of rock is meant to resemble an old woman with a basket on her back. Sometimes you could catch the glimpse of a beaky profile, at other times she could be anything.

"Christ, man, she's more like a hen," the farmer who gave me directions to find her had considered. Of all ancient remains she is the most obstinately pagan, although facts about her ancient worship are few. The legend that she was turned from an old woman into a rock by the priest of Kilcatherine church reveals how Christianity finally defeated her powers as the goddess of fertility and witchcraft. She is the Celtic version of Hecate, associated with sorcery and graveyards and darkness. Although she is chiefly remembered as the old woman, the oldest of all, the *Cailleach Beara*, like Hecate, had three manifestations, one of which was that of the beautiful young moon goddess. Directly below the shoulder of the hill where the stone crouches facing out to sea, there are three small oddly shaped narrow fields. One of them is still known as the Field of the Fair Woman.

Kilcatherine used to be known for seine fishing, and twenty boats worked the bay opposite Illaunbesheen island. Today the almost deserted peninsula, which seldom sees visitors or tourists, remains one of the most beautiful places in West Cork with its majestic views of mountains and sea. A few cottages remain, and the ruin of a tenth-century church located above the *Cailleach Beara* further up the hill. Its position perhaps indicates the victory of Christianity over the older forces. Above the door protrudes a little stone head with a gargoyle face which had been found lying in the graveyard, and was set up by the indefatigable Dan O'Brien.

At Ardgroom, the next harbour on the north side of the coast, there is a bar made of shingle, which is called Cois or Leg, because it looks just like a leg with a shoe on the end kicked out from the shore. Above it a small ring fort is full of children's graves, with one stone slab commemorating an English sailor who was buried among them. "In memory of John Broderick, sailmaker of Gosport, Hants, England, who died on board the R.M.S. *Helen*, and was buried here August, 1869." The name Broderick curiously repeats itself all over the area. The soldier who led the sack of Dursey was named Broderick; so were some of the followers of Puxley after whom Daphne Du Maurier called her fictitious mine owners in Hungry Hill. In 1969, when Gulf Oil plunged into Bantry Bay, the president of the company was Mr E. D. Broderick.

Coming into Ardgroom harbour from the Kilcatherine side, the road passes through rich woodland where massive beeches and chestnuts rise above acres of wild rhododendrons. This is a plantation surrounding the ruins of a house built by a Mrs Puxley shortly after the famine. When the building of the house was in progress, the masons asked her if they might partake of a glass of porter. She seems fully to have shared in the ungracious reputation of her family; refusing their request, she told them briefly: "Go and drink with the ducks in the stream." After that the masons did their best to plaster the outside so badly that the water would drown the place out, but she beat their strategy by lining the walls with slate. However, the house was not to last long. Some years afterwards it became the rectory, but around the turn of the century it fell into disrepair. Now only the trees remain.

Ardgroom is a lonely village with a wide main street full of shuttered empty houses, a curious crenellated church in the Italian style, and a bar with a holly-tree growing inside the window. On the harbour a stone circle overlooks Carrig rock against which a Bearhaven trawler broke up on Christmas Eve, 1967, with the loss of five of its crew. Beyond it are the Ardgroom caves, tunnelled out of the sea; at low tide you can row into them and the sunlight accompanies you inside, reflecting and lighting up the clear water so that the sea urchins and starfish on the bottom are visible as if they were seen through glass.

East of Ardgroom I crossed the line that divides Cork from Kerry. I had intended to confine my journey to West Cork, but the lonely little harbour of Kilmakilloge, just over the Kerry border, had important associations with other places I had seen. In particular, here were the remains of Ardea Castle, which had belonged to the O'Sullivan Beares and brought them a large income from fishing dues; Phillip O'Sullivan, uncle of Donal Cam, received £1900 in tribute from Spanish boats coming up the Kenmare river in search of pilchards. It was to Ardea that Donal Cam travelled to meet the Spanish ship that arrived with supplies for the rebels while Dunboy was being sacked on the other side of the peninsula.

The lushly planted headlands of Kilmakilloge surround Dereen House, once the ancestral seat of the Lansdowne family, which is descended from William Petty. Petty was by far the most able and intelligent of the early settlers who came to Ireland to make their fortunes. He began his career in poor circumstances as a cabin boy on a ship plying between England and the west coast of France. He soon prospered. In business acumen, ruthlessness, dishonesty and inexhaustible energy he resembled Boyle, but although he was just as grasping as the great earl, he still manages to emerge as an attractive personality. His abilities were formidable; he was the all-round Renaissance man, endowed with a remarkable scientific mind filled with curiosity about the way things worked. There were few subjects that did not catch his attention at some time. He produced a dictionary of useful words and wrote Latin poems, including one called *Poema Glanarota* in praise of his Kerry estates, which were called Glanerought. His passion for ships led him to design a paddle boat and a double-bottomed boat which was actually built, but lost afterwards in the Bay of Biscay. Other inventions included a "pacing saddle" and a new sort of carriage which would have been particularly useful to him, since it was "designed to carry an unwieldy infirm and blind carcass over the rocks and bogs of Kerry in all weathers and ways". As a physician Petty considered ways of dealing with drunkenness and the need for setting up hospitals. He once revived a woman who had been hanged for the murder of her child. A highlight of his career was his appointment as Professor of Anatomy at Oxford. Prominent in the Irish College of Physicians, he introduced the new scientific anatomy first expounded by William Harvey into this country. He was deeply interested in politics and trade; not only is he credited with inventing the science of statistics, but his book entitled *Political Arithmetic* laid the foundations for the study of political economy. "If I were a prince," the diarist, John Evelyn, wrote, "I should make him my second counsellor at least".

But Petty is perhaps best remembered as a cartographer. After he came to Ireland in 1652 in Cromwell's wake, as Physician General to the Parliamentary army, he conceived the idea of mapping Ireland in detail with the aid of a team of helpers. And the result of this tremendous undertaking was the Downe Survey, a precursor of six-inch

Dursey Sound

Tim Healy Pass, Glanmore

Calvary Group at the summit of the Tim Healy Pass

mapping, which drew out in detail boundaries and estates in Ireland comprising over two million acres. Before Petty, such detailed cartography had been largely guesswork; now it became a science. He had difficulty in getting paid for his work, and the beginnings of his Irish estates were pieces of land in part-payment from the government. These he described as "refuse ends and talys of lots". In addition he acquired considerable funds by accepting sums of money from owners of estates to draw their ill-defined possessions just a little roughly on his maps—so that they might include this stretch of river, that piece of forest or some other slice of their neighbour's property. His fortunes had a healthy start; later, about the time he was knighted by Charles II in 1662, he added a further thirty thousand acres to his estates by acquiring the confiscated lands of O'Sullivan Mor in the barony of Glanerought.

He set about developing his Kerry estates with great enthusiasm. In 1661 he wrote: "For a great man that would retire, this place would be the most absolute, and the most interesting place in the world, both for improvement and pleasure and healthfulness."

He had little time for the inhabitants, three-quarters of whom, he considered, lived in a brutish nasty condition in cabins with neither chimney, doorway, stairs nor window. But on the land itself he instituted the familiar patterns of civilization begun by other settlers, opening iron-mines, building a fish pallace on the shores of Kilmakilloge harbour, and introducing the seine net to the area with permanent benefit.

The historian, Froude, who stayed at Dereen in 1867, blamed Petty for the destruction of the forests which once covered the peninsula. People still say locally that "a bird could walk from Kilmakilloge to Bearhaven on the tops of trees". It is always difficult to believe in these forests, since the eye has come to accept the barrenness as natural and correct; but if you pass a patch of bog where turf has been lifted, you will see that the squared cavities left behind are littered with whitened tree stumps.

Froude wrote disapprovingly: "The founder of the Lansdowne family secured in his scramble for Irish land for some trifling sum, the lordship of this wilderness of mountains. The woods were hiding places for wolves and rapparees, or worse than both, Jesuits; and the lovers of the picturesque had not come into being, even in England." The iron

o

ore needed charcoal so that the metal could be melted and mixed with red ore from Wales to make it less brittle. Petty was quite aware of the destruction he was causing. He estimated that the woods in Ireland, with the help of Norwegian imports, would only last another seventy years—even this reckoning was over-optimistic. But he considered that he was doing a service in ridding fertile acres of scrubby rapparee-concealing forests. There was a proverb in those times that the Irish could never be subdued while the leaves were on the trees. It is fair to add that he did much replanting of the land, and a descendant continued the work, the results of which are to be seen today. Paradoxically, such estate trees planted by improving landlords are now often objects of dislike, because of their associations with the more recent past.

Like many an Irish landlord, Petty eventually found his estates a burden. The difficulties of running the new industries increased, and six years after he had described Kerry as the most interesting place in the world, he was calling his visits there "the wearies". Now he resented the time he was obliged to spend in "an obscure corner of the world, but such where I am forced to go thro thick and thin. . . ." But he continued to develop and to acquire further lands. At his death in 1687 he is said to have owned in this area alone more than 270,000 acres.

It was time for me to turn southwards once more. I had no desire to drag the rusty bicycle forward into the Kerry ranges and to push up long winding roads where the mist occasionally rolled back to reveal a tourist car or a wet sheep. Bad enough to have to struggle up the long road to the Tim Healy Pass. I walked in sunshine through hills covered in the strident yellow and purple of gorse and heather. Then at last the tunnel at the top and the run downwards towards the clear beauty of Bantry Bay. During the war when the Germans were mapping out Ireland for possible invasion, they mistook the name of the Tim Healy Pass and christened it the Helige Pass instead.

From the summit I could look towards the hundred miles or so of country over which I had travelled. I had seen a succession of landscapes of great beauty, imbued with the most savage and melancholy history. Too many of them were empty now; too many houses were inhabited by lonely old men, or, newly painted and converted, stood with shutters drawn waiting for foreigners to take their summer holidays. The sombre results of emigration, of course, are not confined to West Cork, and the pattern is the same throughout western Ireland. In some ways such extensive emptying of the countryside can be said to have positive advantages. There is little of the atmosphere of threat that one meets journeying through the English countryside, where horizons have factory chimneys and lines of pylons. Pollution is minimal, confined to a limited number of tourist developments, some tar on the beaches, and a few scattered car bodies and rubbish dumps. But the price to pay for the preservation of natural surroundings is desolation. I have seen some of the deserted islands in late summer when their fields and laneways, thick in ragweed and thistles, swarm with butterflies. Other movement is from hares and from cattle brought over by boat to graze beside the ruined cottages. Another threat, even more potent than that of pollution, is the prospect of depopulation until the mainland is as empty as these islands.

Recently two economists who studied in West Cork came to the conclusion that only one farm in ten can be termed a viable unit. It is the amount of unproductive land that makes farming in the region such a heartbreak, when almost half the acreage of any small struggling farm consists of useless rock, gorse and bog. The smallholdings, whose ageing owners struggle to raise a small dairy herd and beef cattle, supplemented perhaps with pigs and poultry, are maintained by government grants and by remittances from relatives who have emigrated and still loyally remember those who remain behind. Many of these farms are unlikely to survive another generation.

There is a little reason for optimism. The census figures for Skibbereen, for example, show that in 1966, for the first time in a hundred and nineteen years, the population remained static and did not decline. Many people will tell you how much better things are than they used to be. Farmers have cars, milking parlours, running water and television; shopkeepers benefit from tourism. Perhaps the recent signs of prosperity have not come too late, like the cable car across the Dursey Sound.

REFERENCES

1 O'Casey, Sean, *I Knock at the Door* (Macmillan, 1939).
2 Corkery, Daniel, *Hidden Ireland* (Gill & Co., 1925).
3 Fleming, Lionel, *Head or Harp* (Barrie & Rockliff, 1965).
4 Freeman, T. W., *Ireland* (Methuen, 1950).
5 Barry, Tom, *Guerilla Days in Ireland* (Irish Press Ltd, 1939).
6 Smith, Cecil Woodham, *The Great Hunger* (Hamish Hamilton, 1962).
7 Wilson, T. G., *Irish Lighthouse Service* (Allen Figgis, 1968).
8 Thomas, Albert, *Wait and See* (Michael Joseph, 1944).

The author has quoted on a number of occasions from *The Pooles of Mayfield* by Rosemary ffolliot (Allen Figgis, 1958). This is a family history and collection of papers.

There are various quotations from the writings of Edith Somerville. Most are from *Notions in Garrison* and *Some experiences of an Irish R.M.* (Longmans).

There are two quotes from *Records of the Somerville Family of Castlehaven and Drishane*, compiled by Edith Somerville and Boyle Townshend Somerville, published privately in 1940, on pages 54 and 58.

BIBLIOGRAPHY

Barry, Tom, *Guerilla Days in Ireland*, Dublin, 1949.

Boland, Michael R., *The Scandal of West Cork*, Skibbereen, 1958.

Chatterton, Lady, *Rambles in the South of Ireland*, London, 1834.

Collis, Maurice, *Edith Somerville and Martin Ross*, London, 1968.

Coombes, Rev. J., *The Benedictine Priory of Ross*, Timoleague, 1964.

Coombes, Rev. J., *Utopia in Glandore*, Timoleague, 1970.

Corkery, Daniel, *Hidden Ireland*, Dublin, 1925.

C.Y.M.S., Clonakilty, *Clonakilty and District, Past and Present*, Skibbereen, 1959.

Cullen, L. M., *Life in Ireland*, London, 1968.

Donovan, Dr D., *Sketches in Carbery*, Dublin, 1876.

Dunbar, Janet, *Mrs. G.B.S.*, London, 1963.

Estyn Evans, E., *Irish Folk Ways*, London, 1957.

Falls, Cyril, *Elizabeth's Irish Wars*, London, 1950.

Fetherstonehaugh, A. J. *The True Story of the Two Chiefs of Dunboy*. Privately printed.

ffolliot, Rosemary, *The Pooles of Mayfield*, Dublin, 1958.

Flanagan, Patrick, *Transport in Ireland 1880–1910*, Wicklow, 1969.

Fleming, Lionel, *Head or Harp*, London, 1965.

Fontaine, James, *Memories of a Huguenot Family*, London, 1874.

Freeman, T. W., *Ireland*, London, 1950.

Freeman, T. W., *Prefamine Ireland*, Manchester, 1957.

Froude, James Anthony, *The Two Chiefs of Dunboy*, London, 1889.

Froude, James Anthony, *Reminiscences of an Irish Journey in 1849*, London, 1882.

Gibbings, Robert, *Sweet Cork of Thee*, London, 1951.

Gibson, Rev. C. B., *At the Feet of Gabriel*, Skibbereen, 1944.

Hall, Mr and Mrs S. C., *Ireland: its Scenery, Character, etc.*, London, 1841.

Haughton, J. P., *The Town of Skibbereen*.

Hayward, Richard, *Munster and Cork*, London, 1964.

Holland, Rev. W., *History of West Cork and the Diocese of Ross*, Skibbereen, 1949.

Jackson, Professor, *Bronze Age Mines on Mount Gabriel*, Dublin.

Journal of the Cork Historical and Archaeological Society.

Journal of the Ivernian Society.

Joyce, Professor P. W., *Irish Place Names*, Dublin, 1883.

Kane, Sir Robert, *Industrial Resources of Ireland*, Dublin, 1845.

Kitching, J. A., *Ecological Studies at Lough Ine*, London, 1969.

Leask, H. G., *Irish Castles*, Dundalk, 1941.

MacDermot, F., *Theobald Wolfe Tone*, London, 1939.

McDowell, R. B., *Social Life in Ireland, 1800–45*, Dublin, 1957.

Maclysaght, E., *Irish Life in the Seventeenth Century*, London, 1939.

du Maurier, Daphne, *Hungry Hill*, London, 1943.

Maxwell, Constantia, *Country and Town Life under the Georges*, London, 1940.

Nicholson, Asanath, *The Bible in Ireland*, London, 1926.

O'Mahony, J., *West Cork and its Story*, Tralee, 1960.

O'Maidin, Padraig, *Pococke's Tour of South and South-West Ireland*, Journal of the Cork Historical and Archaeological Society, July–December, 1959.

O'Riordan, S., *Antiquities of the Irish Countryside*, London, 1942.

O'Sullivan, Phillip, *Historicae Catolicae Iberniae Compendium*, Lisbon, 1621.

Pankhurst, R. K. P., *William Thompson*, London, 1954.

Reilly, A. J., *Father John Murphy, Famine Priest*.

Skibbereen Social Survey, 1964.

Smith, Charles, *State of the County and City of Cork*, Dublin, 1774.

Somerville, Edith, and Martin, Ross, *Some Experiences of an Irish R.M.*, London, 1906.

Somerville, Edith, and Martin, Ross, *Notions in Garrison*, London, 1939.

Somerville, Edith O. E., *Somerville Family Records*, Cork, 1940.

Stafford, Thomas, *Pacata Hibernia*, London, 1633.

Strauss, E., *Sir William Petty*, London, 1954.

Thackeray, William Makepeace, *Irish Sketchbook*, Edition Smith and Elder, London, 1879.

Thomas, Albert, *Wait and See*, London, 1944.

Townsend, Horatio, *Statistical Survey of Cork*, Cork, 1816.

Townshend, Dorothea, *An Officer of the Long Parliament*, London, 1892.

Trench, William Stuart, *Realities of Irish Life*, London, 1868.

Went, A. E. J., *Deposition of Sir William Hull*, Journal of the Cork Historical and Archaeological Society, Jan–June, 1947.

Went, A. E. J., *Pilchards in the South West of Ireland*, Journal of the Cork Historical and Archaeological Society, July 1964.

Woodham-Smith, Cecil, *The Great Hunger*, London, 1962.

Cork Advertiser (1867).
Cork Examiner.
Southern Star.
Skibbereen Eagle.
The Times.
Tuckey's Cork Remembrancer.
The Irish Times.

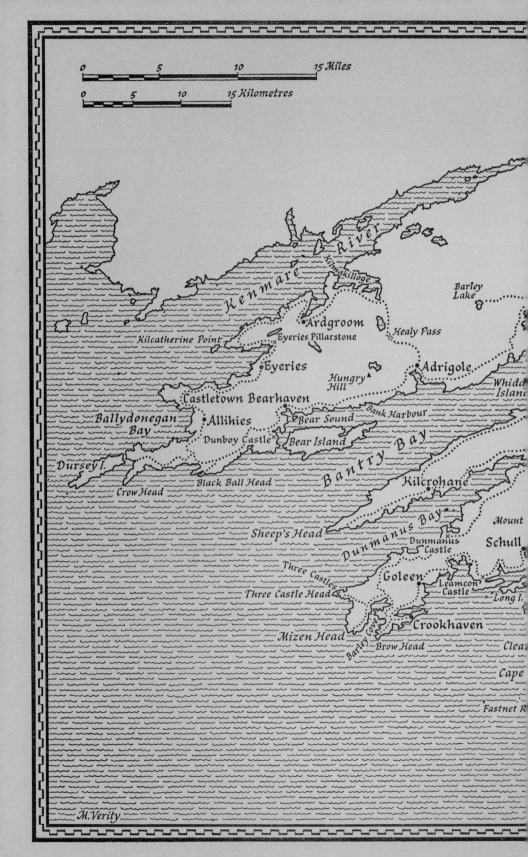